Labour Supply and Microsimulation

Labour Supply and Microsimulation

The Evaluation of Tax Policy Reforms

John Creedy

The Truby Williams Professor of Economics, University of Melbourne, Australia

Guyonne Kalb

Associate Professor at
The Melbourne Institute of Applied Economic and Social Research, University of Melbourne, Australia

Edward Elgar

Cheltenham, UK • Northampton, MA, USA

Published by
Edward Elgar Publishing Limited
Glensanda House
Montpellier Parade
Cheltenham
Glos GL50 1UA
UK

Edward Elgar Publishing, Inc.
136 West Street
Suite 202
Northampton
Massachusetts 01060
USA

A catalogue record for this book is available from the British Library

Library of Congress Cataloguing in Publication Data

Creedy, John, 1949–
Labour supply and microsimulation : the evaluation of tax policy reforms / John Creedy, Guyonne Kalb.
p. cm.
Includes bibliographical references and index.
1. Labor supply–Mathematical models. 2. Labor supply–Effect of taxation on–Mathematical models. 3. Taxation–Mathematical models. I. Kalb, Guyonne. II. Title.

HD5701.6.C737 2006
331.1201'1–dc22 2006007960

ISBN-13: 978 1 84542 881 5
ISBN-10: 1 84542 881 1

Printed and bound in Great Britain by MPG Books Ltd, Bodmin, Cornwall

Contents

Appendices

Figures

Tables

Acknowledgments

The work on which chapters 9 and 11 are based was supported by the Australian Department of Family and Community Services. We are grateful for this support, though of course the views expressed in these chapters are those of the authors and do not represent the views of the Minister for Family and Community Services, the Department of Family and Community Services or the Commonwealth Government. Several of the chapters included in this book are based on material from projects which received funding from ARC Research Grants.

The material in this book is based on work which initially appeared in a number of separate journal papers, although they have in most cases undergone substantial revisions. Chapter 2 is based on Creedy (2004a). Chapters 3 to 5 are an extended version of Creedy and Kalb (2005a). Chapters 6 and 7 are based on Creedy (2004b) and Creedy (2004c) respectively. Chapters 8 and 9 are based on Creedy and Kalb (2005b) and Creedy, Kalb and Scutella (2004). Chapter 10 is based on Creedy and Scutella (2004). Chapter 11 is based on Creedy, Kalb and Kew (2004) and chapter 12 is based on Creedy and Duncan (2005). We are very grateful to our joint authors, Alan Duncan, Hsein Kew and Rosanna Scutella, as well as to the editors of the relevant journals for permission to use the material here.

Part I

Introduction

Chapter 1

Introduction

Microsimulation models are used to examine the effects of hypothetical or actual tax and benefit reforms, using a large cross-sectional data set that reflects the degree of heterogeneity found in the population. The level of disaggregation that can be obtained from microsimulation results, compared with what is possible in general equilibrium modelling, is a major advantage when the interest is, for example, in distributional issues such as inequality or poverty or in the effect on subgroups in the population of reforms to the tax and transfer system. As a result, this type of model has gained popularity in the evaluation of tax and social security policy changes, where it is important to know how different, sometimes quite small, subgroups are affected by policy proposals.

Static or arithmetic microsimulation models, which calculate the 'morning-after' effect of policy changes, provide a wealth of information for a wide variety of potential policy changes. However, when the aim of a policy is to stimulate labour supply by providing incentives for individuals and households to enter the labour market or increase their participation in the labour market, behavioural responses become important. Therefore, behavioural microsimulation models, which are able to simulate potential labour supply responses resulting from a policy change, have been developed. Earlier generations of simulation models used continuous hours labour supply modelling.

However, this book focuses on behavioural microsimulation based on discrete choice labour supply modelling. Discrete hours labour supply models are being widely adopted in tax policy microsimulation because it is relatively easy, compared with the continuous hours approach, to incorporate taxation and social security details in estimation and simulation.

1.1 Main Aims of the Book

The first aim of this book is to provide an introduction to, and review of, behavioural tax microsimulation methods. To reach the stage where a policy change, such as a change in income taxation rates, can be simulated, several steps are needed. First, a model needs to be specified explaining labour supply behaviour. Second, taxation and social security details and individual information on incomes, wages and household composition are needed to calculate net incomes at all possible labour supply levels. Third, the labour supply model is estimated using information on individuals' labour supply, net income at the different labour supply levels and other relevant characteristics. Fourth, once the parameters of the model have been estimated, they can be used to simulate the effect of policy changes. Finally, once the individual effects have been computed, individual and household weights are needed to aggregate the individual results up to the population level. These steps are described in detail in the early chapters of this book. The presentation makes regular use of diagrams and numerical examples, as well as formal derivations.

The second aim is to present new methods of evaluating policy changes. Once the stage has been reached where policy changes can be simulated, it becomes important to analyse the results and provide summary measures which can be used with the output data, where effects for each individual in the sample are available. Interest may, for example, be in the effect on poverty or inequality or in welfare changes which also account for the non-financial change, such as a change in labour supply resulting from a policy change. Naturally, there are many evaluation approaches and the focus of the evaluation may be different depending on the question of interest. This book deals with a limited number of issues related to interpreting the results from microsimulation. The issues included are welfare measurement, income distribution, confidence intervals around the simulated results, and feedback effects on the wage distribution via labour demand, which in turn alters the behavioural labour supply responses. None of these approaches and proposed methods is model-specific. Each of them can be applied to the output of any behavioural microsimulation model.

1.2 Outline of the Book

The substantive chapters of this book are divided into two main Parts. Part II concentrates on the first aim of reviewing behavioural microsimulation methods, where attention is given to the three steps of model specification, estimation and microsimulation, followed by the determination of the appropriate weights. Part III focuses on the second aim of examining policy evaluation methods.

Part II begins in chapter 2 and provides an explanation, relying on the use of diagrams, of some of the important relationships between tax and social security changes and labour supply changes. A more formal framework to explore labour supply is examined in chapter 3, where a basic discrete labour supply model is specified. The next two chapters elaborate on this basic discrete labour supply model. First, chapter 4 focuses on the estimation of the model and illustrates the approach by a simple numerical example. In addition, some possible extensions to the basic model are explored. This is followed in chapter 5 by a description of a simulation procedure which bases its behavioural responses on the labour supply model described in the previous chapters. Here numerical examples are again used to illustrate the approach, followed by a realistic empirical example using Australian data.

Chapter 6, the final chapter in Part II, is concerned with the reweighting of sample surveys. Reweighting may be necessary if the subgroups of interest have not been appropriately weighted to represent the correct aggregate population values. Alternatively, if the data to be used for simulation are too many years out of date, or if aggregation to a hypothetical future population is required, reweighting may assist in transforming the current dataset so that it can represent a population with a different demographic structure. A technical explanation is given of the methodology, followed by an empirical example using New Zealand data.

Part III is concerned with the evaluation of the results after simulating a policy change. The first chapter of Part III, chapter 7, again starts with a diagrammatic representation. This chapter provides an intuitive explanation of the two concepts of welfare changes and excess tax burdens, which represent efficiency losses due to a distortion in choices arising from taxation. These two concepts are important when the benefits arising from a government expenditure, measured by a welfare change, need to be compared with the loss in efficiency, measured by the excess burden. Chapter 8 discusses an approach used to measure welfare changes in labour supply modelling, where budget constraints are often highly nonlinear, making the standard approach unsuitable. The approach is applicable to continuous and discrete hours labour supply models and the chapter illustrates the method with some numerical examples.

The probabilistic outcomes of behavioural microsimulation modelling, obtained when using discrete hours labour supply models, require a special approach to the measurement of inequality and poverty. Chapter 9 describes three alternative approaches and compares the performance of each approach using Monte Carlo experiments. The application of the preferred approach is illustrated using Australian data. Chapter 10 remains in the area of poverty and inequality measurement. Alternative units of analysis and equivalence scales are described. These are used in an empirical example to explore the sensitivity of conclusions regarding changes in poverty or inequality with regard to the choice of unit of analysis, the measure of the economies of scale within households and the degree of aversion to inequality.

Microsimulation models usually provide point estimates of changes in government expenditure or revenue or in aggregate labour supply changes. Chapter 11 describes two approaches to compute a confidence interval for these aggregate values based on the uncertainty associated with the labour supply parameters. One approach is fairly accurate but requires very long computing times whereas the other approach provides an approximation but can be obtained much more quickly. Both methods are applied using Australian data.

Finally, the last chapter aims to allow effects from the demand side of the labour market to influence the microsimulation results which are usually calculated in isolation from other sectors of the economy. Chapter 12 explores an approach which allows labour supply changes to affect wage levels and therefore labour demand, resulting in new equilibrium employment levels and wage levels. Different assumptions regarding the elasticity of labour demand can be made to examine the sensitivity of the microsimulation results to these alternative demand schedules. Again, Australian data are used to illustrate the methodology.

The focus of the book is on the role that microsimulation models can play in supporting rational policy analysis. By this is meant the examination and reporting of the implications of alternative policies, so that policy makers can form their own judgements. It also involves the determination of policies that are implied by the adoption of a range of clearly specified value judgements. Given that no model is without its limitations, it is always necessary to treat the output from microsimulation models with caution. Nevertheless, given the central role of tax and transfer systems, such models can provide a valuable contribution to policy analysis and can thereby help to provide a counterweight against the rhetoric and special pleading that otherwise play a large part in tax policy debates.

The production of behavioural tax microsimulation models represents a considerable challenge and has involved substantial innovations in labour supply modelling. Such models represent a relatively recent development, made feasible by improvements in computing facilities. They offer interesting challenges and considerable potential for further extensions. It is hoped that the present book, by reviewing some behavioural microsimulation methods and presenting new methods of policy evaluation, will stimulate further work.

Part II

Microsimulation Issues

Chapter 2

Continuous Hours Labour Supply

Tax and transfer systems in most countries are highly complex, consisting of a wide range of benefit payments, each with its own set of withdrawal rates and thresholds. Often the different components are not well integrated, so that unplanned effects can arise, especially where piecemeal adjustments to benefit levels and income thresholds are made over a period of time. Policy reforms are typically concerned with balancing the aims of providing income support with the desire to avoid excessive disincentive effects of taxes. In designing reforms, it is useful to have in mind a number of relationships which can conveniently be discussed in diagrammatic terms.

This chapter therefore explores a range of diagrams which are helpful in thinking about the design of tax and transfer systems and their potential effects on labour supply behaviour. Emphasis is given to nonlinear or even nonconvex budget constraints and the resulting wide range of labour supply responses. The analysis of labour supply in the presence of nonlinear budget constraints rapidly becomes complicated, in particular when individuals can choose from an unlimited number of working hours from a continuous range of hours. Optimal labour supply could potentially be found on any of the linear segments or at any of the kinks in the budget constraint. When the budget constraint is not convex, finding optimal labour supply requires checking each linear segment and kink of the budget constraint. For complex tax and transfer systems this is computationally intensive.

The use of diagrams relating gross and net incomes, for specified groups, is described in section 2.1. Section 2.2 first introduces budget constraints and utility maximisation in a simple labour supply framework, followed by a discussion of a variety of piecewise linear budget constraints. The effect of a non-recoverable cost of applying for benefits and its joint effect on take-up and labour supply are briefly examined in section 2.3. Section 2.4 concludes this chapter.

2.1 Net and Gross Incomes

Tax and transfer systems are typically specified in terms of a set of gross income thresholds and associated marginal tax rates applying above the thresholds. The tax rates arise from a combination of income taxes and benefit withdrawal, or taper, rates. The levels of such rates and thresholds generally depend on the particular type of individual or household. A popular way of illustrating the nature of the system is to use a diagram with gross income, from all non-benefit sources, on the horizontal axis and net income on the vertical axis, as in Figure 2.1.

This type of diagram has the advantage that it displays the tax thresholds and rates clearly and applies to all those in the specified demographic group. Along the 45° line, net and gross incomes are equal. Figure 2.1 also shows a simple proportional income tax applied to all income at the rate t. The vertical distance between the tax schedule and the 45° line, at any gross income level, shows the amount of tax paid, ty, and the vertical height of the schedule shows net income, $(1-t)\,y$. The slope of the line therefore measures the proportion of each \$ retained after tax, that is $(1-t)$.

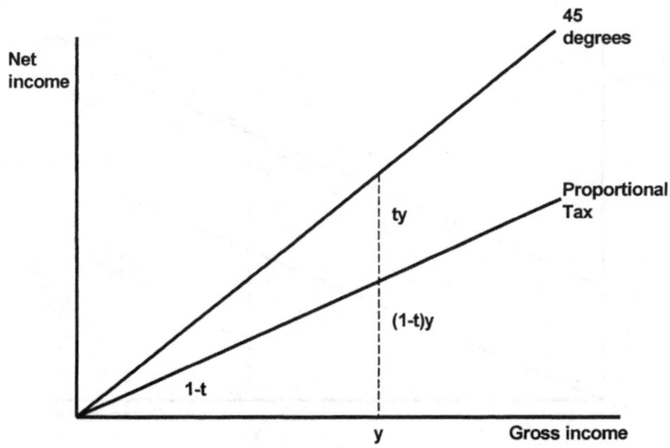

Figure 2.1: Net and Gross Income

2.1.1 A Basic Income–Flat Tax

Figure 2.2 combines the proportional income tax with an unconditional transfer payment equal to B. Hence the relationship between gross and net income is shifted up by an amount, B, at all points. This is the simplest possible tax and transfer system imaginable; it is referred to as a basic income–flat tax, or BI/FT, scheme. It has been referred to by several other names, including negative income tax (NIT), social dividend and linear tax scheme.

The figure shows immediately the break-even income level, y_B, where net and gross income are equal; all those below y_B receive a net gain. The BI/FT need not necessarily be administered as an unconditional benefit combined with a proportional tax. It may involve an integrated system in which those below y_B pay no tax and receive the vertical distance between the tax schedule and the 45° line, while those above the break-even point only pay tax, determined as a fixed proportion of income measured in excess of y_B, so that tax is $t\left(y-y_B\right)$.

There are two policy instruments, B and t, the values of which cannot

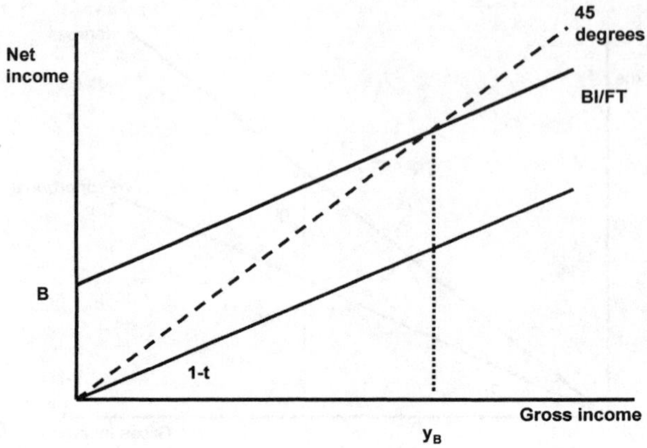

Figure 2.2: A Basic Income–Flat Tax

be chosen independently because of the existence of a government budget constraint. That is, given the choice of B, t is determined by the budget constraint and vice versa. In a pure transfer system, where all tax revenue is redistributed in transfer payments, the tax rate is given by solving $t\sum_i^n y_i = nB$, where n is the number of individuals. Hence $t = B/\overline{y}$, or the ratio of the social dividend to arithmetic mean income, and the break-even point is the arithmetic mean, $y_B = \overline{y}$.

A generous BI/FT scheme therefore requires a relatively high marginal tax rate, t, but the average tax rate (ATR) is less than the marginal tax rate (MTR) for all individuals, and is negative for all those below y_B. The marginal and average rate schedules are shown in Figure 2.3.

This demonstrates that considerable redistribution can be achieved with a tax system having a constant, rather than increasing, marginal rate structure. A progressive tax structure requires only an increasing average tax rate at all income levels. Indeed, in the limit such a system can achieve complete equality if $t = 1$ and $B = \overline{y}$. However, this type of argument requires the assumption that gross incomes are unaffected by the tax structure. When

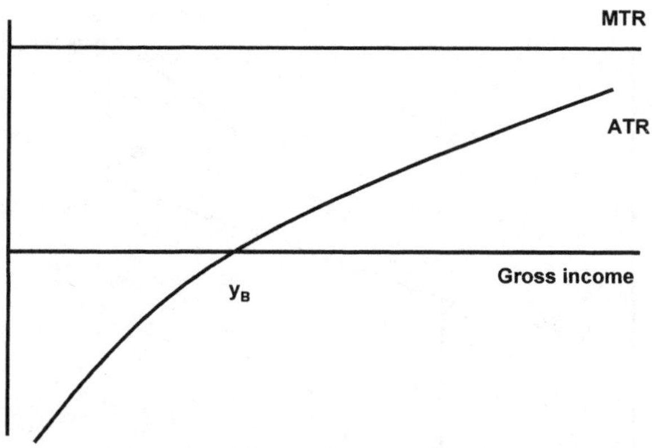

Figure 2.3: Marginal and Average Tax Rates

allowance is made for labour supply incentives, there is a 'trade-off' between 'equity and efficiency', which can considerably limit the redistribution that can be achieved.

Many income tax structures have a tax-free area. Figure 2.4 shows an income tax structure of this kind, where taxation above the threshold, a, is equal to $t\,(y-a)$. The tax schedule thus follows the 45 degree line from the origin until A, and is then AB. However, if AB is extended to the left, it hits the vertical axis at a net income of at. Thus for taxpayers, for whom $y > a$, the tax-free threshold is equivalent to a BI/FT scheme with base income at and tax rate t. An increase in the threshold takes a few individuals out of the tax 'net' but provides an increase in the effective basic income for all taxpayers. Any multi-rate income tax structure, even in the absence of a tax-free area, looks, for those above the first tax rate, like a single rate structure with a tax-free threshold. This tax-free threshold can be expressed as a function of the earlier rates and thresholds similar to at in Figure 2.4.

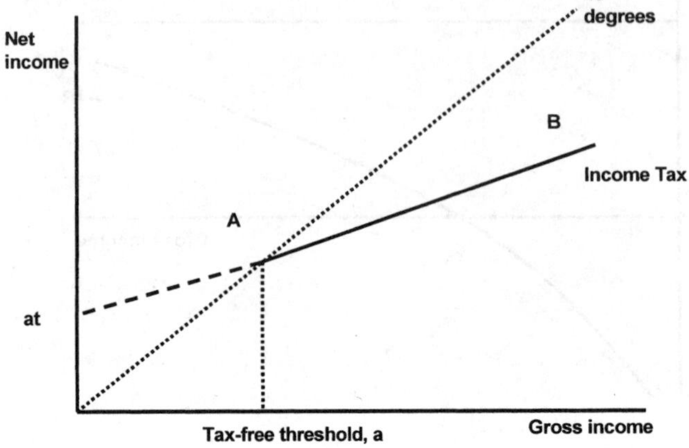

Figure 2.4: A Tax-free Threshold

2.1.2 Means-Tested Benefits

Typically, tax and transfer systems have a degree of means testing whereby benefits are withdrawn as individuals obtain higher gross incomes. A typical system with a benefit level A is shown in Figure 2.5. The tax schedule ABCD has a range AB where there is a benefit withdrawal rate, and a further range CD where the marginal income tax rate is increased. However, the highest marginal effective tax rate is faced by those on the lowest incomes, as is evident from the low gradient of the section AB of the tax schedule. In the means-tested system of Figure 2.5, a further degree of freedom in policy choices is lost because of the need to avoid a discontinuity, particularly at the point B. A discontinuity would produce a sudden, possibly negative, change in net income for a small increase in gross income. In practice, because various benefits are planned independently and thresholds are often adjusted separately, discontinuities exist. For example in 2004/2005 in Australia, an increase in the minimum wage of a full-time single earner in a couple household with children would have been taxed at 104 per cent. This was due

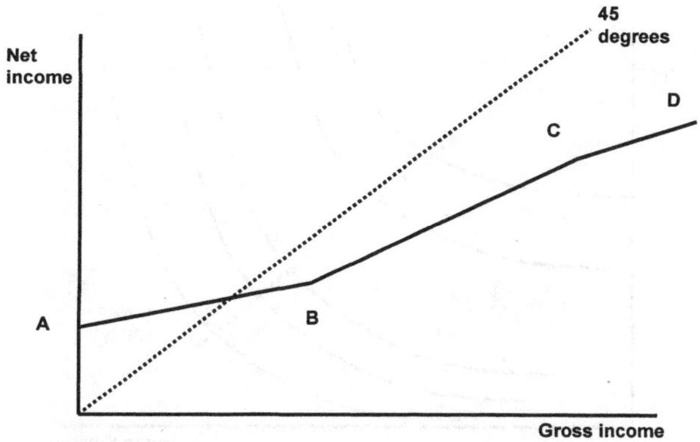

Figure 2.5: A Typical Multi-rate System

to the withdrawal of the partner's parenting payment at 70 per cent, the single earner's own income tax rate of 30 per cent and the withdrawal of the low-income tax rebate at 4 per cent.

The use of a diagram showing the relationship between net and gross income has limitations as a device for examining labour supply incentive effects of taxes. For this, individual budget constraints in combination with individual preference (or utility) functions are needed. Budget constraints show net income against hours of work (or leisure) for a particular individual.

2.2 Taxes and Labour Supply

The discussion in this section assumes that the individual has a fixed gross wage (though there may be an overtime premium) in a single job. Each individual is assumed to maximise utility, which is regarded as a function of net income and leisure. The relative values of leisure and net income may be different for different individuals. An example of an indifference map is shown in Figure 2.6: indifference curves that are further to the north west represent higher utility. In this simple static model, although hours of

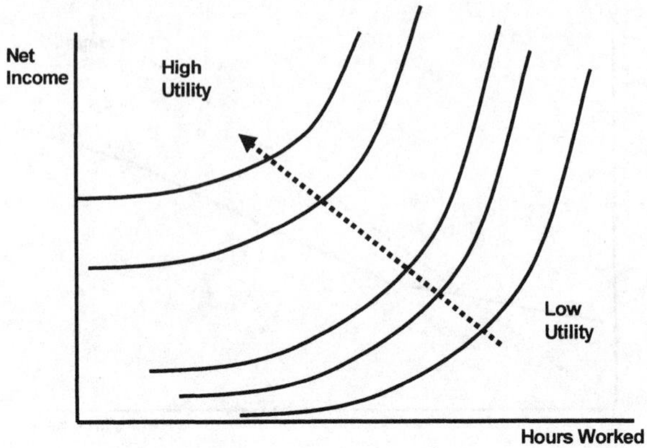

Figure 2.6: An Indifference Map

work are considered, consumption does not take time, there is no household production and leisure is simply enjoyed as time not spent working. The individual trades, at the margin, the disutility arising from working an extra hour with the utility obtained from the consumption of the resulting net income.

Utility is maximised subject to a budget constraint, which depends on the individual's wage rate, as well as some other characteristics, and is thus unique. A basic requirement of any model designed to examine taxes in the presence of labour supply responses is therefore that it is capable of producing the budget constraints for all individuals in the data set on which the model is constructed. The following subsections discuss a variety of budget constraints that could occur.

2.2.1 The Basic Income–Flat Tax Budget Constraint

Figure 2.7 shows the budget constraint for an individual under the BI/FT structure, and facing a gross wage rate per hour of w. The starting point of the constraint, where hours worked equal zero, $h = 0$, corresponds to

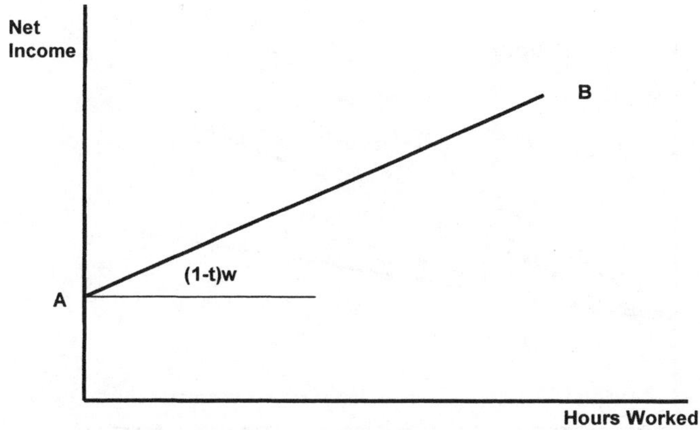

Figure 2.7: Individual Budget Constraint: BI/FT

net income at point A. This includes any benefits, along with all sources of non-wage income (and if the labour supply decision of couples is assumed to involve some kind of joint maximisation process, this may include the net income of the partner).[1] The slope of the budget constraint measures the extra net income obtained from an extra hour of work, and is thus equal to the net wage rate, $w\,(1-t)$.

Maximisation of utility leads either to a corner solution at A, where the individual does not work, or a tangency solution somewhere along AB. Within this framework, the work participation decision is associated with movement away from the corner solution. This corner is more likely to be chosen, when the gross wage is lower and the tax rate is higher, since both tend to make the constraint flatter, decreasing the rewards to work.

Figure 2.8 shows the effect on labour supply of varying the wage rate.

[1] If labour supply is completely jointly determined, a three-dimensional budget constraint and preference function (including the partner's labour supply on the third axis) should be drawn to find the optimal choice. However, if for example female labour supply is decided conditional on the man's labour supply, then the man's income from employment can be treated as a given and can be added to the non-labour income of the female partner's budget constraint.

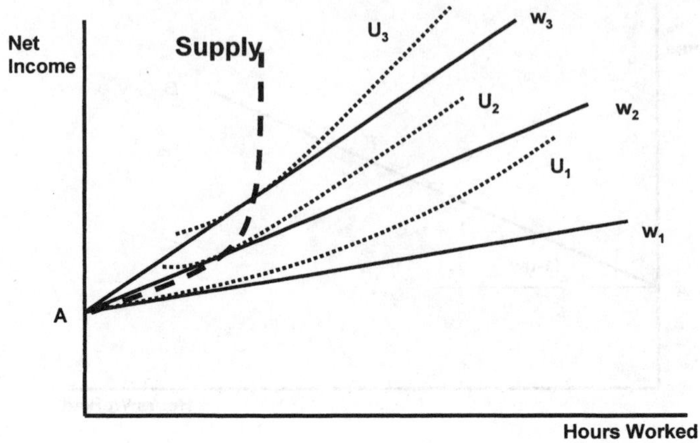

Figure 2.8: Wages and Hours Worked

For the relatively low wage rate of w_1, the optimal position is at the non-participation corner A on indifference curve U_1. As the wage increases to w_2, and then to w_3, the individual moves to tangency positions on indifference curves U_2 and U_3 respectively.

The gross wage is not transparent in Figure 2.8, because the slope of the budget line is the net wage. It is therefore useful to transfer the information to a separate diagram, the labour supply curve, showing hours worked against the gross wage rate. The supply curve associated with this linear budget constraint is shown in Figure 2.9 as AAB. The range AA is associated with the kink point A in Figure 2.7 and reflects wage rates for which the individual remains at the 'non-participation' kink. For higher wages, labour supply expands along the range AB as this pivots about A. Depending on the individual's preferences, the supply curve may bend backwards, as shown by the dashed line.

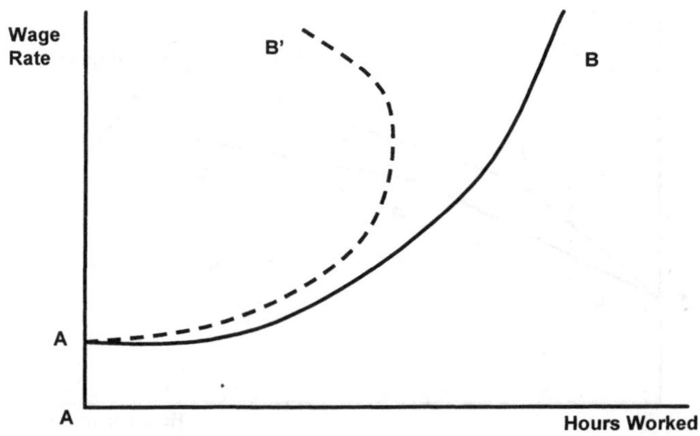

Figure 2.9: Labour Supply with the BI/FT

2.2.2 Piecewise-Linear Convex Budget Constraints

This and the following subsections extend the analysis from the previous subsection to deal with budget constraints made up of several linear segments, each associated with a given marginal tax rate and earnings threshold. Such multi-segment constraints are referred to as piecewise-linear budget constraints.

The effect of an increase in the gross wage on a more complex budget constraint is shown in Figure 2.10. The constraint ABC has a kink at B, reflecting the presence of an earnings threshold where the marginal effective tax rate increases. The budget set is said to be convex: a straight line joining any two points is associated with feasible positions, that is net incomes on this line are less than or equal to the net income along the budget line.

The earnings threshold is not evident from the budget constraint, unlike the net/gross income diagram, since the hours level at which it occurs depends on the wage rate. For a higher wage rate, the budget constraint pivots to AB$'$C$'$, and the kink point B$'$ is to the left of B. This is because a lower hours level is required, at the higher wage, to reach the earnings threshold

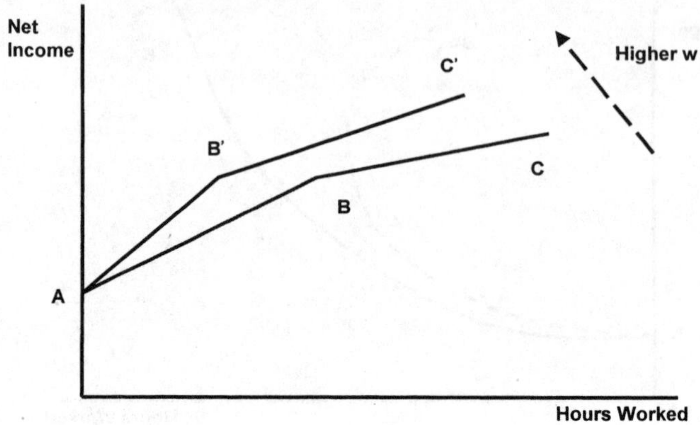

Figure 2.10: A Convex Budget Set

where the marginal rate increases; gross and thus net income remain constant at the kink.

A corner solution is shown in Figure 2.11, where the highest indifference curve just touches the budget constraint at point B. Nevertheless, the optimal position for the individual can be represented as if it were a tangency solution. An artificial budget line can be drawn which is tangential to the indifference curve at the kink, B. This introduces the important concepts of the virtual wage and virtual income. They are taken from the theory of rationing, where corner solutions are important. These new concepts of the virtual wage and virtual income are particularly useful when considering the welfare changes arising from tax reforms.

Before considering the labour supply function implied by the budget constraint in Figure 2.10, it is useful to examine the relationship between gross earnings (that is, the product of hours worked and the gross wage, wh) and the wage rate first. This is shown in Figure 2.12. At very low wages, utility maximisation gives rise to the corner solution at A. When the wage rate exceeds some level (as the section AB of the constraint pivots about A),

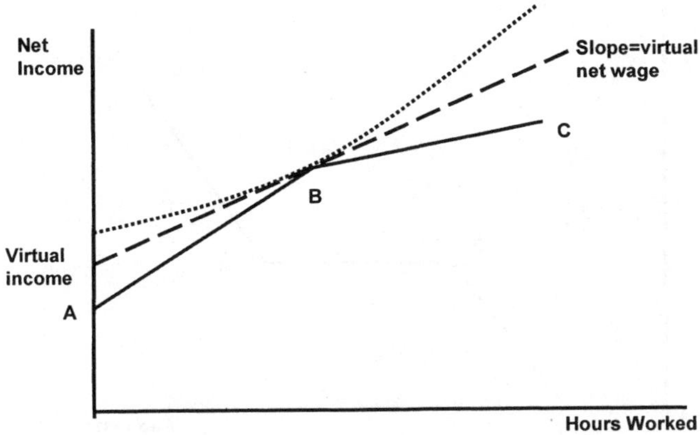

Figure 2.11: A Corner Solution

the individual moves to a tangency position. Increases in the wage induce higher labour supply until the gross earnings threshold is reached at which the marginal effective tax rate increases. A characteristic of this kind of kink in the budget constraint – where there is no tangency solution but a position where the highest indifference curve touches the relevant corner – is that the individual 'sticks' at the corner for a range of wage rates. In this case the gross earnings remain constant as the wage rate rises over a range, although of course the associated hours level falls. Eventually, for a sufficiently high wage rate, the individual moves to a tangency along the range BC of the constraint. The lengths of the flat sections AA and BB, and the nature of the rising sections AB and BC, depend on the individual's preferences. A higher preference for consumption over leisure (flatter indifference curves) results in shorter sections AA and BB in Figure 2.12.

Individuals may face the same tax rates and thresholds, but the variation in non-wage incomes, wage rates and preferences means that each budget constraint and gross earnings/wage schedule is unique. However, the existence of the kink may suggest that some 'bunching' of individuals around the

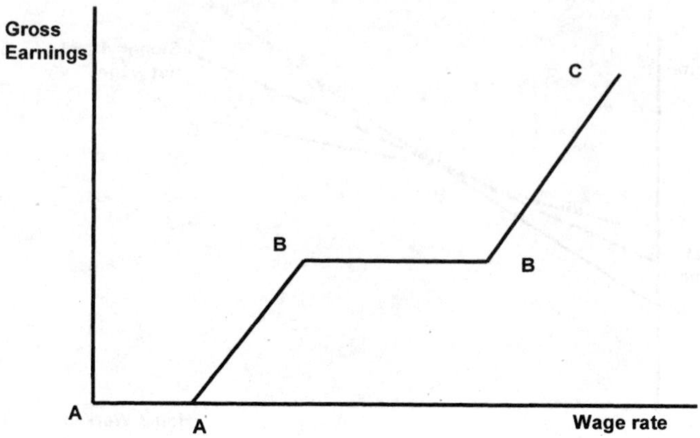

Figure 2.12: Gross Earnings and the Wage Rate

threshold in the distribution of gross earnings should be observed. Due to several other factors playing a role in the labour supply decision, this kind of phenomenon is nevertheless only observed in particular cases. That is, a tax threshold need not produce a 'spike' in the earnings distribution, and modes may in practice correspond to tangency solutions. Hence the distribution of earnings does not necessarily provide any information about the extent of the labour supply effects of taxation.

The range BB in Figure 2.12 is associated with a fixed level of earnings, so that wh is constant. This implies that, in a graph of hours worked plotted against the wage rate, the hours of work would follow a rectangular hyperbola over the relevant range. The labour supply function is shown in Figure 2.13. This property, that the labour supply curve turns sharply backwards, following a rectangular hyperbola, as the wage rate increases over a range, is entirely general and applies to any kink in the budget constraint associated with an increase in the marginal effective tax rate at a threshold level of earnings.

Two important general lessons emerge from this discussion. First, the

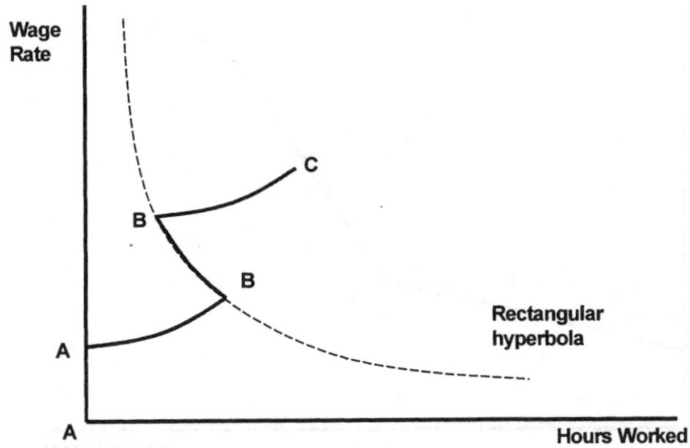

Figure 2.13: Labour Supply Curve

number of hours of work supplied and the net wage are jointly determined. Second, it makes little sense to attempt to describe the labour supply function (hours supplied as a function of the gross wage) in terms of a single elasticity. Even if the ranges AB and BC have a constant elasticity, large variations occur at the kink points, and of course the elasticity changes sign twice at each kink point.

2.2.3 Piecewise-Linear Non-convex Constraints

An example of a budget constraint with a means-tested benefit is given in Figure 2.14, as ABC. The benefit is gradually withdrawn at a relatively high rate until it is exhausted at B, when the individual only pays income tax. Here the budget set is said to be non-convex. This raises the possibility of an indifference curve being simultaneously tangential to both sections of the constraint, for a particular wage rate given the preference function. This is shown in Figure 2.14 by the two tangencies at J and K. A small increase in the wage rate would therefore produce a discrete jump in hours worked from J to K.

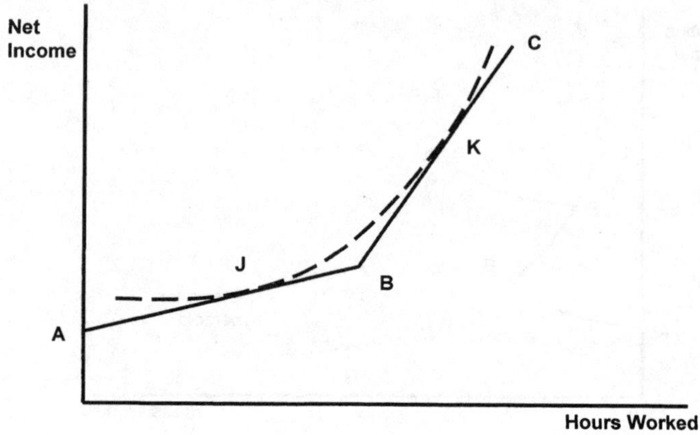

Figure 2.14: Means Testing: A Non-convex Budget Set

A discrete jump of this kind is reflected in the relationship between gross earnings and the wage rate, shown in Figure 2.15. When the wage rate is increased, earnings become positive after a particular wage has been passed and the individual increases labour supply along the range AB. But at a particular wage, the 'switching' wage, the individual jumps to point K along the range BC in Figure 2.14. Further increases in the wage produce a gradual increase in labour supply along KC. The associated labour supply curve is shown in Figure 2.16, where the vertical jump in Figure 2.15 translates into the horizontal range JK of the supply curve. There is a range where the individual is working and receiving benefits along part of AJ; but this is just a proportion of the hours range over which the individual is actually eligible for benefits.

These properties of the relationship between the shape of the budget constraint and the labour supply curve are general. A kink in the budget constraint associated with a rise in the marginal tax rate is associated with a 'backward bending' range along a rectangular hyperbola (where gross earnings are constant), and a kink associated with a fall in the effective marginal

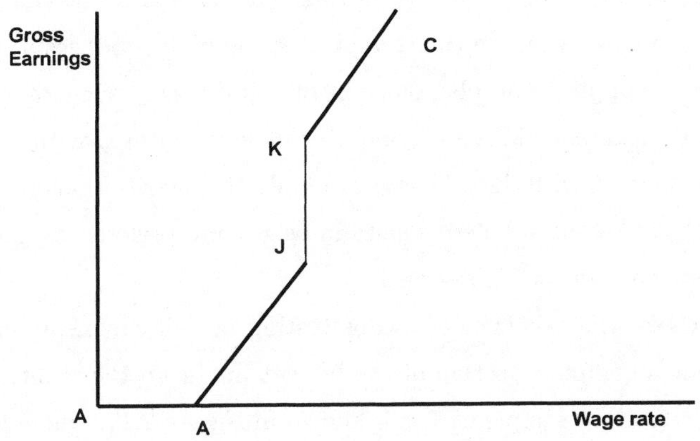

Figure 2.15: Gross Earnings and the Wage Rate

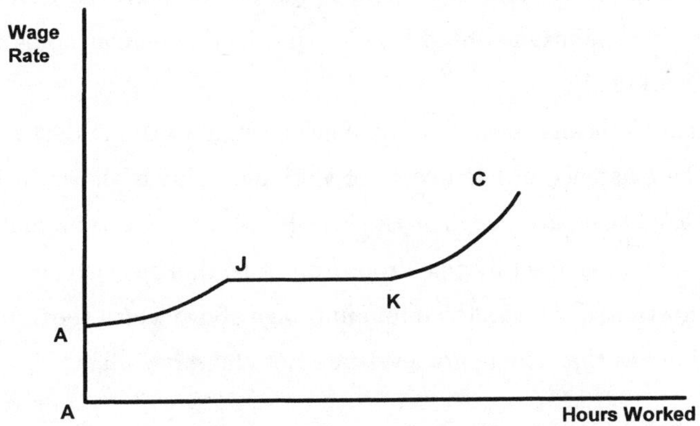

Figure 2.16: Labour Supply Curve

tax rate produces a horizontal range in the supply curve. In the first case the kink produces a degree of rigidity (no movement from the 'travelling' kink as the wage changes), while in the second case the kink produces a discrete jump in labour supply. The phenomenon of a jump may suggest that the earnings distribution should have a 'gap', or at least an area with very low probabilities. But, as with the other type of kink, the distribution of earnings is generated by substantial heterogeneity in wages and preferences, and such a gap may not necessarily be observed.

In some cases, the existence of means testing benefit payments may actually rule out a complete section of the budget line from the point of view of labour supply. An example of this is shown in Figure 2.17, where instead of two tangency positions, the highest indifference curve is shown to give rise simultaneously to a corner solution at A and a tangency at K. Hence the whole range of AB is ruled out, as well as the range BK of BC. The relationship between gross earnings and the wage is shown in Figure 2.18 where the 'switching' wage produces a jump from zero labour supply and thus zero earnings to the point K. This individual would not be observed both working and receiving the means-tested benefit; that is, this person would not be among the 'working poor'.

In addition to means testing, a non-convex range of the budget set may arise from the existence of fixed costs of working. This is shown in Figure 2.19, where fixed costs are shown as the length AB. As soon as an individual enters paid employment net income drops from A to B. The existence of these fixed costs substantially raises the minimum wage above which the individual works, and implies that low hours levels are not chosen at all.

2.2.4 A Multi-rate Tax Structure

Figure 2.20 contains a budget constraint having four marginal tax rates. Means testing of benefits involves an increase in the marginal rate after point

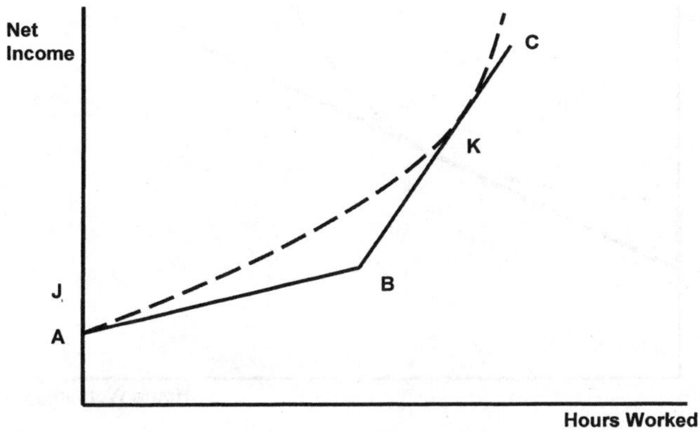

Figure 2.17: Corner and Tangency Solutions

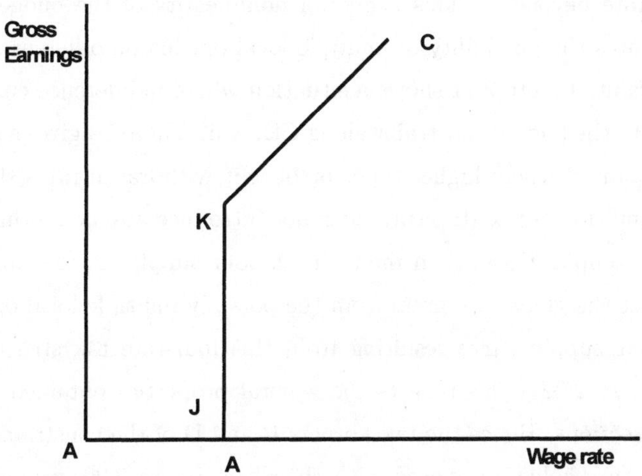

Figure 2.18: Gross Earnings and the Wage Rate

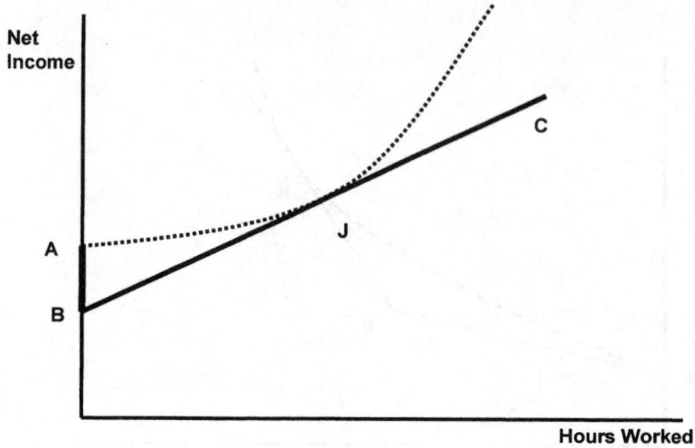

Figure 2.19: Fixed Costs of Working

B, and a subsequent reduction in the marginal rate once benefits have been exhausted at point C. The range DE reflects an increase in the marginal income tax rate beyond D. This degree of nonlinearity of the budget constraint generates the possibility of multiple local optima on different ranges of the constraint. Figure 2.21 shows a situation where indifference curve U_1 is tangential to the budget constraint along CD, while curve U_2 gives a corner solution at point B where higher taper or benefit withdrawal rates start to apply. The multi-rate tax structure does not introduce any new principles, but it raises complications when modelling labour supply, as care must be taken to select the global optimum from the possibly multiple local optima.

The labour supply curve resulting from this four-rate tax structure is shown in Figure 2.22. This reflects the general properties obtained in the previous subsections. Hence the two corners B and D of the constraint (and the earnings thresholds associated with them) in Figure 2.20 generate the two ranges BB and DD of Figure 2.22 which involve reductions in labour supply along rectangular hyperbolae. The flat section of the supply curve JK is associated with the jump from a tangency along BC to a tangency

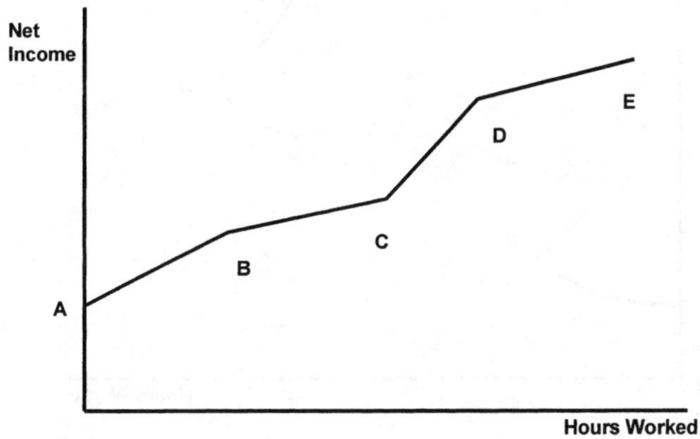

Figure 2.20: A Multi-rate System

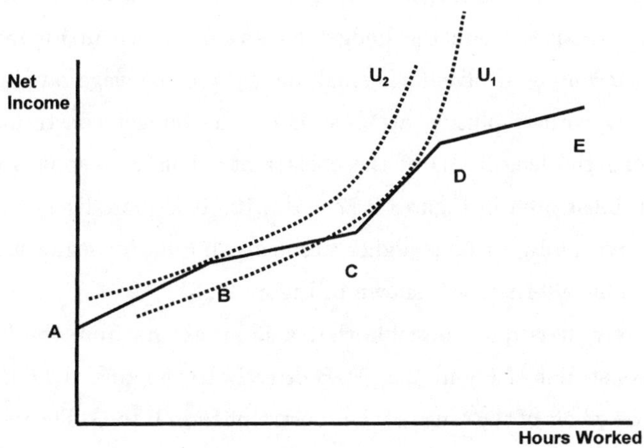

Figure 2.21: Multiple Local Optima

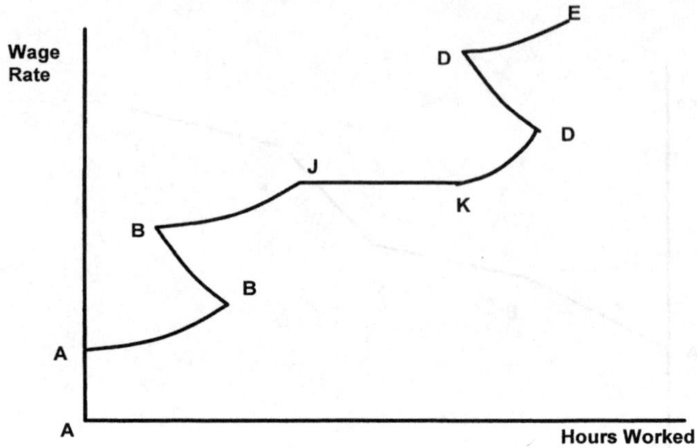

Figure 2.22: Labour Supply with a Multi-rate System (Alternative 1)

along DC of the budget constraint. The rising sections of the supply curve are associated with tangency solutions.

The supply curve need not necessarily take the precise form shown in Figure 2.22. Consider again the budget constraint shown in Figure 2.20. The supply curve may involve, for a small increase in the wage rate, a jump directly from a corner solution at point B on the budget constraint to a tangency along the length CD of the constraint. This corresponds to the type of jump illustrated in Figures 2.17 and 2.18. It is more likely to occur if the benefit withdrawal rate is higher, resulting in a flatter segment AB in Figure 2.20. This alternative is shown in Figure 2.23.

Alternatively, it is quite possible that a jump occurs from the kink in the budget constraint of Figure 2.20 at B directly to the kink at D, thereby leaving out the whole of the range of the constraint from B to D. The resulting labour supply curve is illustrated in Figure 2.24.

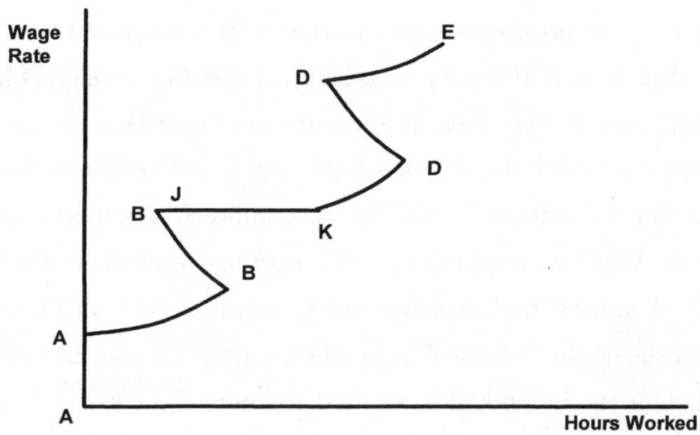

Figure 2.23: Labour Supply with a Multi-rate System (Alternative 2)

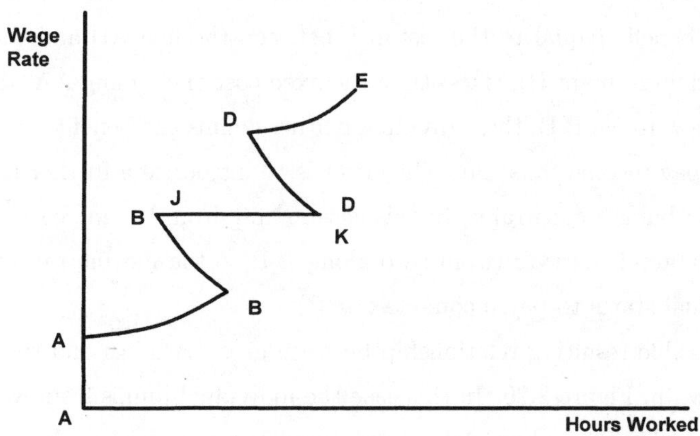

Figure 2.24: Labour Supply with a Multi-rate System (Alternative 3)

2.3 Benefit Take-up

The discussion in the previous sections of this chapter has made the implicit assumption that there is 100 per cent take-up of benefits by eligible individuals. However, suppose that there is a non-recoverable fixed cost of claiming benefits, and consider the simple case of a means-tested benefit with a single taper rate, combined with an income tax, also imposed at a fixed rate above the tax-free threshold corresponding to the earnings level where the benefit is exhausted. The basic budget constraint is shown as ABC in Figure 2.25. The line from the origin to point B indicates net wage income, excluding any benefit, although the individual is entitled to claim the benefit: hence the slope of B′B is equal to the gross wage rate.

The net income obtained by the individual after claiming the benefit is reduced by the fixed cost of claiming, so that the section AB drops down by a vertical distance equal to the cost of claiming. The new effective budget constraint is the line A′B′BC. For hours of work beyond the point B′ the individual is better off by not claiming the benefit because the reduced amount of benefit (equal to the distance between the line AB and the line from the origin to point B), is less than the fixed cost of claiming AA′. Hence along the new range B′B, the individual neither claims the benefit nor earns enough to pay income taxation. The effect is to introduce a further kink in the effective budget constraint, in this case arising from the increase in the effective marginal tax rate (from zero along B′B to the income tax rate as the individual starts to pay income tax at B).

One possible resulting relationship between gross earnings and the wage rate is shown in Figure 2.26. In this case the individual jumps from working and receiving benefits, along A′B′, to working and not claiming benefits or paying income tax, along B′B. This is shown as the jump from J to K in Figure 2.26. Beyond this point the individual increases labour supply, until reaching the kink where there is an associated horizontal section over which

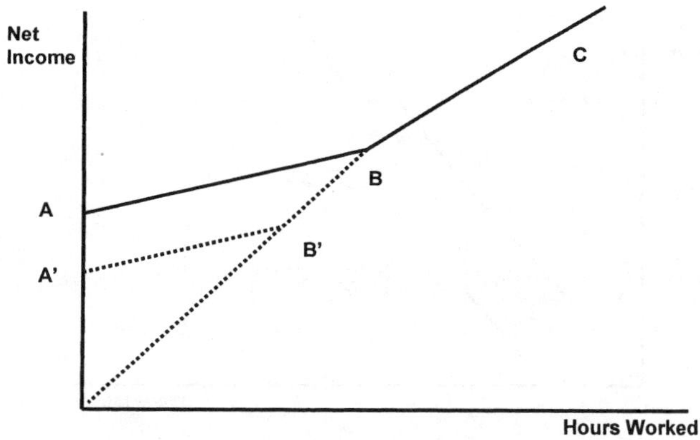

Figure 2.25: A Fixed Cost of Claiming a Benefit

labour supply is reduced. There are other possibilities. For example, an indifference curve may simultaneously touch points A′ and B in Figure 2.25. This means that there is no range where the individual works and receives the means-tested benefit; take-up is complete at the non-participation corner at A′. Or an indifference curve may be tangential to the constraint along A′B′ and touch the corner at B. In this case there is also no range where take-up is incomplete, although there is a range where the individual works and receives the benefit.

2.4 Conclusions

This chapter has illustrated some of the complexities involved in modelling the incentive effects of taxes and transfers, using only basic diagrammatic methods of analysis. It was assumed that individuals can vary their hours of work continuously. A wide range of labour supply responses are shown to result from highly nonlinear budget constraints. A tax or benefit change which improves the labour supply incentives for one group of workers, without making them worse off, may at the same time introduce disincentives facing

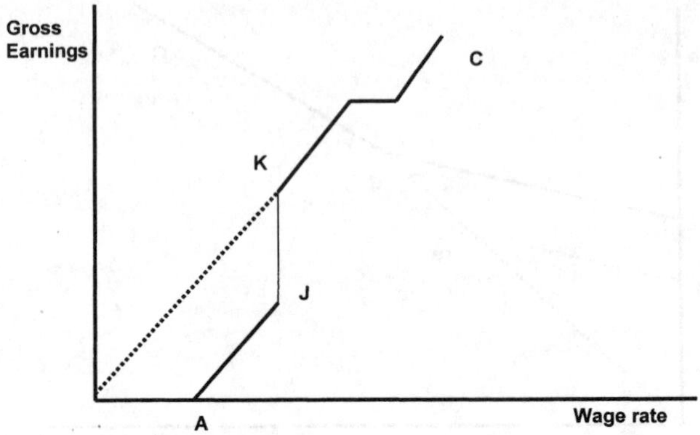

Figure 2.26: Earnings with Incomplete Take-up

another group of workers. Tax policy design inevitably involves difficult trade-offs between the desire to avoid labour supply disincentives and the desire to provide income support.

Several approaches have been adopted in continuous hours labour supply modelling.[2] Often a reasonably flexible labour supply function is estimated relating hours worked to net wage rates, non-wage incomes and a range of individual characteristics. The associated utility function is found by appropriate integration methods. Alternatively, a supply function is derived from either a direct or (more commonly given the greater flexibility allowed) an indirect utility function. However, considerable problems arise because of the fact that net wages and hours are jointly determined, and problems exist concerning the determination of virtual non-wage incomes for each linear

[2] The first generation of labour supply models linearised the budget constraint by taking the average net wage rate or the marginal wage rate in the observed hours. This results in a simple regression model if an appropriate utility function is chosen. This type of model is of limited use when interest is in policy analysis related to the tax and benefit system. The second generation of models examined the full budget constraint when searching for optimal labour supply, allowing for any nonlinearities and nonconvexities. Burtless and Hausman (1978) were the first to use this approach; see Hausman (1979, 1985b) or Moffitt (1986) for a discussion of the approach.

segment of the budget constraint. Indeed, it is extremely difficult to capture the complexities arising from supply behaviour under piecewise linear constraints in empirical continuous hours models. The next chapter discusses a discrete hours labour supply approach.

Chapter 3

Discrete Hours Labour Supply

This chapter provides an introduction to the analytics of discrete hours labour supply modelling. The assumption behind discrete hours labour supply modelling is that utility-maximising individuals choose from a relatively small number of hours levels, rather than being able to vary hours worked continuously. Early influential papers on discrete choice modelling include McFadden (1974a, 1974b) and it seems that the first to use a discrete approach to labour supply modelling were Zabalza, Pissarides and Barton (1980). The discrete approach is perhaps more realistic than the continuous approach, in that typically only a finite number of part-time or full-time working options are available. Van Soest, Woittiez and Kapteyn (1990) and Tummers and Woittiez (1991) showed that a discrete specification of labour supply can improve the representation of actual labour supply compared with a continuous specification. It is assumed that the same set of hours is available to each individual.

The discrete approach also substantially simplifies the information required about the budget set faced by each individual. In the continuous hours context the analysis of choices under piecewise-linear budget lines must deal with the complexities arising from budget sets displaying convex and non-convex ranges, and multiple local equilibria. In practice, the evaluation of the complete range of each individual's unique budget set is cumbersome, given the complexity of most tax and transfer systems. This is further complicated in the case of couples and joint utility maximisation, where the budget constraint is three dimensional. With discrete hours models it is simply a question of evaluating utility at a limited number of points, none of which represents a standard tangency solution. The advantages of discrete hours modelling are perhaps strongest in the context of the empirical estimation of individuals' preference functions. The discrete hours approach can also deal directly with the population heterogeneity that is a fundamental feature of cross-sectional surveys.

The discrete modelling approach described in this chapter is illustrated and reinforced using small numerical examples, for which considerable simplification is obviously required. This chapter is devoted to specification issues. Section 3.1 describes the discrete choice modelling framework. In practice, the determinants of any individual's behaviour can never be known with certainty. A feature of the discrete hours approach is that the stochastics are introduced at the initial modelling stage in the utility function rather than in the derived labour supply model; measured utility differs from true utility as a result of measurement, optimisation and other errors. This generates a probability distribution over the set of hours available for work. Section 3.2 first provides a numerical example of the way in which such a probability distribution is generated, where the error terms follow a hypothetical discrete distribution. This is followed by a more detailed and formal examination of the error specification and its implications for the probability distribution of an individual's hours worked. In section 3.3, a flexible specification is introduced for the utility function. The final section of this chapter presents some conclusions.

3.1 The Basic Model

This section presents the utility maximisation framework and discusses the determination of the probability distribution of hours worked. Subsection 3.1.1 describes the discrete choice model, involving the introduction of a random term reflecting the difference between actual and measured utility for an individual. In contrast with a deterministic approach, this gives rise to a probability distribution of hours worked for each individual, as discussed in subsection 3.1.2. The measurement of labour supply elasticities in this framework is examined in subsection 3.1.3.

3.1.1 Utility Maximisation

Consider an individual with a set of measured characteristics, X. The individual (who faces a fixed gross wage rate) maximises utility by selecting the number of hours worked, h, subject to the constraint that only a discrete number of hours levels, h_i, $(i = 1, ..., n)$ are available for work. Utility is determined by the amount of leisure and net income, is increasing in both arguments, and is bounded by the time and budget constraints. That is, the amount of leisure per week cannot be more than the total amount of time available per week minus the hours of work. Total weekly income is restricted by the available amount of nonlabour and labour income. The latter is the individual's wage rate multiplied by hours worked. Instead of leisure, hours of work are often used as the argument in the utility function because labour supply is typically the key variable of interest in economics.

Most models implicitly allow for home production by assuming that leisure includes home production time. Few articles explicitly allow for home production given the measurement problems. Exceptions are, for example, Becker (1965), Wales and Woodland (1977), Kooreman and Kapteyn (1987), Apps (1994), and Apps and Rees (1996, 1997).

The utility associated with each hours level is denoted U_i^* and is a function of 'measured' utility $U(h_i|X)$ plus an error term, v_i, so that:

$$\begin{aligned} U_i^* &= U(h_i|X) + v_i \\ &= U_i + v_i \end{aligned} \tag{3.1}$$

Although utility is considered to be a function of net income and hours worked, it is not necessary here to refer to net income, since this is determined directly from the associated hours level and the wage and other characteristics of the individual. The term v_i arises from factors such as measurement errors concerning the variables in X, optimisation errors of the individual or the existence of unobserved preference characteristics. Any observation on h is associated with a set of possible draws of the n random variables v_i from their respective distributions. Within this framework, there exists a probability distribution over available hours levels that is influenced by the properties of the v_i. Without these error terms, the model would be deterministic and knowledge of the form of U and the vector X would be sufficient to determine the precise utility-maximising choice of hours level.

The issue considered here is how to generate the probability distribution for labour supply, $p(h = h_i) = p_i$, for $i = 1, ..., n$, given assumptions about the distributions v_i. In the next sections, emphasis is given to the case where the errors are independent and identically distributed.

3.1.2 Probability Distributions

The framework summarised by equation (3.1) involves a distribution of utility for each discrete hours level, depending on the distributions of the v_i. Suppose for convenience that there are only three hours points. The three probability density functions of U_i^*, for $i = 1, 2, 3$, are shown in Figure 3.1, where in each case increasing utility involves moving upwards along each vertical axis. The horizontal axis measures relative frequency. The choice of any particular hours level is associated with draws from these three distributions, where the hours level producing the highest U_i^* is chosen.

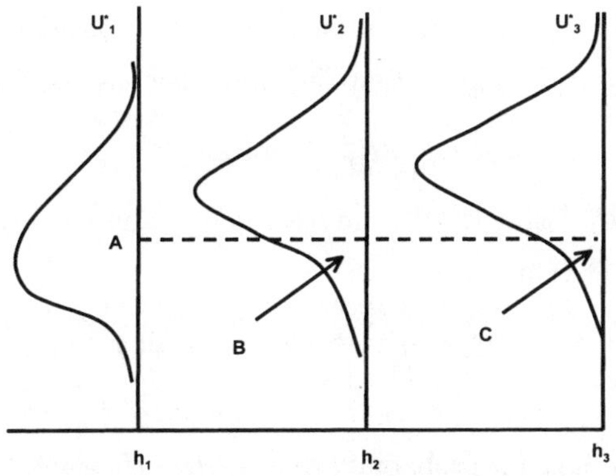

Figure 3.1: Utility Distributions at Three Hours Levels

Consider the probability that hours level h_1 is chosen, given that the value $U_1^* = A$ has been selected from the distribution of U_1^*. This can only be chosen if it is higher than the values of U_2^* and U_3^* selected from their respective distributions. From Figure 3.1, the probability that $U_2^* < A$ is given by the area B. Similarly the probability that $U_3^* < A$ is the area C. The joint probability that h_1 is chosen, given the selection of $U_1^* = A$, is the probability that $U_2^* < A$ **and** $U_3^* < A$. If the draws from the distributions are independent, this probability is the product, BC, of the two areas. The standard rule for independent probabilities is that $P(A \text{ and } B) = P(A)\,P(B)$.

This relates only to one draw, of $U_1^* = A$, from the distribution of U_1^*. It is necessary to consider the overall probability of h_1 being chosen. This is obtained by adding together all the conditional probabilities, for all possible values of U_1^*. The appropriate combination of probabilities here follows the general rule that $P(A \text{ or } B) = P(A) + P(B)$. Even for the higher values of U_1^*, Figure 3.1 suggests that the conditional probabilities of h_1 being selected would in most cases be low. Overall, the probability of h_1 producing maximum utility is small compared with the probability of h_2 or h_3 producing maximum utility.

To explain the above procedure more formally, consider the hours level, i. Utility maximisation implies that this hours level is chosen if:

$$U_i^* \geq U_j^* \qquad \text{for all } j \tag{3.2}$$

Substituting for U_i^*, using (8.29), and rearranging, this condition is equivalent to the requirement that:

$$v_j \leq v_i + U_i - U_j \qquad \text{for all } j \tag{3.3}$$

Hence for any given value of v_i, the probability of U_i^* exceeding all other values is equal to the joint probability that $v_i+U_i-U_1 \geq v_1$ and $v_i+U_i-U_2 \geq v_2$ and so on for all j. If the various distributions are independent, this joint probability is the product of the separate probabilities, $P\left(v_j \leq v_i + U_i - U_j\right)$. Therefore, for any given value of v_i, the probability that hours level i produces maximum utility is equal to:

$$\prod_{j \neq i} P\left(v_j \leq v_i + U_i - U_j\right) \tag{3.4}$$

This is the conditional probability, for a given value of v_i. The overall probability is found by aggregating terms like (3.4) over all possible values of v_i. The analysis of this problem is considerably simplified by assuming that the form of the distribution of v_i for each i is the same. An example is given in the next section, and this is followed by a more detailed and analytical treatment of the error specification. First, it is necessary to consider the concept of the wage elasticity of labour supply in the discrete hours context.

3.1.3 Labour Supply Elasticities

The structural basis of the discrete model means that there is no explicit labour supply function which depends directly on wage and other characteristics of the individual.[1] The estimated parameters are those of the utility

[1]This contrasts with the continuous hours approach where a supply function arises from utility maximisation subject to the budget constraint. However, the need to be able to move between utility and labour supply functions in continuous hours microsimulation places a severe restriction on the range of functions used.

function, which determine labour supply in terms of a distribution of hours worked. This raises the question of how the concept of the (uncompensated) wage elasticity of labour supply can be applied in the discrete hours context.

An elasticity measure may be based on expected hours worked. Consider an individual with known characteristics, including the hourly wage and the net incomes associated with each hours point, from which the probabilities of being at each of the discrete hours points can be calculated, as shown in more detail in section 3.2. Using these probabilities the expected value of labour supply can be computed. Next, the individual's gross wage is increased by a small amount, keeping all other characteristics the same, and the new expected labour supply is calculated. An elasticity can be produced by dividing the percentage change in expected labour supply by the imposed percentage change in the wage. Such elasticities in general vary according to the initial wage rate and the individual's characteristics, as well as the net incomes at the hours points, which are determined by the tax and benefit system.

In some models with more complex error specifications (as discussed in section 4.4), it is not possible to determine the probabilities analytically. However, a simulation approach can be taken. Values from the relevant error distributions are drawn for all labour supply points, after which the optimal choice of labour supply can be determined by finding the highest U^*. If this process is repeated several times the distribution of labour supply for a particular individual can be determined by counting the number of times each discrete point is the optimal point. Given the probabilities at each of the discrete hours points, the expected value of labour supply can be calculated and the process of deriving wage elasticities is then the same as described above.

A variation on this approach uses the individual's observed hours at the actual wage rather than the expected hours.

3.2 Hours Probabilities

This section shows how the probability distribution of an individual's hours of work is derived, first using a simple hypothetical numerical example in subsection 3.2.1, followed by a more general derivation in subsection 3.2.2 and the use of a specific error distribution in subsection 3.2.3.

3.2.1 A Numerical Example

Suppose for the purposes of this example that v takes only discrete values, a_k, for $k = 1, ..., K$. In general, let $f(a_k)$ denote the proportion of values equal to a_k and let $F(a_k)$ denote the proportion less than or equal to a_k. The value of p_i (the probability of h_i producing the highest utility) is thus obtained as the addition of terms corresponding to (3.4):

$$p_i = \sum_{k=1}^{K} \left\{ \prod_{j \neq i} F(a_k + U_i - U_j) \right\} f(a_k) \tag{3.5}$$

Consider a situation in which there are just four levels of labour supply available, so that $n = 4$. The values of U_i associated with each hours level, h_1 to h_4, are respectively 5, 7.5, 10 and 9. For the purpose of this example for a single individual, it is not necessary to specify either the form of the function, U, or the precise discrete hours levels. Clearly, without the stochastic component of utility, h_3 would be chosen.

Suppose that all values for v are drawn independently from the same discrete distribution with four possible outcomes, so $K = 4$, and let v take the values shown in Table 3.1. In this hypothetical example the arithmetic mean value of v is non-zero.

The selection of an hours level is, as explained in section 3.1, associated in this case with the random draws from the four distributions, each identical to the one shown in Table 3.1. For example, a set of random values for v_1 to v_4 may be, say, 2, 0, -2 and 2 respectively. These give rise to utilities, U_i^*, of

Table 3.1: Hypothetical Discrete Distribution of the Error Term

k	1	2	3	4
a_k	−2.0	0.0	2.0	3.5
$f(a_k)$	0.1	0.3	0.4	0.2
$F(a_k)$	0.1	0.4	0.8	1.0

7, 7.5, 8, and 11 for the hours levels h_1 to h_4 respectively. Hence h_4 is chosen in this case. Given a draw of -2 from the distribution of v_3, the option h_4 can dominate h_3 (that is, $U_4^* > U_3^*$) if v_4 takes either of the values 0, 2 or 3.5. The conditional probability of h_4 dominating, given this selection from v_3, is thus $0.3 + 0.4 + 0.2 = 0.9$, found by adding the relevant values of $f(v)$ in Table 3.1. The enumeration of all possible combinations of this type is most efficiently carried out following the approach underlying equation (3.5).

Consider the probability of selecting hours level h_3. The relevant values are shown in Table 3.2. The second column, headed $U_3 - U_j$, shows the differences in the values of U; these are all positive, as hours level 3 has, by assumption, the highest value of U. The column headed $k = 1$ relates to the values and probabilities when a_1 is drawn for v_3. The first row shows that when $k = 1$, that is when $v_3 = a_1 = -2$, the term v_1 must be less than $a_1 + U_3 - U_1 = 3$ in order to ensure that hours level 3 has a higher value of U^*. From the assumed distribution in Table 3.1, there is a probability of 0.8 that v is less than 3. This is shown in the second row of Table 3.2. Similarly, when $k = 1$, hours level h_3 gives higher utility than h_4 only if $v_4 < -1$; this has a probability of 0.1.

The conditional probability that h_3 is chosen, when $v_3 = -2$, is therefore $(0.8)(0.4)(0.1) = 0.032$. The final column of Table 3.2 shows that when $k = 4$, so that $v_3 = a_4 = 3.5$, hours level 3 always dominates and the conditional probability of it being chosen is 1. The overall probability p_3 is

Table 3.2: Conditional Probabilities for Hours Level 3

j	$U_3 - U_j$		$k=1$	$k=2$	$k=3$	$k=4$
1	5	$a_k + U_3 - U_1$	3	5	7	8.5
		$F(a_k + U_3 - U_1)$	0.8	1	1	1
2	2.5	$a_k + U_3 - U_2$	0.5	2.5	4.5	6
		$F(a_k + U_3 - U_2)$	0.4	0.8	1	1
4	1	$a_k + U_3 - U_4$	−1	1	3	4.5
		$F(a_k + U_3 - U_4)$	0.1	0.4	0.8	1
Conditional probability that $U_3^* > U_1^*$ and $U_3^* > U_2^*$ and $U_3^* > U_4^*$			0.032	0.320	0.800	1.0

thus given by:

$$\begin{aligned} p_3 &= \sum_{\substack{k=1\\k\neq 3}}^{4} P(U_3^* > U_j^*, \text{for all } j \neq 3 \mid v_3 = a_k)\, p(v_3 = a_k) \\ &= \sum_{\substack{k=1\\k\neq 3}}^{4} \left(\prod_{j\neq 3} F(a_k + U_3 - U_j) \right) f(a_k) \\ &= (0.032)(0.1) + (0.32)(0.3) + (0.80)(0.4) + (1.0)(0.2) \\ &= 0.619 \end{aligned} \tag{3.6}$$

Similar calculations show that $p_1 = 0.003$, $p_2 = 0.080$ and $p_4 = 0.298$. The resulting probability distribution of hours clearly depends in a complex way on the distribution of the error term.

This example has been constructed in order to illustrate the way in which the hours distribution for an individual is derived from the underlying stochastic specification and utility levels. In practice more structure has to be imposed by specifying a precise form for the error distribution, $f(v)$.

3.2.2 Specification of a Continuous Error Distribution

This subsection defines the general probability of hours worked for a continuous specification of the error distribution $f(v)$. The discrete error distribution in the previous section was used only for illustrative purposes, and it is first necessary to restate the problem where v is considered to be a continuous random variable. Hence, $f(v)$ and $F(v)$ are now the density and distribution functions respectively of v. It is possible to convert the result in equation (3.5) into the following form for continuous v, remembering that hours continue to be discrete:

$$p_i = \int_{-\infty}^{+\infty} \left\{ \prod_{j \neq i} F(v_i + U_i - U_j) \right\} f(v_i)\, dv_i \tag{3.7}$$

The expression in (3.7) takes all the possible conditional probabilities, represented by $\prod_{j \neq i} F(v_i + U_i - U_j)$, and integrates v_i out to obtain the required marginal distribution p_i. Given that the conditional probabilities require the product of distribution functions, $F(.)$, it cannot be expected that an arbitrary choice of $f(v)$ would be tractable. A special case using a continuous distribution is examined in the next subsection, which is necessarily more technical than the previous discussion.

3.2.3 A Special Case: The Extreme Value Distribution

This subsection considers a special case generating a highly convenient form for the hours distribution.

Suppose the distribution of v is described by the following density function:

$$\begin{aligned} f(v) &= e^{-v} e^{-e^{-v}} \\ &= \exp\left(-v - e^{-v}\right) \end{aligned} \tag{3.8}$$

for which the distribution function is:

$$F(v) = e^{-e^{-v}} \tag{3.9}$$

The choice of this thin-tailed distribution has the obvious advantage that no further parameters need to be estimated.[2] This is known as an Extreme

[2] If, instead of the additive form used here, the multiplicative form $U_i^* = U_i v_i$ were adopted, with $f(v) = \frac{1}{v} \exp\left(-\frac{1}{v}\right)$, equivalent results would be obtained, as can be seen by taking logarithms and transforming the distribution.

(Maximum) Value Type I distribution, often abbreviated simply to 'extreme value' distribution. This is because it has been found useful in many applications involving extreme values. If a process which generates values for a variable is observed over a period and the maximum value observed is set equal to x, the resulting distribution of x can often be described by the above form. The more general form is $f(x) = \frac{1}{\beta}\exp\left(-\frac{x-\mu}{\beta}\right)\exp\left(-e^{-\frac{x-\mu}{\beta}}\right)$. The standardised form therefore has $\mu = 0$ and $\beta = 1$. This distribution is also referred to as a Gumbel, or double exponential, or Fisher–Tippett Type I distribution. There is a corresponding extreme minimum value distribution. It is highly tractable in the present context. These qualities have generally been taken as sufficient justification for its use, though section 4.4 briefly discusses some alternatives.

The arithmetic mean of this distribution is non-zero, being equal to 0.5772 (Euler's number); the mode is zero and the median is $-\ln(\ln 2)$. The shape of the distribution is illustrated in Figures 3.2 and 3.3, showing the density and distribution functions respectively. In Figure 3.3, the distribution function used in the numerical example of section 3.2.1 is shown for comparison: this is obviously a step function for the discrete distribution.

Substitution into $\left[\prod_{j\neq i} F(v_i + U_i - U_j)\right] f(v_i)$ gives:

$$\exp\left(-v_i - e^{-v_i}\right)\prod_{j\neq i}\exp\left(-e^{-v_i}e^{-U_i+U_j}\right) \tag{3.10}$$

Noting that the logarithm of $\prod_{j\neq i}\exp\left(-e^{-v_i}e^{-U_i+U_j}\right)$ can be expressed as $-e^{-v_i}\sum_{j\neq i}e^{-U_i+U_j} = -e^{-v_i}e^{-U_i}\sum_{j\neq i}e^{U_j}$, and using $x = \exp(\log x)$, the expression in (3.10) becomes:

$$\exp\left[-v_i - e^{-v_i}\left(1 + e^{-U_i}\sum_{j\neq i}e^{U_j}\right)\right] \tag{3.11}$$

Furthermore:

$$\begin{aligned} 1 + e^{-U_i}\sum_{j\neq i}e^{U_j} &= e^{U_i}e^{-U_i} + e^{-U_i}\sum_{j\neq i}e^{U_j} = e^{-U_i}\sum_{j=1}^{n}e^{U_j} \\ &= e^{\lambda_i} \end{aligned} \tag{3.12}$$

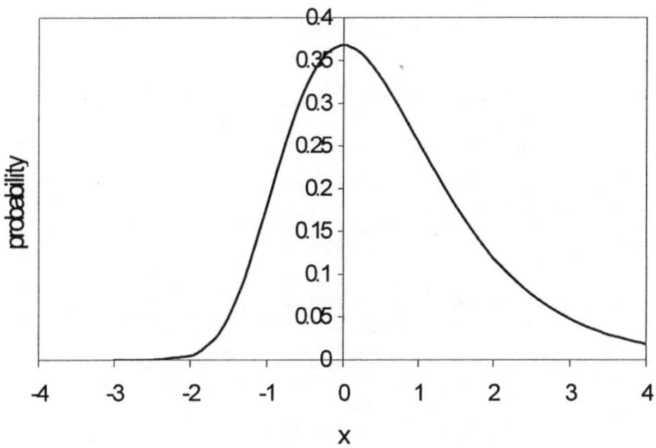

Figure 3.2: Extreme Value Probability Density Function

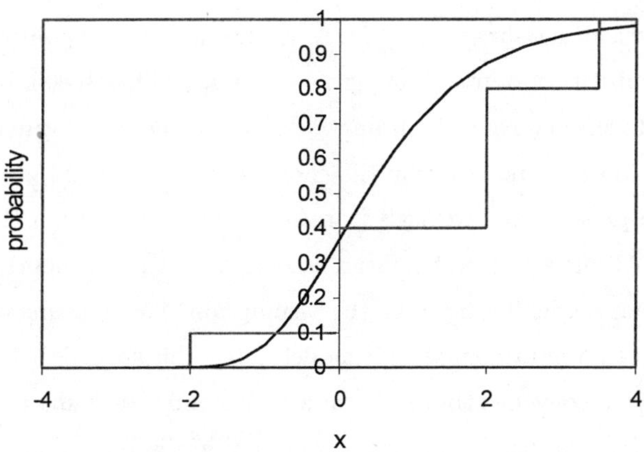

Figure 3.3: Extreme Value Cumulative Distribution Function and the Discrete Distribution from Table 3.1

Hence (3.11) can be rewritten more succinctly as $\exp\left[-v_i - e^{-(v_i-\lambda_i)}\right]$. Thus:

$$p_i = \int_{-\infty}^{+\infty} \exp\left[-v_i - e^{-(v_i-\lambda_i)}\right] dv_i \tag{3.13}$$

Further simplification is achieved using the transformation, $v_i' = v_i - \lambda_i$, so that $v_i = v_i' + \lambda_i$ and $dv_i = dv_i'$, whereby:

$$\begin{aligned} p_i &= \int_{-\infty}^{+\infty} \exp\left[-v_i' - \lambda_i - e^{-v_i'}\right] dv_i' \\ &= e^{-\lambda_i} \int_{-\infty}^{+\infty} \exp\left[-v_i' - e^{-v_i'}\right] dv_i' \\ &= e^{-\lambda_i} \int_{-\infty}^{+\infty} f\left(v_i'\right) dv_i' \\ &= e^{-\lambda_i} \\ &= \frac{e^{U_i}}{\sum_{j=1}^{n} e^{U_j}} \end{aligned} \tag{3.14}$$

In this special case, the probability distribution of hours of work for an individual depends in a convenient way on the measured utility levels associated with each hours level. For the numerical example considered earlier, the hypothetical measured utility levels for the four hours points are 5, 7.5, 10 and 9. Substitution into (3.14) gives the probabilities 0.005, 0.056, 0.686 and 0.253. In the deterministic framework, monotonic transformations of the utility function have no effect on the choice of optimal hours worked. However, in the present context such transformations (other than the addition of a constant) affect the probabilities associated with each hours level. The discrete choice model flowing from the assumption of an extreme value distribution is called a multinomial logit model. Thus this special distribution for the error terms conveniently results in a multinomial logit model for utility. This type of model has been used extensively in discrete choice modelling. More on the logit model and alternative discrete choice models can be found in Maddala (1983).

3.3 Specification of the Utility Function

An advantage of the discrete hours framework, in contrast to the continuous approach, is that it can be applied to any legitimate direct utility function, offering considerable flexibility in the form of utility function that can be used. For the moment, utility is assumed to be independent of an individual's characteristics except for hours worked, wage and other income. Appropriate allowance for dependence on characteristics is discussed in chapter 4. In this section, all individuals have the same utility function with the same parameters. This does not mean that all individuals are expected to have the same optimal level of hours. First, people with different wage levels have different levels of income at the hours points and so optimal hours are located at different points. Second, the error term v which is added to the utility, as described in section 3.1.1, introduces random differences in utility caused by unobserved factors.

Suppose the utility functions take the simple linear form:

$$U = \beta_h h + \beta_y y \tag{3.15}$$

This implies that the marginal utility of net income is constant and equal to β_y and the marginal utility of hours worked is constant and equal to β_h. The latter coefficient is expected to be negative. For each individual, the chosen hours point is observed and the value of y for each discrete labour supply point h can be calculated, given information on the gross wage of each individual and knowledge of the tax and transfer system.

This linear form is obviously highly restrictive. The assumption of constant marginal utilities is implausible and in empirical applications, utility functions usually allow for diminishing marginal utility. A popular choice in applied work is the quadratic utility function:

$$U = \beta_y y + \beta_h h + \alpha_y y^2 + \alpha_h h^2 + \alpha_{yh} yh \tag{3.16}$$

where the marginal utility of income is:

$$\frac{\partial U}{\partial y} = \beta_y + 2\alpha_y y + \alpha_{yh} h \tag{3.17}$$

For example, Keane and Moffitt (1998) have used this specification. An alternative is the translog specification in which the arguments of utility are income and leisure ($l = T - h$), rather than income and hours worked:

$$U = \beta_y \ln y + \beta_l \ln(T-h) + \alpha_y (\ln y)^2 + \alpha_l (\ln(T-h))^2 + \alpha_{yl} \ln y \ln(T-h) \tag{3.18}$$

where the marginal utility of income is:

$$\frac{\partial U}{\partial y} = \frac{\beta_y + 2\alpha_y \ln y + \alpha_{yl} \ln(T-h)}{y} \tag{3.19}$$

This specification was used by, for example, Van Soest (1995).

Both specifications allow for diminishing returns through the quadratic terms. Thus if α_y is negative the marginal utility of income decreases with the amount of income. Furthermore the cross-product term allows for complementarity between income and leisure, when α_{yh} is negative or α_{yl} is positive, or substitutability, when α_{yh} is positive or α_{yl} is negative. For example, the value of income may decrease if less leisure time is available; that is extra income may be appreciated less if there is no time for consumption.

Neither the translog nor the quadratic utility function is automatically quasi-concave across the full range of possible parameter values. This is not a problem as long as the optimal parameter values result in a utility function that is quasi-concave in the observed labour supply points. This contrasts with continuous hours labour supply modelling, where the necessary restriction of the parameter space may bias substitution effects upwards and income effects downwards, and which in addition is cumbersome in maximum likelihood estimation; as explained in MaCurdy, Green and Paarsch (1990). In discrete hours labour supply modelling, it is sufficient to check for quasi-concavity after estimation, which involves two necessary conditions, discussed by Van Soest (1995). The first is the basic requirement that utility increases with income. The second condition is more complicated but straightforward to check.

The quadratic and translog utility functions can both be easily extended to allow for households consisting of couples, where both partners simultaneously determine labour supply. This is achieved by assuming that the couple maximises one utility function, which seems a reasonable assumption for households where the members pool their incomes. However, a common criticism of this type of model is that the assumption of one common utility function for the household as a whole is not realistic. Unfortunately, alternatives using bargaining models and other types of non-unitary collective models require detailed data and their own set of assumptions which are needed, for example, to divide consumption into shared and private goods or to construct a sharing rule for income. This approach was used in, for example, Chiappori (1988), Bourguignon and Chiappori (1994), Browning *et al.* (1994), Apps and Rees (1997) and Blundell *et al.* (2001). Such models need to be simplified in other areas. As a result, researchers who focus on tax and benefit policy issues and are interested in incorporating the full detail of tax and benefit systems have mostly chosen unitary utility functions.

The quadratic utility function for a couple can be written as:

$$\begin{aligned} U &= \beta_y y + \beta_m h_m + \beta_f h_f + \alpha_y y^2 + \alpha_m h_m^2 + \alpha_f h_f^2 \\ &\quad + \alpha_{ym} y h_m + \alpha_{yf} y h_f + \alpha_{fm} h_f h_m \end{aligned} \tag{3.20}$$

where the index m denotes hours and parameters of the male and the index f denotes hours and parameters of the female, and y represents joint income. The parameter α_{fm} indicates whether the male's and female's labour supply are complements or substitutes.

3.4 Conclusions

This chapter has provided an introduction to the specification of a basic discrete hours labour supply model to be used in microsimulation and has given several numerical examples to illustrate the more technical exposition of the methods used in this research field. The field is of course subject to continual development. For example, several extensions are occurring with regard to the specification of the different random error terms in the utility function, which are aimed at increasing the flexibility of the labour supply model. Alternative models relax the assumption of particular restrictive patterns in the variance–covariance matrices of the error terms in use, such as independence between the different labour supply choices. An increase in computing power has made some of these extensions feasible, although they are often still quite burdensome to carry out. These and other extensions are discussed in the next chapter.

Chapter 4

Estimation of Discrete Hours Models

The previous chapter examined the specification of the discrete choice model underlying an individual's labour supply behaviour. The basic assumption in the labour supply model is that individuals maximise utility, which depends on two arguments, income and hours of work. Utility is expected to increase with income and to decrease with hours of work (or increase with the complement of working hours, leisure and home production time). This chapter discusses how the model can be estimated with the help of data, using the maximum likelihood method. The extreme value error distribution, examined in detail in the previous chapter, is again used. The construction of the likelihood function is described in section 4.1 and its maximisation is considered in section 4.2. An advantage of the discrete hours framework, in contrast to the continuous approach, is that it can be applied to any legitimate direct utility function. Hence no explicit assumption about utility functions is made when discussing estimation.

A numerical example of estimation, based on a very simple utility function, is given in section 4.3. Alternative specifications of the basic discrete hours model are discussed in section 4.4, followed by alternative error distributions in section 4.5. Section 4.6 concludes.

4.1 The Likelihood Function

The notation used in the previous chapter did not need to distinguish between individuals, since only a single individual was examined. However, estimation uses information from a cross-section of individuals. Suppose there are M individuals and the index k is used to refer to individuals $k = 1, ..., M$. There are, as before, n discrete hours levels h_i, for $i = 1, ..., n$. It is first necessary to indicate the optimal hours level for the kth person; denote this by h_{i_k}, so that i_k indicates the chosen value of i (the hours index) for person k. The probability of selecting this hours level is p_{i_k} and the corresponding optimal utility level is $U^*_{i_k,k}$. All other utility levels (associated with other hours levels) are denoted $U^*_{j,k}$ for $j = 1, ..., n$.

Using this notation:

$$p_{i_k} = P\left(U^*_{i_k,k} \geq U^*_{j,k} \text{ for all } j\right) \tag{4.1}$$

Thus when all v_i are assumed to follow the extreme value distribution discussed in section 3.2.3, the probability associated with the optimal hours chosen by person k is expressed as:

$$p_{i_k} = \frac{e^{U_{i_k,k}}}{\sum_{j=1}^{n} e^{U_{j,k}}} \tag{4.2}$$

The joint probability that individual 1 selects h_{i_1} **and** individual 2 selects h_{i_2} **and** individual 3 selects h_{i_3} and so on, is given, assuming that the decisions are made independently, by the product:

$$P(h_{i_1}, ..., h_{i_M}) = p_{i_1} p_{i_2} ... p_{i_M} = \prod_{k=1}^{M} \frac{e^{U_{i_k,k}}}{\sum_{j=1}^{n} e^{U_{j,k}}} \tag{4.3}$$

This joint probability concerns the probability of the set of hours levels, h_{i_k} for $k = 1, ..., M$, being chosen by the M individuals, given their preferences and other personal characteristics, and assuming that all v follow identical extreme value distributions.

Researchers do not know the parameters of the assumed form of preference functions, but have information about the hours worked by each individual in a random sample taken from the population. In addition, data are available on personal characteristics and net incomes of each individual at each discrete hours point. The net incomes are not observed directly but are obtained from knowledge of each individual's wage rate and the details of the tax and transfer system. The taxation and benefit rules are applied to the gross income of each individual at each of the discrete points to obtain the associated net income. Depending on the complexity of the rules and the data available, it may not be possible to include all benefits. Furthermore, the wage rates of those who are not in employment at the time of the survey cannot be observed, so it is necessary to impute wage rates for non-workers using estimated wage functions. An alternative is to estimate a joint wage and labour supply model; see, for example, Gerfin (1993).

The probability in (4.3) can be viewed from another perspective. Given an assumption about the general form of the utility functions, it is possible to find parameter values that, if true, would produce the highest probability of observing the actual hours values. The expression in (4.3) is reinterpreted as being a function of the unknown parameter values, for a given set of observed hours. Since the framework is one in which a particular true set of parameters is assumed to exist, and any variations are attributed to sampling variations, it is not appropriate, when discussing the function in terms of parameters, to refer to a probability of parameters taking particular values. Rather, it is correct to refer to the probability of observing this particular sample of individuals (with their combinations of characteristics and hours worked) conditional on the parameter values. Suppose that each individual's utility function depends on a vector of coefficients β, with elements β_ℓ, for

$\ell = 1, ..., S$. The probability statement in (4.3) can be rewritten as:

$$L(\beta_1, ..., \beta_S) = \prod_{k=1}^{M} \frac{e^{U_{i_k,k}}}{\sum_{j=1}^{n} e^{U_{j,k}}} \tag{4.4}$$

where $L(\beta_1, ..., \beta_S)$, a function of the unknown parameters (for a given sample of individuals for whom hours worked are observed), is referred to as the likelihood function. Here the fixed parameters are effectively treated as if they were variables. The estimates, $\widehat{\beta}_1, ..., \widehat{\beta}_S$, produced by finding values for $\beta_1, ..., \beta_S$ that maximise the value of this function, are referred to as maximum likelihood estimates.

Taking logarithms gives the log-likelihood for this model:

$$\log L = \sum_{k=1}^{M} \left[U_{i_k,k} - \log \left(\sum_{j=1}^{n} e^{U_{j,k}} \right) \right] \tag{4.5}$$

This monotonic transformation does not affect the maximum likelihood estimates but, by converting products into sums, makes analysis much easier.

4.2 Maximum Likelihood Estimation

The log-likelihood is maximised when the following first-order conditions are satisfied:

$$\frac{\partial \log L}{\partial \beta_\ell} = 0 \text{ for all } \ell = 1, ..., S \tag{4.6}$$

The second-order sufficient conditions for the solution to represent a maximum are not examined here. Remembering that $\partial \log x / \partial x = 1/x$, and using the function of a function rule, differentiation of (4.5) gives:

$$\begin{aligned} \frac{\partial \log L}{\partial \beta_\ell} &= \sum_{k=1}^{M} \left[\frac{\partial U_{i_k,k}}{\partial \beta_\ell} - \left(\frac{1}{\sum_{j=1}^{n} e^{U_{j,k}}} \right) \sum_{j=1}^{n} \frac{\partial e^{U_{j,k}}}{\partial \beta_\ell} \right] \\ &= \sum_{k=1}^{M} \left[\frac{\partial U_{i_k,k}}{\partial \beta_\ell} - \sum_{j=1}^{n} \left(\frac{e^{U_{j,k}}}{\sum_{j=1}^{n} e^{U_{j,k}}} \right) \frac{\partial U_{j,k}}{\partial \beta_\ell} \right] \end{aligned} \tag{4.7}$$

In considering the terms in (4.7) it should be remembered that, even if every individual has the same general form of utility function, the individual utilities depend on the personal characteristics in X.

Using (4.6) and (4.7), to rewrite the first-order conditions, gives for all ℓ:

$$\sum_{k=1}^{M}\left[\frac{\partial U_{i_k,k}}{\partial \beta_\ell} - \sum_{j=1}^{n} p_{j,k}\frac{\partial U_{j,k}}{\partial \beta_\ell}\right] = 0 \tag{4.8}$$

This has the interpretation that the aim of this method is to make the first derivatives of utility in the observed hours points on average equal to the weighted average of derivatives of utility over all possible hours points. The weights for each individual are equal to the probabilities of each discrete hours level. Although this is an interesting interpretation of the first-order conditions, it does not provide practical help in trying to solve the nonlinear set of equations.

The solution, giving the set of maximum likelihood estimates for all β_ℓs, can be obtained using numerical methods involving a sequence of iterations which lead efficiently from an arbitrary starting point to the solution. In particular, Newton's method involves repeatedly solving the following matrix equation, where $\beta^{[I]}$ denotes the vector of parameters in the Ith iteration:

$$\beta^{[I+1]} = \beta^{[I]} + \left[-\frac{\partial^2 \log L}{\partial \beta_\ell \partial \beta_s}\right]^{-1}_{\beta^{[I]}} \left[\frac{\partial \log L}{\partial \beta_\ell}\right]_{\beta^{[I]}} \tag{4.9}$$

and the first and second derivatives are evaluated using the parameters $\beta^{[I]}$. Furthermore, it can be shown that the inverse of the matrix of second derivatives at the final iteration provides an estimate of the variance–covariance matrix of parameter estimates. Further discussion of Newton's method, which is often used to solve nonlinear equations, can be found in Appendix A.

The application of Newton's method in the present context requires the second derivatives of the likelihood function. Differentiating (4.8) again with respect to parameter β_s, gives:

$$\frac{\partial^2 \log L}{\partial \beta_\ell \partial \beta_s} = \sum_{k=1}^{M} \left[\frac{\partial^2 U_{i_k,k}}{\partial \beta_\ell \partial \beta_s} - \sum_{j=1}^{n} \left\{ p_{j,k} \frac{\partial^2 U_{j,k}}{\partial \beta_\ell \partial \beta_s} + \frac{\partial U_{j,k}}{\partial \beta_\ell} \frac{\partial p_{j,k}}{\partial \beta_s} \right\} \right] \tag{4.10}$$

where:

$$\frac{\partial p_{j,k}}{\partial \beta_s} = p_{j,k} \left[\frac{\partial U_{j,k}}{\partial \beta_s} - \sum_{t=1}^{n} p_{t,k} \frac{\partial U_{t,k}}{\partial \beta_s} \right] \tag{4.11}$$

An example using this procedure is described in the following section.

4.3 A Numerical Example of Estimation

This section illustrates the application of the maximum likelihood method using a simple numerical example involving a linear form of utility function; see equation (3.15) in section 3.3. Although this example is obviously unrealistic as it has few individuals and a simple utility specification, the very simplicity helps to concentrate on the mechanics of the method: the general approach is no different in a more realistic empirical context. Utility is assumed to be independent of an individual's characteristics except for hours worked, wage and other income. Appropriate allowance for dependence on characteristics is discussed in section 4.4. Here, all individuals have the same utility function with the same parameters. This does not mean that all individuals are expected to have the same optimal level of hours. First, people with different wage levels have different levels of income at the hours points and so optimal hours are located at different points. Second, the error term v introduces random differences in utility caused by unobserved factors.

Suppose that there are only three individuals, whose details are shown in the top section of Table 4.1. There are just three hours levels available for work: 0, 20 and 40 hours, corresponding to not working at all, working part time and working full time respectively. The observed gross wage rates, conditional on the observed hours of work for each individual, give the gross income shown in the final column. In this example, the individual with the highest wage rate works longer hours. If allowance were made for other characteristics, unobserved heterogeneity, and measurement or optimisation errors, an economic model could be derived where this does not always need to be the case. Some low-wage individuals may prefer long hours, and some high-wage individuals may prefer shorter hours, depending on their characteristics.

Table 4.1: Three Individuals and Three Hours Levels

Person	Gross wage	Chosen hours	Gross income
1	4	0	0
2	8	20	160
3	10	40	400
Incomes at alternative hours			
		Hours	Income
1	4	20	80
	4	40	160
2	8	0	0
	8	40	320
3	10	0	0
	10	20	200

Assuming for simplicity that there are no income taxes or benefit payments, the net income is simply equal to gross income. Estimation requires information about the net incomes at all the possible hours levels for each individual. In the present example the required values are easily obtained, as shown in the lower section of Table 4.1. Where there is a complex tax and transfer system, the required net incomes are obtained by applying the rules of the system, along with an assumption regarding the take-up of benefits, at each hours level.

The simplified form of utility function in (3.15) means that the required derivatives of U with respect to parameters are easy to evaluate, given that $\partial U/\partial \beta_h = h$ and $\partial U/\partial \beta_y = y$. Appropriate substitution of these values, along with values from Table 4.1, into the first-order conditions in (4.8) gives:[1]

$$\begin{aligned}\left[\frac{\partial \ln L}{\partial \beta_h}\right]_{\widehat{\beta}} &= 0 - \frac{20\exp(\widehat{\beta}_h 20 + \widehat{\beta}_y 80) + 40\exp(\widehat{\beta}_h 40 + \widehat{\beta}_y 160)}{1 + \exp(\widehat{\beta}_h 20 + \widehat{\beta}_y 80) + \exp(\widehat{\beta}_h 40 + \widehat{\beta}_y 160)} \\ &\quad +20 - \frac{20\exp(\widehat{\beta}_h 20 + \widehat{\beta}_y 160) + 40\exp(\widehat{\beta}_h 40 + \widehat{\beta}_y 320)}{1 + \exp(\widehat{\beta}_h 20 + \widehat{\beta}_y 160) + \exp(\widehat{\beta}_h 40 + \widehat{\beta}_y 320)} \\ &\quad +40 - \frac{20\exp(\widehat{\beta}_h 20 + \widehat{\beta}_y 200) + 40\exp(\widehat{\beta}_h 40 + \widehat{\beta}_y 400)}{1 + \exp(\widehat{\beta}_h 20 + \widehat{\beta}_y 200) + \exp(\widehat{\beta}_h 40 + \widehat{\beta}_y 400)} \\ &= 0 \end{aligned} \tag{4.12}$$

$$\begin{aligned}\left[\frac{\partial \ln L}{\partial \beta_y}\right]_{\widehat{\beta}} &= 0 - \frac{80\exp(\widehat{\beta}_h 20 + \widehat{\beta}_y 80) + 160\exp(\widehat{\beta}_h 40 + \widehat{\beta}_y 160)}{1 + \exp(\widehat{\beta}_h 20 + \widehat{\beta}_y 80) + \exp(\widehat{\beta}_h 40 + \widehat{\beta}_y 160)} \\ &\quad +160 - \frac{160\exp(\widehat{\beta}_h 20 + \widehat{\beta}_y 160) + 320\exp(\widehat{\beta}_h 40 + \widehat{\beta}_y 320)}{1 + \exp(\widehat{\beta}_h 20 + \widehat{\beta}_y 160) + \exp(\widehat{\beta}_h 40 + \widehat{\beta}_y 320)} \\ &\quad +400 - \frac{200\exp(\widehat{\beta}_h 20 + \widehat{\beta}_y 200) + 400\exp(\widehat{\beta}_h 40 + \widehat{\beta}_y 400)}{1 + \exp(\widehat{\beta}_h 20 + \widehat{\beta}_y 200) + \exp(\widehat{\beta}_h 40 + \widehat{\beta}_y 400)} \\ &= 0 \end{aligned} \tag{4.13}$$

The result is two nonlinear equations in the two unknowns $\widehat{\beta}_y$ and $\widehat{\beta}_h$. Using an iterative solution procedure, as described in section 4.2, the maximum likelihood estimates were found to be $\widehat{\beta}_h = -15.41$ and $\widehat{\beta}_y = 1.93$. The iterative process was started from a value of 0.01 for both parameters. The only prerequisite for starting values is that the function is defined for those values. When dealing with exponentials, as in this example, large starting values are not recommended because of potential overflow problems. No standard deviations are calculated given that the example consists of three individuals only; the matrix of second derivatives is poorly conditioned.

[1] This specification for v automatically takes care of the scaling of utility, because $\frac{\exp(U_1)}{\exp(U_1)+\exp(U_2)} \neq \frac{\exp(aU_1)}{\exp(aU_1)+\exp(aU_2)}$. Therefore no normalisation is needed when using this approach.

Consider the wage elasticity of labour supply for person 2, defined as in subsection 3.1.3 in terms of changes in expected hours. At the observed wage level, the hours and corresponding net incomes (equal to gross incomes since by assumption there are no taxes in this example) in Table 4.1 are used, with the parameter estimates, to obtain the utilities corresponding to each hours point, by appropriate substitution in $U_{i2} = \widehat{\beta}_h h_i + \widehat{\beta}_y y_{i2}$. From these, the probabilities of being at each of the labour supply points are given by $p_{i2} = \exp(U_{i2})/\sum_j \exp(U_{j2})$ and expected labour supply $E(h(2))$ is calculated using $E(h(2)) = \sum_i p_{i2} h_i$. In this example $E(h(2)) = 0.16 \times 0 + 0.30 \times 20 + 0.54 \times 40 = 27.6$.

After increasing the wage by 1 per cent, new net incomes and hence new utilities for each discrete hours point are obtained. Using the resulting new probabilities, expected hours are found to be 39.5. This implies an elasticity of 43. In this simplified example, with just three individuals, two positive hours levels and linear utility, a small change in the wage rate for this individual leads to a very high probability of working for 40 hours. In practice, given the substantial heterogeneity in populations, considerable differences in individual elasticities are typically found. Studies based on continuous hours models typically report only a single elasticity evaluated at the sample averages of relevant variables, so care should be taken in making comparisons.

4.4 Alternative Specifications

This section presents a number of alternative specifications of the basic model discussed in the previous sections and in chapter 3. The discussion in this section is meant as an overview only and provides much less detail than the discussion of the basic model. However, the basic approach to estimation remains similar for several of these alternative specifications.

In this section, the quadratic utility function presented in section 3.3 is taken as the starting point in the first two subsections. First, allowance for participation in welfare programmes, often described in terms of the take-up of benefits, is examined in subsection 4.4.1. Alternative ways in which allowance may be made for individuals' personal characteristics are discussed in subsection 4.4.2. The effect of differences in the particular discrete hours points being offered to individuals or the relative attractiveness of different hours points is described in subsection 4.4.3. The final subsection discusses the important issue of childcare costs.

4.4.1 Welfare Participation

The standard utility function, discussed in chapter 3, can be extended through addition of a term for welfare participation, or benefit take-up, following Moffitt (1983). The choice between discrete labour supply points is then extended to a choice between discrete labour supply points with and without welfare participation, whenever relevant. It is expected that disutility is attached to participation in welfare programmes, which could be caused for example by the costs of applying for benefits. These could be pecuniary costs or non-pecuniary costs, such as the time needed to travel to a social security office, or by a psychological effect, where people on welfare feel stigmatised. The latter explanation is more likely to be important when participation in welfare is clearly noticeable to the outside world, such as through payment in shops with Food Stamps in the U.S.

A simple way of adding welfare participation to the utility function is through the addition of a dummy variable for participation. Examples of this approach can be found in Fraker and Moffitt (1988), Hoynes (1996), Hagstrom (1996), Smith (1997), Keane and Moffitt (1998) and Kalb (1999, 2000). Let $d_w = 1$ if the person participates and $d_w = 0$ if the individual does not take up the benefit, even if entitled to it. The coefficient on this variable indicates the disutility associated with participation in welfare; that is, a larger negative value indicates greater disutility. For the quadratic utility function, the specification is therefore:

$$U = \beta_y y + \beta_h h + \alpha_y y^2 + \alpha_h h^2 + \alpha_{yh} yh + \phi d_w \tag{4.14}$$

The participation parameter can be made dependent on individual characteristics in the same way as for the preferences for work or income. This is described in the following subsection.

An alternative approach is to estimate an unordered model of moving from one choice to another, where the amount of labour supply and participation in the welfare programme jointly determine choice. In this specification there is no explicit welfare participation parameter, but the gain in utility from a choice with welfare participation compared with a choice without welfare participation can be determined conditional on the income gain associated with the move between these choices and other individual characteristics. Bingley and Walker (1997, 2001) estimated a three-point labour supply model where at all, some or none of the labour supply points there is the additional option of participation in a welfare programme.

4.4.2 Personal Characteristics

For simplicity of exposition, consider again the linear utility function:

$$U^* = \beta_h h + \beta_y y + v \tag{4.15}$$

The approach discussed in this section is straightforward to apply to the more flexible utility function presented in chapter 3. This can be extended to make the preference parameters dependent on personal and household characteristics, such as education, number and age of children or an individual's own age, which are likely to influence the preference for work and income. Including these characteristics in the preference for work parameter, the utility function could be written as follows:

$$U^* = (\beta_{h1} + \beta_{h2} age + \beta_{h3} d)\, h + \beta_y y + v \tag{4.16}$$

where, say, $d = 1$ if the age of the youngest child is 0 to 4, and $d = 0$ otherwise. In this case, two extra parameters for the preference for work are included, so the likelihood now depends on four unknown parameters which need to be estimated.

This specification is more flexible than in the numerical example of section 4.3, where just one preference parameter for work was estimated. For example, individuals with young children are allowed to have different preferences compared with individuals without young children. This approach can be used to estimate the effect of an individual's characteristics on preferences and may help to explain differences in behaviour between individuals with similar wages but different personal characteristics.

This addition means that the effects on wage elasticities of labour supply (as defined above in terms of expected hours worked) of characteristics like age or household composition can be examined. Expected labour supply can be calculated for two individuals who are the same except for the characteristic of interest. There is thus scope for a wide range of elasticities, which provide information on the effect of specific characteristics.

The approach reflected in equation (4.16) does not incorporate unobserved heterogeneity of individuals because allowance is made only for the measured characteristics. This can be overcome by adding unobserved heterogeneity to the preference parameters. Hence the coefficient on h is written as:

$$\beta_h = \beta_{h1} + \beta_{h2} age + \beta_{h3} d + \varepsilon \tag{4.17}$$

This introduces an additional error term, ε, which is typically assumed to be normally distributed. This addition complicates the method of estimation somewhat, so that the method of simulated maximum likelihood is now required. However, estimation of such models, including correlated error terms in the different preference terms, remains fairly straightforward using this method; as is explained, for example, in Van Soest (1995).

4.4.3 Characteristics of Hours Points

It is often observed that the probability of obtaining a job offer depends on the desired number of hours of work. Euwals (2001) showed that there is a discrepancy between observed and desired hours of work, which converge only to some extent over time. This indicates that some individuals work a suboptimal number of hours, which is however preferred over not working. For example, finding a job of 5 hours per week may be more difficult than finding a 40-hour job. As a result some discrete hours points are not well represented by the standard labour supply model, which does not allow for demand-side restrictions. For example, it is often found that labour supply models overpredict part-time hours of work. Several methods have been used to overcome this lack of fit to the observed labour supply. Some examples of alternative approaches are discussed briefly here. In this subsection, not all of the examples imply an alternative specification of the utility function.

First, an *ad hoc* approach of including a penalty parameter for particular hours of work in the utility function has been used to reduce the utility at certain hours points, so that the probability at these hours points is reduced; examples include Van Soest (1995), Callan and Van Soest (1996) and Kalb (2000). A second approach involves the inclusion of the probability of a job offer at the different discrete hours points in the model, which can be applied when desired hours of work are known. For example, Woittiez (1991) used the hours restrictions as a way of specifying a discrete model; that is, only a subset of discrete points have positive probability of being in the choice set of the individual. The possible choices in this subset can be determined from the actual hours, because all other available job offers must have had a lower utility. Alternatively, Euwals and Van Soest (1999) took desired labour supply as given and examined the probability of obtaining job offers at the different hours points separately.

Third, a parameter measuring the fixed cost of working can be subtracted from net income in a quadratic utility function; see, for example, Duncan and Harris (2002a). This approach is similar to the first approach but is expressed in dollars rather than units of utility. Thus it is intuitively more appealing, although the costs represented by this parameter are both pecuniary and non-pecuniary costs.

In the fourth approach, the number of job offers in an interval associated with the discrete point is directly used to weight the probabilities derived by using the extreme value distribution; see Aaberge, Dagsvik and Strøm (1995), Aaberge, Colombino and Strøm (1999) and Kornstad and Thoresen (2002, 2004), who used this approach. A final approach, by Duncan and Harris (2002b), adapts the multinomial logit model to allow for captivity at particular discrete hours points. This increases the probability of observing an individual at particular hours points. It allows some hours points to have a high probability, which does not need to depend on an individual's characteristics. This may, for example, be expected at the standard full-time 40-hours point.

4.4.4 Accounting for Childcare Costs

In the previous subsection, an implicit approach accounting for the fixed cost of working was described. This subsection discusses one of the most important contributions to the cost of working for families with children, in particular preschool children, which are childcare costs. Several papers have tried to allow for this important cost explicitly.

Discussions of the provision of childcare services and policies among policy makers and researchers generally presume a strong link between childcare costs and availability on the one hand, and labour supply, especially that of the mother, on the other hand. However, results based on overseas research suggest that this link is more complicated and harder to estimate than was at first believed. In some cases, estimated labour supply responses have been smaller than expected. Empirical research based on local data, incorporating the institutions and policies in place, is necessary to shed light on the importance of this relationship and the effectiveness of policies related to childcare. Cobb-Clark, Liu and Mitchell (2000) pointed out the large degree of heterogeneity in the structure of costs, prices and forms of childcare. This highlights the importance of modelling different kinds of childcare and allowing for possible endogeneity of prices.

Apps and Rees (2000) looked at costs of children within the household and household decisions on the consumption of goods and the allocation of time. The costs of children are internal and based on the children's share of consumption as well as the opportunity cost of parental time spent in childcare. Australian data on time use allow them to separate the nonmarket time spent on leisure from parental childcare. They find that the value of parental time devoted to childcare is a substantial component of total childcare costs.

Apps and Rees focused on the internal cost of parental childcare while many other papers deal with the external costs of childcare services. The implicit assumption being made in the latter models is that one hour of leisure by a parent is equivalent, in terms of household utility, to one hour of parental care either directly from enjoyment in caring for one's children or indirectly through the input in the children's development. As long as childcare subsidies are directed solely at childcare services provided outside the home, this approach would be appropriate for the simulation of the effects of policy changes in childcare subsidies. However, this simplified specification of the behaviour of the household and the lack of data on internal costs mean that the childcare costs estimated in this type of paper constitute only part of the total costs. Clearly a framework that captures both components of the costs would be an important extension.

The issue of quantity constraints linking hours of childcare and hours of work in joint labour supply childcare demand models has received little attention, with most studies using an unrestricted model of both hours of work and childcare use. Exceptions are Connelly (1992) and Kornstad and Thoresen (2002) in which it was assumed that hours of work and childcare use must be equal; Blundell *et al.* (2000), who estimated the relationship between hours of work and hours of childcare for different groups; Duncan, Paull, and Taylor (2001a), who relaxed the assumption of equal hours of labour supply and childcare by allowing childcare use to exceed the mother's hours of work; and Doiron and Kalb (2005), who estimated demand for childcare as a function of labour supply and then imputed childcare demand separately at the different discrete levels of labour supply including non-participation. The latter two approaches recognised that childcare may be seen as beneficial to the child and is not solely purchased to allow mothers to work. Results from some of these studies suggest that imposing quantity constraints directly on childcare demands has potentially large effects on parameter estimates. However, there is still much contention over the appropriate form which should be used to model this constraint.

In the empirical work to date, a problem is that many of the data sets only include information on childcare for those households in which mothers work. Explaining the relationship between childcare demand and the decision to participate has been much more difficult because of this feature of the data. The issue of informal care, which is often provided without financial cost, has also been problematic because of the lack of information needed to explain availability and attributes of such care. Blau and Hagy (1998) and Michalopoulos, Robins and Garfinkel (1992) are two rare studies which modelled jointly the employment decision and the choice of mode of childcare.

Empirical results based on U.S. and U.K. data sets vary considerably with the particular approach used as well as the data set. Generally, it has been found that policies which reduce the costs of childcare induce an increase in both labour supply and childcare use; for an overview see Doiron and Kalb (2005). The responses in labour supply are quite small on average but they are stronger for people at the bottom of the income distribution so that progressive measures generally elicit a larger reaction. Anderson and Levine (1999) reviewed econometric studies and concluded that the overall elasticity of labour force participation of mothers with regard to childcare prices lies between -0.05 and -0.35. Women with few skills are more affected than higher-skilled women. Use of childcare by employed mothers is more price sensitive than for unemployed mothers. Formal childcare is also more sensitive to price and wage effects than informal care. Little effect of policy reforms on substitution towards higher-quality childcare can be found. Also, quality and quantity appear to be substitutes at least for formal care but there are indications that existing measures of quality are not adequate in capturing important features of the trade-offs being made in this respect.

In order to simulate the effects of specific childcare policy reforms on labour supply, a model with endogenous childcare demand and labour supply must be estimated. Furthermore, this model must incorporate detailed information on the relationship between policy parameters and the household decisions regarding labour supply and childcare use. Doiron and Kalb (2005) estimated costs of and demands for childcare conditional on labour supply and on household characteristics based on the Child Care Survey data. These estimates are then used to impute revised net incomes (the original incomes minus the imputed childcare costs) for the households in another data set, the Survey of Income and Housing Costs. Labour supply parameters are then estimated taking into account the parameters of the childcare demand and cost functions.

Two different models of childcare costs are used. In the first, the costs are estimated directly without separating the parameters of the demand functions from the prices paid by the households. This yields a more precise and simpler model of costs, but it also limits the policy reforms that can be simulated since this approach does not provide estimates of adjustments in childcare use to price changes. Many childcare policies could not be explicitly incorporated since they depend on the price rather than the total costs to the households. The second model consists of a system of demands for hours of childcare, which are then used to estimate childcare costs. The estimation of demands is complicated by the endogeneity of hourly costs faced by the households. Therefore data on fees charged by childcare centres are used to capture exogenous variations in prices in the market for childcare services.

Controlling for variations in quality and the resulting endogeneity of prices has been an important issue in several recent overseas studies. Most of the studies on childcare demand are based on household surveys and these rarely include measures of quality or other attributes of the childcare service. Hence the correction for endogeneity in prices has been achieved by using some of the variables as instruments for price variations or by merging information from other sources. Blau and Robins (1988, 1989) used regional variations in expenditures to measure price and quality changes. Kimmel (1998) and Ribar (1992, 1995) used regional variations in childcare regulations and wage levels. Blau and Robins (1988) and Leibowitz, Klerman and Waite (1992) imputed information on wages of childcare workers by state, while Duncan, Paull and Taylor (2001a, 2001b) matched information on availability of services by local authority. Other researchers have matched information from household surveys to information from care providers on fees and other attributes of care. This method uses variations from the supply side of the market to capture variations in the price–quality packages of childcare services available to households. Walker (1992), Blau and Mocan (1999), Blau and Hagy (1998) and Hagy (1998) are examples of studies using this approach.

4.5 Alternative Error Distributions

The use of the extreme value distribution contains an assumption that has, in previous sections, remained implicit. This form assumes that there is no correlation between the error terms of the different hours alternatives. This is usually referred to as the 'independence of irrelevant alternatives' property, and means that taking out one of the choices would not affect the odds ratios of the other choices. For example, suppose that individuals can initially choose between 0, 5, 10, 15, ..., 45 and 50 hours of work. Taking out the 10 hours choice, it seems unlikely that the relative probabilities of the other choices would not change. If 10 hours were no longer an option, it seems likely that individuals previously preferring this discrete point would move to the neighbouring labour supply points, thus changing the odds between the choices. An obvious but unpopular approach is to extend the extreme value distribution with fixed mean and variance to a version where these two parameters are estimated, allowing for correlation between the choices.

Some authors have chosen an alternative to the extreme value distribution used to specify the random term added to measured utilities. This usually complicates estimation and a sign of the larger complexity is that in such cases it has been possible to distinguish at most three discrete hours points. This contrasts with around ten hours points for each individual, when using the extreme value distribution. This remains possible even when labour supply is estimated jointly for couples. However, the advantage of the alternative approaches is that greater flexibility is allowed in modelling the relationship between the labour supply of two members of a couple or between labour supply and welfare participation.

A model related to the multinomial logit described in the previous sections is the nested multinomial logit. Hagstrom (1996) showed that this specification allows for correlation between some of the decisions in the model. In his application, correlation between the wife's labour supply choice and welfare participation within the husband's labour supply choice is allowed. This relaxes the independence assumption between all alternatives in the standard multinomial logit model, although some structure is still imposed on the covariance matrix. In addition, a distinction is made between choice-specific variables and individual-specific variables, imposing more structure on the way characteristics influence the different choices by individuals.

An alternative to the extreme value distribution is a normal distribution, which would lead to a probit-type model instead of the logit-type model. However, multivariate probit models are difficult to estimate, even for as few as three categories. An additional problem is that it is impossible analytically to determine the limits of integration which indicate which discrete hours point is preferred. With the recent development of simulation techniques combined with more powerful computers, this type of model has become more feasible and some researchers have explored this option. Fraker and Moffitt (1988) estimate labour supply and participation in two welfare programmes for female heads of household in a reduced form model. Three levels of labour supply are distinguished. The choice for these levels of income depends on the preference parameter for work, which depends on an individual's characteristics, and an unobserved factor which is assumed to be normally distributed. No error terms are added directly to the utility function. The model can be estimated because the ranges for the preference parameter where each hours point is optimal can be written down. The calculation of these boundaries is based on two indifference curves. The first obtains bounds such that $U(0, y_0) = U(20, y_{20})$ and the second imposes $U(20, y_{20}) = U(40, y_{40})$. This approach only works when the budget constraint is not too nonconvex, which might otherwise make it impossible for part-time work to be optimal in this specification of the model. The problem of finding the limits of integration, which determine which discrete labour supply point and whether welfare participation is chosen, necessitated the reduced form approach by Fraker and Moffitt. A similar specification using a structural approach can be found in Keane and Moffitt (1998), who overcame the problems with the limits of integration by using advanced simulation techniques. With the simulation approach there is no need to determine analytically the limits of integration. However, estimation is cumbersome and time consuming.

Bingley *et al.* (1995) used an approach where the difference between utility levels is modelled rather than the utility function itself. Under the assumption of normally distributed error terms on the utility function, a multinomial probit model can be derived. They distinguish three discrete points and model the probability of preferring non-participation over part-time employment and the probability of preferring non-participation over full-time employment. Thus the distributions of the differences in utility between non-participation and part-time employment and between non-participation and full-time employment are modelled. They allow for correlation across the choices. The variance–covariance matrix is normalised by assuming that the variance of the difference between the part-time and full-time error term has a variance of one. When more than three choices are specified, simulation techniques are needed for the estimation.

Finally, a flexible non-parametric approach was taken by Hoynes (1996), who added unobserved heterogeneity to the preference parameters for labour supply of husband and wife and for welfare participation. This approach uses a discrete factor representation, where sets of M different pairs of unobserved heterogeneity for the husband's and wife's preferences for work parameter and for the preference for welfare participation $(\theta_{hk}, \theta_{wk}, \mu_k)$ are observed with a probability π_k where $k = 1, ..., n$ and $\sum_{k=1}^{M} \pi_k = 1$. The flexibility of this approach is appealing, but it adds a large number of additional parameters to be estimated ($4M - 1$ in addition to the number of parameters in a multinomial specification). For large M, any correlation between the different error terms can be represented by this specification. In addition to this discrete probability distribution, which is meant to capture the correlation between the different preference terms, normally distributed independent error terms are added to the preference for welfare participation and the observed hours of work. The use of error terms for the hours is an interesting approach to circumvent the need to group observed hours in categories with more or less arbitrary boundaries. Inputs in Hoynes's model are continuous hours, and the difference between these continuous observed hours and the discrete labour supply points is accounted for through a multiplicative factor $\exp(\varepsilon)$, where ε is normally distributed with mean $-\sigma^2/2$ and variance σ^2. Hence zero hours are observed with certainty but positive hours are observed with an error. Although the intuition behind this model is simple, estimation of the model is difficult, particularly for large M.

4.6 Conclusions

This chapter has examined the estimation, using iterative maximum likelihood methods, of the parameters of preference functions in structural discrete hours labour supply models. A simple numerical example was provided to illustrate the approach. The field is of course subject to continual development, and some extensions were discussed. For example, several extensions are occurring with regard to the specification of the different random error terms in the utility function, which are aimed at increasing the flexibility of the labour supply model. Alternative models relax the assumption of particular restrictive patterns in the variance–covariance matrices of the error terms in use, such as independence between the different labour supply choices. An increase in computing power has made some of these extensions feasible although they are often burdensome to carry out.

Chapter 5

Simulation with Discrete Hours

The previous two chapters have concentrated on the specification and estimation of the discrete hours labour supply model. This chapter turns to the use of such models in behavioural tax microsimulation. Policy changes for which this can be done are mostly of a financial type, such as a change in the amount of benefits, the withdrawal rate, eligibility for benefits or the range of income where a withdrawal rate applies. Such changes result in a change in net income at each of the discrete hours points, which may produce a shift in the optimal choice for an individual. These changes contrast with, for example, modifications to rules regarding the duration of benefits, residence requirement, willingness to accept training, the ability to refuse job offers and reasons for job loss. These are important design features of a social security system but are difficult to accommodate in microsimulation.

First, section 5.1 describes the method of calibration used to place individuals at their observed discretised hours level under the tax system in operation at the time of the survey. The generation of a post-reform probability distribution of hours worked for each individual, conditional on them being at their observed pre-reform hours, is also described. Second, section 5.2 provides a small numerical example of a tax reform, based on the three hypothetical individuals used in the illustration of maximum likelihood estimation in chapter 4. A realistic example, based on Australian data, is given in section 5.3. Conclusions are given in section 5.4.

5.1 Individual Calibration

Once the parameters of the specified preference functions have been estimated, they can be used to simulate the effects on labour supply of policy changes. A common approach is to use a base data set and start from the labour supply observed in this data set to obtain a starting point for simulation based on the observed labour supply under a particular tax and benefit system. This is achieved by calibration. To calibrate, error terms representing the random utility component, allowing for example for optimisation errors, are drawn from the relevant distribution (for example, the extreme value distribution) and added to the deterministic utility in each of the hours points. If this results in the observed labour supply being the optimal choice for the individual, the draw is accepted; otherwise another set of error terms is drawn and checked. This is repeated until the required number of sets of error terms are drawn.

These sets of error terms, with values leading to the observed labour supply, are then used to compute a distribution of labour supply after a specified reform. The more error terms that are drawn, the more accurate is the computed distribution, especially for those points with low probability. Given the individual's characteristics and draws for the error term, utility at each hours level after the change can be determined. In this way, a probability of being in each of the discrete hours points, conditional on the observed pre-reform labour supply, can be derived for each individual. A more formal statement of calibration is provided in Appendix B.

5.2 A Numerical Example

This section presents a small tax policy simulation using the numerical example from the previous chapter (subsection 4.3) in order to illustrate the calibration procedure described above. Utility for all individuals is given by the estimated utility function $U = -15.41h + 1.93y$. In the simulation, a linear tax and benefit system is introduced. Individuals without earnings receive 15 units of income. Gross income, excluding this basic income of 15, is taxed at 20 per cent. As discussed in chapter 2, this is sometimes described as a basic income–flat tax structure, a social dividend scheme or a negative income tax. Table 5.1 presents income and measured utility at the three discrete hours points for all three individuals before and after the reform.

Table 5.1: Utility Pre- and Post-reform

h	y_1	U_1	y_2	U_2	y_3	U_3
			Pre-reform			
0	0	0	0	0	0	0
20	80	−153.8	160	0.6	200	77.8
40	160	−307.6	320	1.2	400	155.6
			Post-reform			
0	15	28.9	15	28.9	15	28.9
20	79	−155.7	143	−32.2	175	29.5
40	143	−340.4	271	−93.4	335	30.2

From the table it is clear that the introduction of the tax system has made work much less attractive. Adding random draws from the extreme value distribution to the estimated utility function, in order to obtain the U^*s, results in different utility levels for each draw. Here only the draws are stored that result in the observed hours being the optimal choice for the relevant individual. Table 5.2 presents, for each individual, ten sets of draws from the extreme value distribution which result in the observed hours being the optimal choice for each individual. The corresponding utility levels are presented below each value of v, where U^{*0} indicates utility pre-reform.

Calculation of the utility conditional on these draws, after the reform has been introduced, results in the post-reform utility levels indicated by U^{*1}. From the measured utility levels, U, in Table 5.1, individuals 1 and 2 are most likely not to participate whereas individual 3 has utility levels at 0, 20 and 40 hours of work which are relatively close to each other. In Table 5.2 it can be seen that, for individual 3, post-reform utility in draw 9 is highest for 20 hours of work and in draw 4 it is highest at zero hours of work, whereas in the other draws the utility is highest when the person is working full time. For the other two individuals, non-participation always results in the highest utility.

The results from these ten draws can be summarised in a transition table. Table 5.3 presents such a matrix for this example. The last column presents the distribution of labour supply before the reform and the last row presents this distribution after the reform. The distribution before the reform consists of the percentages of individuals observed in each of the hours points. The distribution after the reform is constructed from the individual probabilities of being at each of the discrete hours points. After the reform an individual cannot be assigned to one of the discrete hours points but has a positive probability of being at each of the hours points. However, some of these probabilities may be close to zero. All these probabilities for an individual add up to one. The numbers inside the matrix are row percentages indicating the probability of individuals moving from one discrete hours point to another. Thus the probability of moving from zero hours is nil, the probability of moving from 20 hours to zero hours is 100 per cent and the probability of remaining at 40 hours is 80 per cent. There is a 10 per cent probability of moving from 40 to zero hours and the probability of reducing labour supply from 40 to 20 hours is also 10 per cent.

Instead of simulating the probabilities, the unconditional probability can also be calculated. The predicted unconditional probability of person 3 being at zero hours, 20 hours and 40 hours is 15.4 per cent, 28.1 per cent and

Table 5.2: Utility Pre-reform and Post-reform for Ten Sets of Accepted Draws from the Extreme Value Distribution

	Person 1			Person 2			Person 3		
	$h=0$	20	40	0	20	40	0	20	40
$v_1^{(a)}$	-1.07	1.36	0.18	3.00	3.49	0.23	1.17	1.03	2.43
U^{*0}	-1.07	-152.44	-307.42	3.00	4.09	1.43	1.17	78.83	158.03
U^{*1}	27.88	-154.37	-340.23	31.95	-28.72	-93.15	30.12	30.58	32.58
v_2	-0.80	0.44	-0.01	0.78	0.24	-1.42	0.91	-0.78	5.68
U^{*0}	-0.80	-153.36	-307.61	0.78	0.84	-0.22	0.91	77.02	161.28
U^{*1}	28.15	-155.29	-340.42	29.73	-31.97	-94.77	29.86	28.77	35.83
v_3	0.23	-0.74	0.034	-0.17	1.28	0.08	0.80	1.23	0.99
U^{*0}	0.23	-154.54	-307.56	-0.17	1.88	1.28	0.80	79.03	156.59
U^{*1}	29.18	-156.47	-340.37	28.78	-30.92	-93.29	29.75	30.78	31.14
v_4	2.55	2.40	-0.02	-0.64	1.63	0.52	2.07	1.25	0.46
U^{*0}	2.55	-151.40	-307.62	-0.64	2.23	1.72	2.07	79.05	156.06
U^{*1}	31.50	-153.33	-340.43	28.31	-30.57	-92.85	31.02	30.80	30.61
v_5	-0.02	0.66	1.26	0.71	3.74	2.41	-0.71	-0.40	-0.33
U^{*0}	-0.02	-153.14	-306.34	0.71	4.34	3.61	-0.71	77.40	155.27
U^{*1}	28.93	-155.07	-339.15	29.66	-28.47	-90.96	28.23	29.15	29.82
v_6	0.06	1.63	-1.27	0.11	2.43	-0.41	-1.24	-0.67	-0.53
U^{*0}	0.06	-152.17	-308.87	0.11	3.03	0.79	-1.24	77.13	155.06
U^{*1}	29.01	-154.10	-341.68	29.06	-29.78	-93.78	27.71	28.88	29.61
v_7	-0.62	1.08	-0.55	1.20	0.84	-1.50	1.77	1.12	2.31
U^{*0}	-0.63	-152.72	-308.15	1.206	1.44	-0.30	1.77	79.32	157.91
U^{*1}	28.32	-154.65	-340.96	30.15	-31.37	-94.87	30.72	31.07	32.46
v_8	0.14	1.23	0.17	-0.51	1.85	1.04	-1.35	-0.55	1.12
U^{*0}	0.14	-152.57	-307.43	-0.51	2.45	2.24	-1.35	77.24	156.72
U^{*1}	29.09	-154.50	-340.24	28.44	-30.35	-92.33	27.60	28.99	31.27
v_9	2.75	-0.53	0.36	0.16	1.04	-0.22	0.63	0.43	-0.69
U^{*0}	2.75	-154.33	-307.24	0.16	1.64	0.98	0.63	78.23	154.90
U^{*1}	31.69	-156.26	-340.05	29.11	-31.17	-93.59	29.58	29.98	29.45
v_{10}	1.73	-0.33	-1.19	-1.24	1.48	-0.86	-0.50	0.19	0.23
U^{*0}	1.73	-154.13	-308.79	-1.24	2.08	0.34	-0.50	77.99	155.83
U^{*1}	30.68	-156.06	-341.60	27.71	-30.73	-94.23	28.45	29.74	30.38

note a: v_i indicates the error term for draw i, which is added to the calculated utility level before and after the reform

Table 5.3: Labour Supply Transition Matrix

	Hours post-reform			
Hours pre-reform	0	20	40	Distribution
0	100	0	0	33.333
20	100	0	0	33.333
40	10	10	80	33.333
Distribution	70.000	3.333	26.667	100

56.5 per cent respectively. These probabilities are calculated by computing $P(h_1) = \frac{\exp(U_{1,1})}{\exp(U_{1,1})+\exp(U_{2,1})+\exp(U_{3,1})} = \frac{\exp(28.9)}{\exp(28.9)+\exp(29.5)+\exp(30.2)} = 0.154$, and similar expressions for the other hours points. These are unconditional probabilities, but given the large difference between utility at the different hours levels in the starting situation and the observed hours being the optimal hours, there should not be much difference between the conditional and unconditional probabilities in this case, because most draws from the extreme value distribution would be accepted. The simulation method using draws from the extreme value distribution provides results that are different from these expected probabilities. Table 5.3 shows that these were 10, 10 and 80 per cent respectively for 0, 20 and 40 hours of work. However, by increasing the number of draws in the simulation method the approximation becomes more accurate. For example for 1000 draws, the percentages at 0, 20 and 40 hours are 15.8, 29.5 and 54.7 per cent respectively.

Table 5.4: Expected Hours and Wage Elasticities of Labour Supply: Simulated Approach

	Person 1	Person 2	Person 3
Wage rate	4	8	10
	Calibrated results		
Expected hours at original wage	0	20	40
Expected hours after 1% wage increase	0	38.42	40
Wage elasticity of labour supply	0	92.1	0
	Non-calibrated results		
Expected hours at original wage	0	27.72	40
Expected hours after 1% wage increase	0	39.66	40
Wage elasticity of labour supply	0	43.1	0

Using a similar simulation approach, wage elasticities can be calculated for the three individuals in the example. These can be computed with and without calibration. Table 5.4 shows the results of using the alternative methods for each individual in the pre-reform situation. At the wage levels of persons 1 and 3 a small change does not have any effect on the relative utility levels at each of the hours points. Therefore no change in labour supply is expected. However, for person 2 the utility levels of the three hours points are closer to each other. As a result, a small change in the wage level has a large effect on expected labour supply. It is only for person 2 that calibration has an effect on the outcomes. For the other two persons, nearly all possible draws of the error term result in the observed labour supply choice, whereas for person 2 the error term can shift the optimal outcome from one point to another. Here it is shown that calibration can make a difference to the result. Using calibration in this example, the expected wage elasticity is about twice as large as without calibration. This example produces large elasticities because only two positive hours levels are used and the utility levels at those hours levels are close together.

5.3 An Empirical Example

This section presents a realistic example of microsimulation methods using Australian data. The results presented here concentrate on labour supply effects, but of course it is also possible to evaluate the implications for government taxes and expenditures or to examine inequality and poverty effects. In examining revenue implications, the average values over the successful calibration draws for each individual are used. The simulation results were obtained using the Melbourne Institute Tax and Transfer Simulator, which is described briefly in Appendix C.

First the tax change examined is described, followed by some examples of summary results. The Australian tax and transfer system has a large number of means-tested benefits. The hypothetical policy change analysed here reduces the benefit taper or abatement rates in the 1998 tax structure to 30 per cent. All taper rates of 50 per cent and 70 per cent are reduced to 30 per cent, while leaving all basic benefit levels unchanged. The exception is the withdrawal rate on parental income for people receiving Youth Allowance or AUSTUDY, which remains at 25 per cent. A 30 per cent taper rate means that for every dollar of additional income in the household, the benefit payment is reduced by 30 cents.

In this empirical example, a few individuals are dropped from the simulation and fixed at the observed hours of work, because they cannot be put at their observed labour supply within a reasonable number of tries. This occurs 521 times, which in addition to the 121 rejected cases because of unrealistic wages, represents 6.5 per cent of all individuals in the database.

The effect on labour supply of this reduction in the taper rates is equivocal because it does not automatically mean a reduction in effective marginal tax rates for all individuals. This is an inevitable consequence of flattening the marginal rate structure while keeping basic benefit levels unchanged. A summary of the labour supply effects is given in Table 5.5 for the five demographic groups; for further details on the effects and results of this policy reform see Creedy, Kalb and Kew (2003). After the reform, more sole parents are expected to participate in the labour market since very few women move from work to non-participation, whereas a substantial proportion moves into work from non-participation. The net effect is more than 8 per cent. However, there is a relatively small negative effect for a subgroup caused by the 1.8 per cent of sole parents who decrease their labour supply, which is partly counteracted by the 1.3 per cent of sole parents who increase their working hours after the reform. Nevertheless, the resulting average weekly hours are still increased by nearly 3 hours, showing that the overall effect is positive.

The changes in the probability of working, for several categories, are presented in Table 5.6. Since actual labour supply points are rounded to the nearest discrete labour supply point, the definition of non-participation depends on the number of discrete labour supply points that are used. In this case, it is working less than 3 hours for women and for men it is working less than 10 hours. Sole parents are predicted to have a larger increase in the probability of working as a result of reduced taper rates than other groups.

Table 5.5: Summary of Labour Supply Responses

Behavioural Response	Couples		Single	Single	Sole
	Men	Women	men	women	parents
Workers[a] (per cent, base)	56.93	40.63	52.29	43.56	41.28
Workers[a] (per cent, reform)	57.49	40.24	52.55	43.44	49.54
Non-work–>work (per cent)	1.29	1.72	0.33	0.07	8.3
Work–>non-work (per cent)	0.73	2.10	0.06	0.18	0.03
Workers working more	0.08	0.37	1.07	0.42	1.29
Workers working less	2.60	1.43	0.01	0.44	1.81
Average hours change	-0.37	-0.49	0.32	-0.10	2.88

Note a: self-employed workers are not included in the 'workers' group

Table 5.6: Changes in Work Probability

	Percentage point change						
	Decrease of			Increase of			
	10-50	2-10	0	2-10	10-50	>50	Mean
Income unit type							
Couple	2	18	72	5	3	-	-0.37
Couple+dep.child	-	6	19	55	12	8	0.60
Single	0	3	96	1	0	0	0.09
Sole parent	0	0	46	12	41	-	8.27
Number of children							
None	1	11	84	3	1	0	-0.14
One	4	17	59	9	12	-	1.46
Two	4	14	64	10	8	-	0.85
Three	4	10	67	10	8	-	1.05
Four	4	6	65	12	12	-	2.15
Five	-	3	64	8	25	-	5.48
Six	-	2	79	9	9	-	1.54

Table 5.7: Labour Supply Transition Matrix: Sole Parents (Row Percentages)

Pre-	Post-reform hours										
reform	0	5	10	15	20	25	30	35	40	45	50
0	85.9	0.0	0.3	0.8	1.0	1.9	1.8	1.7	2.1	2.2	2.5
5	-	89.2	0.3	0.4	1.0	0.7	1.7	1.9	1.6	2.3	0.8
10	-	-	86.3	0.6	0.5	1.4	1.5	2.7	2.1	2.4	2.5
15	-	0.1	0.1	91.7	0.3	0.7	1.4	1.1	1.7	1.4	1.6
20	-	-	-	0.1	95.0	0.2	1.1	0.9	0.8	1.3	0.7
25	0.0	-	-	-	-	97.8	0.0	0.3	0.4	0.6	0.9
30	-	0.4	0.3	0.3	0.5	1.1	95.2	0.2	0.7	0.8	0.4
35	-	0.2	0.3	0.7	1.0	1.6	0.5	94.7	0.2	0.6	0.3
40	0.2	0.3	0.6	1.6	1.7	2.5	1.7	0.3	90.8	0.2	0.2
45	0.4	0.3	0.4	1.0	1.9	1.8	2.0	1.9	1.1	87.9	1.3
50	0.1	0.3	0.4	0.8	1.1	1.0	1.1	1.3	0.9	0.4	92.5
Total	50.5	2.7	2.2	3.3	4.6	5.2	4.7	5.1	12.7	2.5	6.5

This sensitivity to work incentives is found in several other studies (Blundell *et al.*, 2000; Blundell and Hoynes, 2001). Families with more children seem also more likely to participate in the labour market after the reform.

An example of a transition matrix, produced following the method described in the previous section, is shown in Table 5.7. This is for sole parents, who can be seen to experience both increases and decreases in labour supply as a result of the change. Compared with singles and couples (not shown here), sole parents are more likely to change labour supply, particularly at the lower and upper end of the hours range. Sole parents working fewer than 25 hours seem most likely to increase their hours whereas sole parents working 35 hours or over are more likely to reduce their hours.

5.4 Conclusions

This chapter has provided an introduction to the way in which a behavioural tax policy simulation can be carried out in a model based on a discrete hours approach to labour supply. A numerical example was used to illustrate the method of calibration, in which individuals are placed at their observed discretised labour supply. Finally, an empirical example was given to illustrate the kind of information that can be provided in order to enhance policy debates. In microsimulation it is easy to calculate effects for subgroups because all effects are calculated at the individual level before being aggregated into the population level or alternatively into subgroups of the population with particular characteristics. This provides a large degree of flexibility in the way the results can be presented. The microsimulation approach also allows a wide variety of effects to be calculated, as long as the base sample has sufficient information for the calculation. Here the effect on labour supply was shown. However, other effects such as the effect on government expenditure on benefit payments or government revenue from income taxation, or the effect on inequality in the population could be calculated using this approach. The microsimulation method also provides a convenient way to analyse the effect of separate components of complex policy changes.

Chapter 6

Reweighting of Sample Surveys

Tax microsimulation models are based on large-scale cross-sectional survey data. Each individual and household has a sample weight provided by the statistical agency responsible for collecting the data. The typical starting point is to use weights that are inversely related to the probability of selecting the individual in a random sample, with some adjustment for non-response. It has become common for agencies, using minimal adjustments, to produce revised weights to ensure that, for example, the estimated population age/gender distributions match population totals obtained from other sources, in particular census data. Such calibration methods are well known among survey statisticians, a highly influential paper being that by Deville and Särndal (1992).[1]

Users of official data usually take the weights as given when grossing up from the sample in order to obtain estimates of population values. This applies not only to simple aggregates, such as income taxation, or the number of recipients of a particular social transfer, or the number of people in

[1] A detailed description of calibration and generalised regression methods used in Belgium is given in Vanderhoeft (2001), who also describes the SPSS-based program g-CALIB-S. Bell (2000) describes methods used in the Australian Bureau of Statistics' household surveys, involving the SAS software GREGWT. Statistics Sweden uses the SAS software CLAN, described by Andersson and Nordberg (1998) and also used by the Finnish Labour Force Survey. All results in the present chapter were obtained using specially written Fortran programs.

a particular age group, but the weights are also used in the estimation of measures of population inequality or poverty. However, there is no guarantee that weights calibrated on demographic variables produce appropriate revenue, expenditure and income distribution results.

One aim of this chapter is therefore to describe the basic calibration approach to survey reweighting. This may be needed, for example, if population aggregates, used for official calibrations, are not sufficiently close to population values obtained from other data sources, such as tax and benefit administration data. A further important reason for wanting to reweight the data arises when a survey from one year is used to examine the likely implications of, say, a tax and transfer policy in a later year. This need can arise if cross-sectional surveys are not carried out every year or if there are long delays in releasing data. Nevertheless, other administrative data may be available at more frequent intervals and could be used in reweighting procedures. It is also useful to be able to allow for changes in, say, the age distribution of the population or in aggregate unemployment rates over time.

When carrying out any kind of reweighting exercise, it should always be borne in mind that reweighting may cause non-calibrated variables to change in undesirable ways. This means that various other checks need to be made on those other variables. Furthermore, the distribution (rather than simply the sum) of important variables, for example alternative sources of income, may be led to change as a result of reweighting. Hence in practice, serious attention needs to be given to these possibilities, involving various comparisons of alternative distributions.[2] In addition, the precision of some survey estimates may be lowered, particularly where many calibration constraints are used. Examples can be found in Skinner (1999); see also Kalton and Flores-Cervantes (2003).

The basic problem of obtaining minimum distance weights is described

[2]While these are important, they do not present special analytical problems and are therefore not discussed in detail here; an example is given in Creedy and Tuckwell (2004).

formally in section 6.1. A specific case uses the chi-square distance function resulting in an explicit solution, which is derived in section 6.2.[3] A more general class of distance measures is discussed in section 6.3, where iterative solutions are needed. Numerical examples are used to compare alternative distance functions, based on a small hypothetical sample. These three sections provide a simplified exposition, with derivations of some of the results stated by Deville and Särndal (1992), whose more sophisticated and comprehensive treatment concentrated on statistical inference issues.[4] Finally, an illustration is provided in section 6.4, where the methods are applied to New Zealand Household Economic Survey (HES) data.

6.1 Obtaining Minimum Distance Weights

For each of K individuals in a sample survey, information is available about J variables; these are placed in the vector:

$$x_k = \begin{bmatrix} x_{k,1} \\ \cdot \\ \cdot \\ \cdot \\ x_{k,J} \end{bmatrix} \tag{6.1}$$

For present purposes these vectors contain only the variables of interest for the calibration exercise (rather than all measured variables). Many of the elements of x_k are likely to be 0/1 variables. For example $x_{k,j} = 1$ if the kth individual is in a particular age group (or receives a particular type of social transfer), and $x_{k,j} = 0$ otherwise. The sum $\sum_{k=1}^{K} x_{k,j}$ therefore gives the number of individuals in the sample who are in the age group (or who receive the transfer payment). In some cases x_k may represent a variable such

[3]The link between this method and generalised regression estimators of population totals is discusssed briefly at the end of the section. See especially Särndal, Swensson and Wretman (1992).

[4]Deville and Särndal (1992) used fewer than two pages to state the results discussed here.

as earnings from a particular source. This applies only where reweighting is strictly appropriate. In other words, if the data simply require a uniform adjustment rather than a redistribution, for example in the case of inflation, it is more appropriate to 'uprate' the data directly.

Let the sample design weights provided by the statistical agency responsible for data collection be denoted s_k for $k = 1, ..., K$. These weights can be used to produce estimated population totals, $\widehat{t}_{x|s}$ based on the sample, given by the J-element vector:

$$\widehat{t}_{x|s} = \sum_{k=1}^{K} s_k x_k \tag{6.2}$$

The problem examined in this chapter can be stated as follows. Suppose that other data sources, for example census or social security administrative data, provide information about 'true' population totals, t_x. The problem is to compute new weights, w_k, for $k = 1, ..., K$ which are as close as possible to the design weights, s_k, while satisfying the set of J calibration equations:

$$t_x = \sum_{k=1}^{K} w_k x_k \tag{6.3}$$

It is thus necessary to specify a criterion by which to judge the closeness of the two sets of weights.

In general, denote the distance between w_k and s_k as $G(w_k, s_k)$. The aggregate distance between the design and calibrated weights is thus:

$$D = \sum_{k=1}^{K} G(w_k, s_k) \tag{6.4}$$

The problem is therefore to minimise (6.4) subject to (6.3). The Lagrangean for this problem is:

$$L = \sum_{k=1}^{K} G(w_k, s_k) + \sum_{j=1}^{J} \lambda_j \left(t_{x,j} - \sum_{k=1}^{K} w_k x_{k,j} \right) \tag{6.5}$$

where λ_j for $j = 1, ..., J$ are the Lagrange multipliers, and $t_{x,j}$ represents the jth element of the vector of known population aggregates, t_x. The following two sections consider methods of obtaining values of w that minimise (6.5).

6.2 The Chi-Square Distance Measure

The constrained minimisation problem stated above has an explicit solution for a distance function based on the chi-square measure. This is discussed in subsection 6.2.1. A small numerical example is examined in subsection 6.2.2.

6.2.1 An Explicit Solution

Consider the chi-square type of distance measure, where the aggregate distance is given by:

$$D = \frac{1}{2} \sum_{k=1}^{K} \frac{(w_k - s_k)^2}{s_k} \tag{6.6}$$

The Lagrangean in (6.5) can be written as:

$$L = \frac{1}{2} \sum_{k=1}^{K} \frac{(w_k - s_k)^2}{s_k} + \sum_{j=1}^{J} \lambda_j \left(t_{x,j} - \sum_{k=1}^{K} w_k x_{k,j} \right) \tag{6.7}$$

Differentiation of (6.7) gives the set of K first-order conditions:

$$\frac{\partial L}{\partial w_k} = \left(\frac{w_k}{s_k} - 1 \right) - \sum_{j=1}^{J} \lambda_j x_{k,j} = 0 \tag{6.8}$$

for $k = 1, ..., K$, along with the J conditions in (6.3). Rewriting $\sum_{j=1}^{J} \lambda_j x_{k,j}$ as $x_k' \lambda$, where the prime indicates transposition, and multiplication of each equation in (6.8) by s_k gives, after rearrangement:

$$w_k = s_k \left(1 + x_k' \lambda\right) \tag{6.9}$$

for $k = 1, ..., K$.

To solve for the Lagrange multipliers, pre-multiply (6.9) by x_k and rearrange, so that:

$$w_k x_k - s_k x_k = s_k x_k x_k' \lambda \tag{6.10}$$

Summing (6.10) over all K, and making use of the calibration equations, gives:

$$t_x - \widehat{t}_{x|s} = \left[\sum_{k=1}^{K} s_k x_k x_k' \right] \lambda \tag{6.11}$$

where the term in brackets on the right hand side of (6.11) is a J by J square matrix. Hence, if this matrix can be inverted, the vector of Lagrange multipliers is given by:

$$\lambda = \left[\sum_{k=1}^{K} s_k x_k x_k' \right]^{-1} \left(t_x - \widehat{t}_{x|s} \right) \tag{6.12}$$

The resulting values of λ are substituted into (6.9) to obtain the new weights.

Write (6.9) as $w_k = s_k (1 + \lambda' x_k)$ and (6.12) as $\lambda' = \left(t_x - \widehat{t}_{x|s} \right)' T^{-1}$ with T as the symmetric matrix $\sum_{k=1}^{K} s_k x_k x_k'$. Given sample observations on the variable y_k, an estimate of the population total, $\widehat{t}_y$, can be obtained as $\sum_{k=1}^{K} w_k y_k$. Substituting for w_k gives the result in Deville and Särndal (1992, p.377) that $\widehat{t}_y = \sum_{k=1}^{K} s_k y_k + \left(t_x - \widehat{t}_{x|s} \right)' B$, where $B = T^{-1} \sum_{k=1}^{K} s_k x_k y_k$. This provides the link between reweighting and the generalised regression estimator. The production of asymptotic standard errors is often based on this estimator, in view of the result that other distance functions are asymptotically equivalent; see Deville and Särndal (1992, p.378). The present discussion concentrates only on finding appropriate new weights.

6.2.2 An Example

The above procedure may be illustrated using a simple example. Suppose there are four variables, $x_{k,j}$ (for $j = 1, ..., 4$) of concern, for which population values t_x are available. The hypothetical data, for a sample of 20 individuals, are shown in Table 6.1. Suppose variable 1 refers to age, so that $x_{k,1} = 1$ for those who are 'young' and is zero otherwise, while $x_{k,2} = 1$ for those who are unemployed and zero otherwise. Variable 3 measures earnings from employment, while variable 4 is another categorical variable referring to location ($x_{k,4} = 1$ if the individual lives in a city and is zero otherwise).[5] Given the sample design weights shown in the penultimate column of Table 6.1, the estimated population totals are equal to $\widehat{t}_{x|s} = [44, 24, 213, 32]'$.

[5] The number of variables needed is of course one less than the number of categories of each type, otherwise singularity problems arise.

Table 6.1: Sample Values and Calibrated Weights

k	$x_{k,1}$	$x_{k,2}$	$x_{k,3}$	$x_{k,4}$	s_k	w_k
1	1	1	0	0	3	2.753
2	0	1	0	0	3	2.109
3	1	0	2	0	5	5.945
4	0	0	6	1	4	4.005
5	1	0	4	1	2	2.484
6	1	1	0	0	5	4.589
7	1	0	5	0	5	5.752
8	0	0	6	1	4	4.005
9	0	1	0	0	3	2.109
10	0	0	3	1	3	3.120
11	1	0	2	0	5	5.945
12	1	1	0	1	4	3.985
13	1	0	3	1	4	5.019
14	1	0	4	0	3	3.490
15	0	0	5	0	5	4.678
16	0	1	0	1	3	2.345
17	1	0	2	1	4	5.070
18	0	0	6	0	5	4.614
19	1	0	4	1	4	4.967
20	0	1	0	0	3	2.109

The symmetric matrix $\sum_{k=1}^{K} s_k x_k x_k'$ and its inverse are given in Table 6.2. The zero elements reflect the property of the basic data, that only individuals who work (for whom $x_{k,2} = 0$) are assumed to receive positive earnings, $x_{k,3}$. Suppose that the known population totals are $t_x = [50, 20, 230, 35]'$, reflecting a younger population than in the sample weights and a lower unemployment rate. Using the approach described in subsection 6.2.1, new weights can be computed. The resulting calibrated weights are shown in the final column of Table 6.1.

The required adjustments to the weights are clearly consistent with expectations, given the calibration requirements and the characteristics of the individuals. For example, the weights for individuals 2, 9 and 20 fall by a relatively large amount (from 3 to 2.109), since these individuals are all

Table 6.2: Matrix $\sum_{k=1}^{K} s_k x_k x_k'$ and Its Inverse

$\sum_{k=1}^{K} s_k x_k x_k'$			
44.000	12.000	101.000	18.000
12.000	24.000	0.000	7.000
101.000	0.000	981.000	101.000
18.000	7.000	101.000	32.000
$\left[\sum_{k=1}^{K} s_k x_k x_k'\right]^{-1}$			
0.037	-0.016	-0.003	-0.008
-0.016	0.053	0.003	-0.011
-0.003	0.003	0.002	-0.005
-0.008	-0.011	-0.005	0.053

unemployed, old and living in rural locations. The aggregates for all these characteristics are required to fall. The weights for individuals 1 and 6 do not drop so far because, although these are unemployed and in a rural location, they are young. The weight for person 12 falls by a small amount because, although unemployed, this person is young and in a city. The weights for individuals 13, 17 and 19 increase by relatively large amounts as they are young, employed and living in a city.

6.3 Alternative Distance Functions

The chi-square distance function is convenient because it enables an explicit solution for the calibrated weights to be obtained, requiring only matrix inversion. However, a modified form of the same approach can be applied to a range of alternative distance functions, as shown in this section. These functions belong to a class of functions having two features: the first derivative with respect to w can be expressed as a function of w/s and its inverse can be obtained explicitly. An iterative solution procedure is required for the calculation of the Lagrange multipliers. The general case of this class is presented in subsection 6.3.1. An iterative approach based on Newton's method is described in subsection 6.3.2. Several weighting functions are described in subsection 6.3.3 and illustrated by examples in subsection 6.3.4.

6.3.1 The General Case

The Lagrangean for the general case is given in equation (6.5). Suppose that $G(w_k, s_k)$ has the property, shared with the chi-square distance function, that the differential with respect to w_k can be expressed as a function of the ratio w_k/s_k, so that:

$$\frac{\partial G(w_k, s_k)}{\partial w_k} = g\left(\frac{w_k}{s_k}\right) \tag{6.13}$$

The K first-order conditions for minimisation can therefore be written as:

$$g\left(\frac{w_k}{s_k}\right) = x_k'\lambda \tag{6.14}$$

Write the inverse function of g as g^{-1}, so that if $g(w_k/s_k) = u$, say, then $w_k/s_k = g^{-1}(u)$. In the case of the chi-square distance function used above, $g(w_k/s_k) = w_k/s_k - 1$, and the inverse takes a simple linear form. In general, from (6.14) the k values of w_k are expressed as:

$$w_k = s_k g^{-1}(x_k'\lambda) \tag{6.15}$$

If the inverse function, g^{-1}, can be obtained explicitly, equation (6.15) can be used to compute the calibrated weights, given a solution for the vector, λ.

As before, the Lagrange multipliers can be obtained by post-multiplying (6.15) by the vector x_k, summing over all $k = 1, ..., K$ and using the calibration equations, so that:

$$t_x = \sum_{k=1}^{K} w_k x_k = \sum_{k=1}^{K} s_k g^{-1}(x_k'\lambda) x_k \tag{6.16}$$

Finally, subtracting $\widehat{t}_{x|s} = \sum_{k=1}^{K} s_k x_k$ from both sides of (6.16) gives:

$$t_x - \widehat{t}_{x|s} = \sum_{k=1}^{K} s_k \left\{g^{-1}(x_k'\lambda) - 1\right\} x_k \tag{6.17}$$

The term $s_k \{g^{-1}(x'_k\lambda) - 1\}$ is of course a scalar, and the left hand side is a known vector. In general, (6.17) is nonlinear in the vector λ and so must be solved using an iterative procedure, as described in the following subsection.

6.3.2 An Iterative Procedure

Writing $t_x - \widehat{t}_{x|s} = a$, the equations in (6.17) can be written as:

$$f_i(\lambda) = a_i - \sum_{k=1}^{K} s_k x_{k,i} \{g^{-1}(x'_k\lambda) - 1\} = 0 \tag{6.18}$$

for $i = 1, ..., J$. The roots can be obtained using Newton's method, described in Appendix A. This involves the following iterative sequence, where $\lambda^{[I]}$ denotes the value of λ in the Ith iteration:[6]

$$\lambda^{[I+1]} = \lambda^{[I]} - \left[\frac{\partial f_i(\lambda)}{\partial \lambda_\ell}\right]^{-1}_{\lambda^{[I]}} [f(\lambda)]_{\lambda^{[I]}} \tag{6.19}$$

The Hessian matrix $[\partial f_i(\lambda)/\partial \lambda_\ell]$ and the vector $f(\lambda)$ on the right hand side of (6.19) are evaluated using $\lambda^{[I]}$.

The elements $\partial f_i(\lambda)/\partial \lambda_\ell$ are given by:

$$\frac{\partial f_i(\lambda)}{\partial \lambda_\ell} = -\sum_{k=1}^{K} s_k x_{k,i} \frac{\partial g^{-1}(x'_k\lambda)}{\partial \lambda_\ell} \tag{6.20}$$

which can be written as:

$$\frac{\partial f_i(\lambda)}{\partial \lambda_\ell} = -\sum_{k=1}^{K} s_k x_{k,i} x_{k,\ell} \frac{dg^{-1}(x'_k\lambda)}{d(x'_k\lambda)} \tag{6.21}$$

Starting from arbitrary initial values, the matrix equation in (6.19) is used repeatedly to adjust the values until convergence is reached, where possible.

As mentioned earlier, the application of the approach requires that it is limited to distance functions for which the form of the inverse function,

[6] The approach described here differs somewhat from other routines described in the literature, for example in Singh and Mohl (1996) and Vanderhoeft (2001). However, it provides extremely rapid convergence in few iterations.

$g^{-1}(u)$, can be obtained explicitly, given the specification for $G(w, s)$. Hence the Hessian can easily be evaluated at each step using an explicit expression for $dg^{-1}(x_k'\lambda)/d(x_k'\lambda)$. As these expressions avoid the need for the numerical evaluation of $g^{-1}(x_k'\lambda)$ and $dg^{-1}(x_k'\lambda)/d(x_k'\lambda)$ for each individual at each step, the calculation of the new weights can be expected to be relatively quick, even for large samples.[7] However, it must be borne in mind that a solution does not necessarily exist, depending on the distance function used and the adjustment required to the vector $t_x - \widehat{t}_{x|s}$.

6.3.3 Some Distance Functions

One reason why the chi-square distance function produces a solution is that no constraints are placed on the size of the adjustment to each of the survey weights. It is therefore also possible for the calibrated weights to become negative. Deville and Särndal (1992) suggested the following simple modification to the chi-square function to avoid negative values, although then the explicit solution for the chi-square case is no longer available and the iterative method must be used.

Suppose it is required to constrain the proportionate changes to certain limits, which may be different for increases compared with decreases in the weights. Define r_L and r_U such that $r_L < 1 < r_U$. The objective is to ensure that, for increases, the proportionate change, $w/s - 1$, is less than $r_U - 1$, or that $r_U > w/s$. For decreases, the aim is to ensure that $1 - w/s$ (or the negative of the proportional change) is less than $1 - r_L$, so that $r_L < w/s$.

For the chi-square distance function, it was shown that $g^{-1}(u) = 1 + u$, where $u = x'\lambda$ and $g^{-1}(u)$ solves for w/s. Hence if $g^{-1}(u) = w/s$ is outside the specified range, it is necessary to set it to the relevant limit, either r_U or r_L, rather than allow it to take the value generated. Since $g^{-1}(u) - 1 = w/s - 1 = u$, it is clear that the limits are exceeded if $u < r_L - 1$ and if

[7] Using numerical methods to solve for each $g^{-1}(u)$ and $dg^{-1}(u)/du$, for $u = x_k'\lambda$, for every individual in each iteration, would increase the computational burden substantially.

$u > r_U - 1$. In each case where the value of $g^{-1}(u)$ has to be set to the relevant limit, the corresponding value of $dg^{-1}(u)/du$ is zero. This approach ensures that weights are kept within the range $r_L s_k < w_k < r_U s_k$. Hence negative values of w are avoided simply by setting r_L to be positive.[8]

It has been seen in subsection 6.3.2 that the solution procedure requires only an explicit form for the inverse function $g^{-1}(u)$, from which its derivative can be obtained. It is not necessary to start from a specification of $G(w, s)$. Deville and Särndal (1992) suggest the simple form:

$$g^{-1}(u) = \left(1 - \frac{u}{2}\right)^{-2} \tag{6.22}$$

The gradient function, $g(w/s)$, is given by solving (6.22) for u, so that:

$$g\left(\frac{w}{s}\right) = u = 2\left(1 - \left(\frac{w}{s}\right)^{-1/2}\right) \tag{6.23}$$

and the form of an alternative distance function can be obtained by integrating (6.23). Hence it is required to obtain $2\int\left\{1 - \left(\frac{w}{s}\right)^{-1/2}\right\} dw = 2\left(w - 2\sqrt{s}\sqrt{w}\right)$, which can be written as $2\left(w + s - 2\sqrt{s}\sqrt{w}\right) - 2s$ and, dropping the last term, which is a constant, this is equal to $2\left(\sqrt{w} - \sqrt{s}\right)^2$. This is referred to as Case A, and its properties are given in the first row of Table 6.3. The second row of the table provides details of Case B, where $g^{-1}(u) = (1 - u)^{-1}$, and the final row gives the corresponding properties of the basic chi-square function.[9] A feature of these functions is that they do not require any parameters to be set.

Deville and Särndal (1992) also suggest the use of an inverse function $g^{-1}(u)$ of the form:[10]

$$g^{-1}(u) = \frac{r_L(r_U - 1) + r_U(1 - r_L)\exp\alpha u}{(r_U - 1) + (1 - r_L)\exp\alpha u} \tag{6.24}$$

[8] This is much more convenient than imposing inequality constraints and applying the more complex Kuhn–Tucker conditions. In addition, it is desirable to restrict the extent of proportional changes even where they produce positive weights.

[9] Deville and Särndal (1992) discuss the use of a normalisation whereby $g^{-1\prime}(0)$ is set to some specified value, but this is not necessary for the approach.

[10] Singh and Mohl (1996), in reviewing alternative calibration estimators, refer to this 'inverse logit-type transformation' as a Generalised Modified Discrimination Information method.

Table 6.3: Alternative Distance Functions

Case	$G(w,s)$	$g(w/s)$	$g^{-1}(u)$	$dg^{-1}(u)/du$
A	$2\left(\sqrt{w}-\sqrt{s}\right)^2$	$2\left(1-\left(\frac{w}{s}\right)^{-1/2}\right)$	$\left(1-\frac{u}{2}\right)^{-2}$	$\left(1-\frac{u}{2}\right)^{-3}$
B	$-s\log\left(\frac{w}{s}\right)+w-s$	$1-\left(\frac{w}{s}\right)^{-1}$	$(1-u)^{-1}$	$(1-u)^{-2}$
χ^2	$(w-s)^2/2s$	$\frac{w}{s}-1$	$1+u$	1

where r_L and r_U are as defined above and:

$$\alpha = \frac{r_U - r_L}{(1-r_L)(r_U-1)} \tag{6.25}$$

Thus $g^{-1}(-\infty) = r_L$ and $g^{-1}(\infty) = r_U$, so that the limits of w/s are r_L and r_U. This function therefore has the property that adjustments to the weights are kept within the range $r_L s_k < w_k < r_U s_k$, although, unlike the chi-square modification, no checks have to be made during computation.

The derivative required in the computation of the Hessian is therefore:

$$\frac{dg^{-1}(u)}{du} = g^{-1}(u)\left\{r_U - g^{-1}(u)\right\}\frac{(1-r_L)\,\alpha\exp\alpha u}{(r_U-1)+(1-r_L)\exp\alpha u} \tag{6.26}$$

Since $g^{-1}(u)$ solves for w/s, (6.24) can be rearranged, by collecting terms in $\exp\alpha u$, to give:

$$\frac{\frac{w}{s}-r_L}{1-r_L} = \frac{r_U-\frac{w}{s}}{r_U-1}\exp\alpha u \tag{6.27}$$

so that the gradient of the distance function is:

$$g\left(\frac{w}{s}\right) = u = \frac{1}{\alpha}\left[\log\left(\frac{\frac{w}{s}-r_L}{1-r_L}\right) - \log\left(\frac{r_U-\frac{w}{s}}{r_U-1}\right)\right] \tag{6.28}$$

The special nature of this gradient function is illustrated by the line D-S in Figure 6.1, which shows the profile of (6.28) for the wide range where $r_U = 4.1$ and $r_L = 0.01$. The first characteristic of the D-S function that is evident is the restriction of w/s to the range specified. Figure 6.1 also shows the function $g(w/s)$ for the other cases discussed above. In all cases, the slope is zero, corresponding to a turning point of the distance function, when

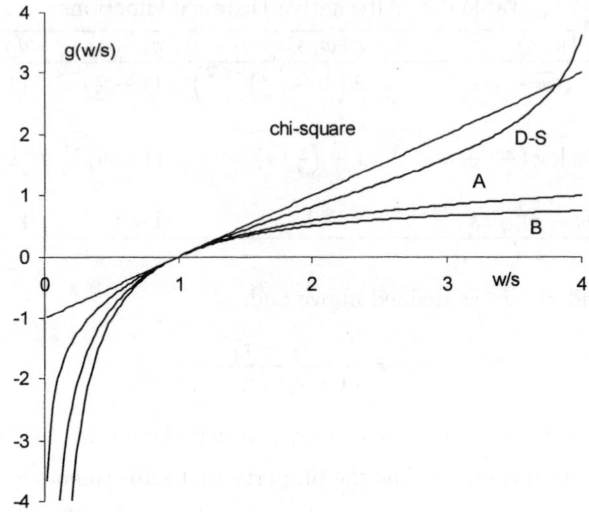

Figure 6.1: Alternative Gradient Functions

$w/s = 1$. Given the quadratic U-shaped nature of the chi-square distance function, the gradient increases at a constant rate, being negative in the range $w/s < 1$. Cases A and B also imply U-shaped distance functions, but with the gradient increasing more sharply for $w/s < 1$ and more slowly than the chi-square function in the range $w/s > 1$.

The distance function is given by integrating (6.28) with respect to w. It is most convenient to apply the variate transformation $x = w/s$, so that $dw = sdx$, and it is required to obtain:

$$\frac{s}{\alpha}\int\left[\log\left(\frac{x-r_L}{1-r_L}\right)-\log\left(\frac{r_U-x}{r_U-1}\right)\right]dx \tag{6.29}$$

Using the result that:

$$\int\log\left(\frac{x-a}{b}\right)dx=(x-a)\left[\log\left(\frac{x-a}{b}\right)-1\right] \tag{6.30}$$

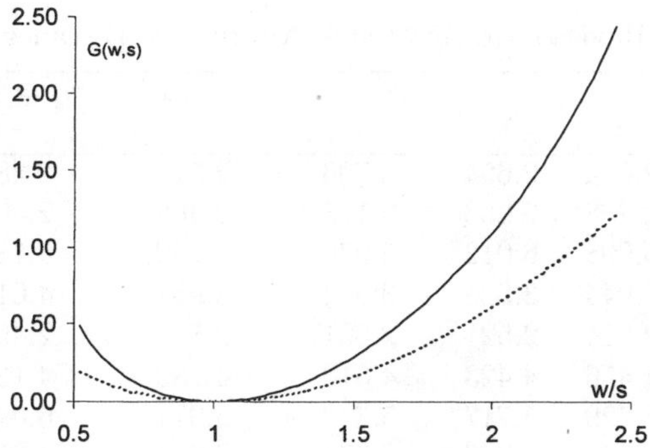

Figure 6.2: Deville–Särndal Distance Functions

and:

$$\int \log\left(\frac{a-x}{b}\right)dx = -\left(a-x\right)\left[\log\left(\frac{a-x}{b}\right)-1\right] \tag{6.31}$$

substitution and rearrangement gives s/α multiplied by:

$$G\left(w,s\right) = \left(r_U - \frac{w}{s}\right)\log\left(\frac{r_U - \frac{w}{s}}{r_U - 1}\right) + \left(\frac{w}{s} - r_L\right)\log\left(\frac{\frac{w}{s} - r_L}{1 - r_L}\right) \tag{6.32}$$

plus a term $(r_U - r_L)\,s/\alpha$, which, since it is a constant, may be dropped without loss. Equation (6.32) is the result stated without proof by Deville and Särndal (1992, p.378). Examples of this distance function are shown in Figure 6.2.[11]

6.3.4 Further Numerical Examples

The application of the distance functions presented in the previous subsection to the hypothetical sample used earlier gives the results shown in Table 6.4, where the simple (unrestricted) chi-square results are added in the last column for comparison. In cases where limits are imposed on the degree of

[11] Folsom and Singh (2000) proposed a variation on this, which they call a 'generalised exponential model', in which the limits are allowed to be unit-specific. In practice they suggest the use of three sets of bounds for low, medium and high initial weights.

Table 6.4: Revised Weights Using Alternative Distance Functions

k	s_k	A	B	$r_U = 3$ $r_L = 0.2$	$r_U = 1.3$ $r_L = 0.8$	$r_U = 1.25$ $r_L = 0.8$	Chi-square
1	3.000	2.674	2.654	2.706	2.513	2.483	2.753
2	3.000	2.228	2.260	2.178	2.408	2.400	2.109
3	5.000	5.998	6.012	5.976	6.162	6.187	5.945
4	4.000	3.944	3.926	3.974	3.951	4.019	4.005
5	2.000	2.514	2.521	2.501	2.534	2.493	2.484
6	5.000	4.456	4.423	4.510	4.189	4.138	4.589
7	5.000	5.729	5.717	5.747	5.911	6.094	5.752
8	4.000	3.944	3.926	3.974	3.951	4.019	4.005
9	3.000	2.228	2.260	2.178	2.408	2.400	2.109
10	3.000	3.086	3.074	3.106	3.213	3.325	3.120
11	5.000	5.998	6.012	5.976	6.162	6.187	5.945
12	4.000	3.814	3.762	3.897	3.645	3.769	3.985
13	4.000	5.108	5.136	5.065	5.094	4.990	5.019
14	3.000	3.490	3.487	3.494	3.604	3.680	3.490
15	5.000	4.665	4.666	4.665	4.442	4.314	4.678
16	3.000	2.370	2.380	2.355	2.428	2.408	2.345
17	4.000	5.191	5.232	5.128	5.115	4.993	5.070
18	5.000	4.603	4.604	4.600	4.366	4.237	4.614
19	4.000	5.028	5.043	5.001	5.069	4.986	4.967
20	3.000	2.228	2.260	2.178	2.408	2.400	2.109

adjustment of the weights, it cannot be expected that a solution will always be available. For this reason, care is needed in the choice of r_L and r_U, as discussed below.

The values of $r_U = 3$ and $r_L = 0.2$ were initially selected as being well outside the range of ratios obtained using the other distance functions. When the range was reduced to the potentially restrictive values of $r_U = 1.3$ and $r_L = 0.8$, none of the ratios obtained was actually at the limits specified. Nevertheless, the change to the weighting function produces a different set of weights, as shown by comparisons in Table 6.4: some actually move further away from their initial, or survey, weights.

The choice of $r_U = 1.25$ and $r_L = 0.8$, shown in the penultimate column of the table, actually places some adjustments to the weights at the lower limit of the range: for individuals 2, 9 and 20, the value of w/s is equal to 0.8. However, no adjustments are at the upper range specified. If r_L is raised to 0.82 (with r_U unchanged), unreported results show that individual 16 is placed at the lower limit, along with 2, 9 and 20 as before; in addition individuals 5, 13, 17 and 19 are pushed to the upper limit of 1.25. The attempt to raise r_L to 0.83 results in no solution being possible. However, if r_U is set to the higher value of 3.0, then $r_L = 0.83$ is found to be the highest value (where the range of variation is limited to the second decimal point) of r_L for which a solution is possible. The two highest ratios needed in this case are for persons 13 and 17, who have w/s values of 1.328 and 1.376 respectively. If r_L is kept at this value of 0.83, the lowest value of r_U for which a solution exists is $r_U = 1.26$. In this case individuals 1, 2, 6, 9, 16 and 20 are placed at the lower limit and individuals 5, 13, 17 and 19 are placed at the upper limit. Clearly, some care needs to be exercised in the choice of upper and lower limits.

While these examples help to explore the characteristics of the different approaches, a practical implementation of the method using an actual data set is carried out in the following section to illustrate the approaches more fully.

6.4 The New Zealand Household Economic Survey

This section applies the above approaches to the New Zealand Household Economic Survey 2000/01, which was the latest survey available at the time of this analysis. The aim is to illustrate the application of the approach in a practical context, and to compare the performance of the alternative distance functions. The variation in the survey weights provided by Statistics New Zealand for the period 2000/01 is illustrated in Figure 6.3, where the weights are arranged in ascending order for a sample of 2808 households. These are integrated weights, not the original weights. For a discussion of the use of integrated weighting, as described by Lemaître and Dufour (1987), by Statistics New Zealand, see Statistics New Zealand (2001). It can be seen that the majority of these weights are within a fairly narrow range, although some are substantially higher, suggesting a considerable degree of under-representation of these household types in the sample.

For present purposes, new weights were obtained using calibration values derived from the New Zealand population in 2003/04, therefore allowing for population changes between 2000/01 and 2003/04. In total, 36 calibration equations were used, covering the total numbers in the following categories: 11 family composition types; 16 age/sex types; 2 unemployment benefit types; 2 domestic purpose benefit types; 2 invalidity benefit types; 2 sickness benefit types; and 1 widow's benefit type. For each of these types, there is of course one additional category not used. The motivation for selecting these variables involved the use of the data for projecting taxes and benefit expenditures. For a general discussion of variable selection, see Nascimento Silva and Skinner (1997). Given that the calibration conditions only relate to the numbers in various categories, in practice it is necessary to carry out further checks on the actual expenditure levels for various demographic groups. The calibration conditions refer in some cases to households, as in whether or not a particular benefit is received, while in other cases they refer to individuals, as with the population age distribution.

The calibrated weights obtained using the basic chi-square distance function are shown in Figure 6.4, where households are arranged in the same order as in Figure 6.3 (although the vertical axis has been truncated at 2,500). The corresponding ratios of calibrated to survey weights, w/s, are displayed in increasing order in Figure 6.5. This clearly shows considerable variability in the weights, with some negative weights resulting. Using the modified chi-square distance function, allowing the ratio of weights, w/s, to be restricted with

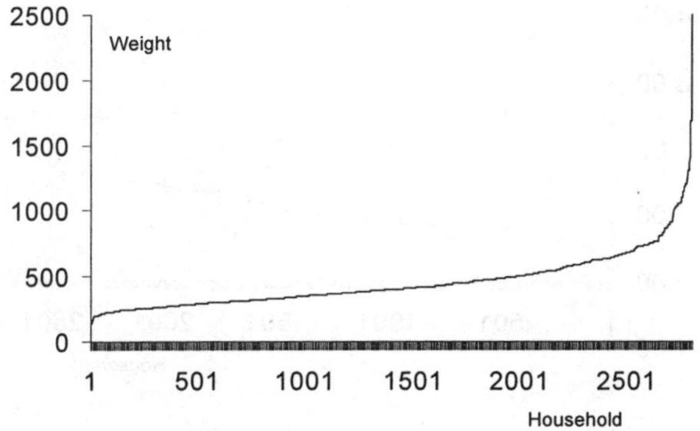

Figure 6.3: Survey Weights: Statistics New Zealand

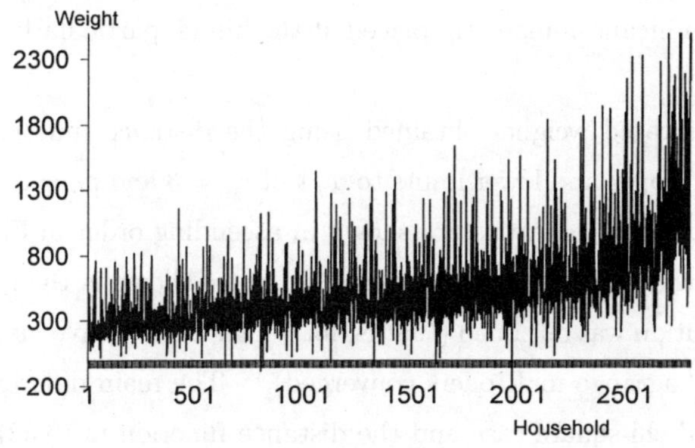

Figure 6.4: Calibrated Weights for Chi-Square Function: Household Order Same as in Figure 6.3

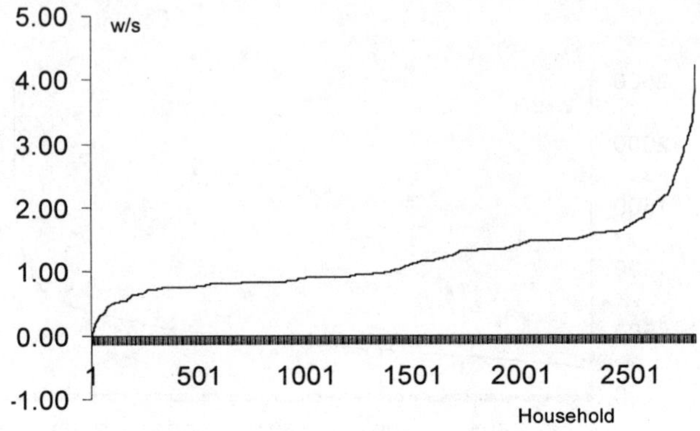

Figure 6.5: Ratio of Calibrated to Survey Weights for Chi-Square Function

the limits $r_U = 3.0$ and $r_L = 0.4$, resulted in values displayed in Figure 6.6. The effects of the adjustment can clearly be seen in the extent to which the new weights are restricted to a range of variation around the initial profile. The top and bottom of the profile in Figure 6.6 are substantially smoothed; clearly a significant number are placed at the limits, particularly at the lower limit.

The calibrated weights obtained using the distance function in (6.32), allowing for upper and lower limits to w/s of $r_U = 3$ and $r_L = 0.4$, are shown in Figure 6.7, and the ratios are shown in ascending order in Figure 6.8. In both cases where limits were imposed, the range shown is the narrowest for which a solution was obtained (that is, for which the iterative method used to obtain the Lagrange multipliers converged).[12] The main difference between the modified chi-square case and the distance function in (6.32) is that the former appears to push more values to the lower edge of the profile.

The use of the other two distance functions failed to produce solutions.

[12]Where a solution was not available, the procedure 'exploded' relatively quickly, after just a few iterations. Otherwise convergence was achieved rapidly.

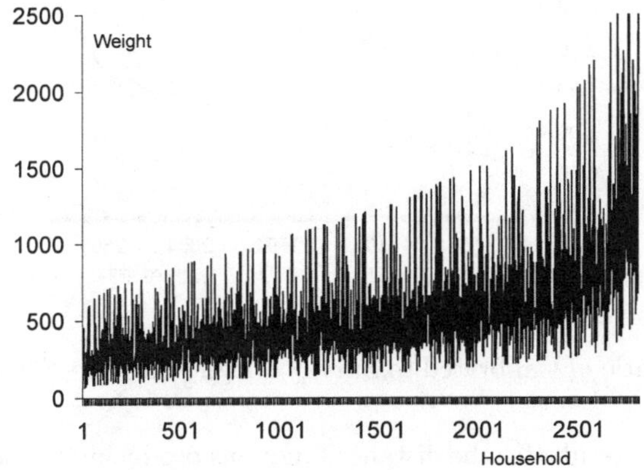

Figure 6.6: Calibrated Weights: Modified Chi-Square Function

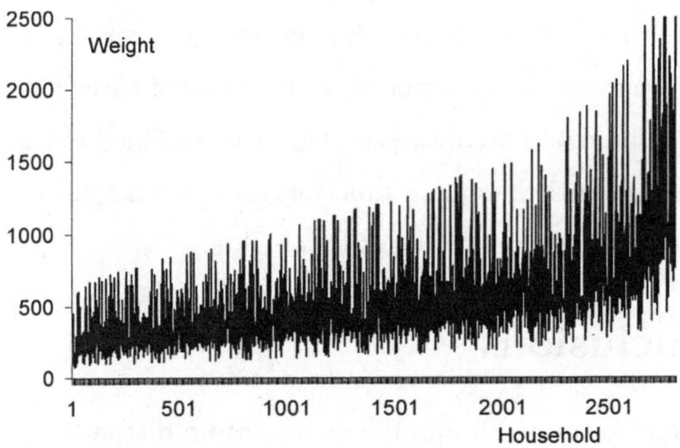

Figure 6.7: Calibrated Weights: Deville–Särndal Function

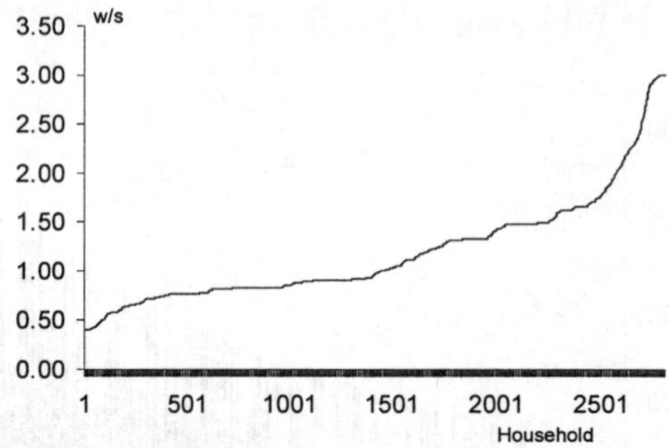

Figure 6.8: Ratio of Calibrated to Survey Weights: Deville–Särndal Function

Comparing the results for the distance functions producing solutions, it seems that the only serious contenders are the two cases imposing constraints on the proportionate changes in weights. The numerical values of the limits which can be imposed, while still obtaining a solution, appear to be the same for the adjusted chi-square function and the function in equation (6.32). Where solutions are available, there seems little on which to base a choice between those two cases. However, in further experiments using a larger number of calibration equations, it was found that no solution was available using the distance function in (6.32), however wide the range of variation allowed. Nevertheless a solution could be obtained using the modified chi-square distance function. The standard chi-square function also gave a solution, as expected, but this produced a number of negative weights.

6.5 Conclusions

This chapter has examined a number of minimum distance methods used to compute new weights for the large cross-sectional surveys used in microsimulation modelling. The methods involve the use of extraneous information about a range of population variables, for calibration purposes. The distance functions explored in this chapter were restricted to those for which the first derivative can be expressed as a function of the ratio of the new weights to the survey weights, and for which that function can be inverted explicitly. In general, an iterative solution procedure is required. An approach based on Newton's method was described and numerical examples were given for several distance functions.

The performance of the approaches, using different distance functions, was examined using the New Zealand Household Economic Survey. Rapid convergence of the iterations was obtained, although care needs to be taken when imposing limits on the proportional adjustments to sample weights. Since the same basic approach can easily examine a range of distance functions and, using Newton's method, convergence is extremely quick, the cost of considering the full range of distance measures is relatively low. However, convergence cannot be expected for each measure in all circumstances.

Finally it is worth remembering that reweighting may cause the distribution of important variables, in particular alternative sources of income, to change. Checks on changes for a range of distributions are therefore recommended.

Part III

Evaluation of Policy Changes

Chapter 7

Welfare Changes and Tax Burdens

Taxation imposes welfare costs on individuals which, expressed in money terms, exceed the tax paid. This gives rise to the idea of the excess burden of taxation, which is one of the most important concepts in public economics. It represents an efficiency loss caused by the distortion in choices arising from a change in relative prices. Tax revenue is used to finance government expenditure on a range of projects as well as paying for transfer payments, such as benefits to specified low-income households. Since the burden imposed on taxpayers exceeds the tax they pay, it is important to ensure that the perceived benefits arising from government expenditure are sufficient to outweigh the efficiency losses.

The aims of this chapter are to explain the concepts of welfare change and excess burden used in the public finance literature, and to demonstrate the result that an approximation to this burden depends on the square of the tax rate. The discussion relies largely on diagrams, though further details are given in Appendix D. For more technical and wide-ranging treatments, see for example Auerbach (1985), Auerbach and Hines (2002), Blundell, Preston and Walker (eds) (1994) and Creedy (1998).

Section 7.1 introduces the main concepts of a money measure of welfare change and the excess burden. It concentrates on the welfare loss imposed on a single individual arising from a tax on a single good. Importantly, general equilibrium effects are ignored. Section 7.2 derives the approximation for this burden using a diagrammatic argument. The next section elaborates on the basic analysis looking at the special context of an income tax, which complicates matters through the fact that it reduces the opportunity cost of leisure. Section 7.4 concludes.

7.1 A Money Measure of Welfare Change

This section explains the concept of welfare change used to examine tax burdens. These concepts apply to welfare changes arising from any set of price changes, but here the price change is assumed to arise purely from a tax change, so that the excess burden concept is relevant. This section defines the equivalent and compensating variations, and the excess burden for the case of a tax on a single good.

7.1.1 A Tax on One Good

Consider a single individual who is maximising utility subject to a fixed budget. There are two goods, X and Y. Good Y may be considered as a composite of all other goods, with the price set equal to unity. Hence units of Y are equivalent to money units. In the initial situation, the budget line, with a slope equal to the relative price of X to that of Y, is shown as AB in Figure 7.1. The optimal position is E_1, a tangency position on indifference curve U_0. Suppose a selective tax is imposed on good X. This causes the price of X to increase so that the budget line pivots to AC. The new optimal position is E_2 on indifference curve U_1.

There is a reduction in the individual's welfare as a result of the tax, as indicated by the move from U_0 to the lower indifference curve U_1. However, the difference $U_0 - U_1$ does not provide a useful measure of welfare change because utility is an ordinal concept. The utility levels themselves are arbitrary

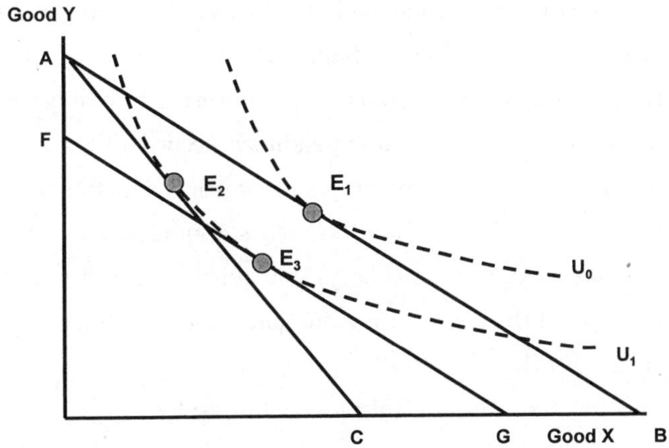

Figure 7.1: A Tax on Good X

and the utility function provides simply a preference ordering of alternative bundles. The ordering is only assumed to have some standard properties, such as transitivity and decreasing marginal rates of substitution.

7.1.2 The Equivalent Variation

Welfare changes are instead based on the change in the cost of reaching a particular indifference curve as relative prices change. This cost is not affected by the arbitrary utility number assigned to the indifference curves. Figure 7.1 shows that utility level U_1 can be attained at the pre-tax prices if the individual faces budget line FG, which is parallel to AB. The optimal position along this hypothetical constraint is E_3. Hence a variation in the individual's budget is equivalent to the tax imposed on X, in the sense that the individual would be indifferent between that budget variation (at the old prices) and the tax. This equivalent variation, denoted EV, is measured in terms of a quantity of good Y by AF, the vertical distance between the two budget lines AB and FG. Another way of describing the EV is that it represents the maximum amount the individual would be prepared to pay to avoid the tax and associated price change.

The utility function can in principle be converted into another function that describes the minimum total expenditure needed to reach a specified indifference curve at a given set of prices. Such a function is called the expenditure function, $E(P, U)$, and has as its arguments, not the amounts of the goods consumed, as with $U(x, y)$, but prices and utility. For an early analysis of the role of the expenditure function in public finance, see Diamond and McFadden (1974).

Given this function, the equivalent variation is:

$$EV = E(P_1, U_1) - E(P_0, U_1) \tag{7.1}$$

where P_0 and P_1 are the vectors of pre-tax and post-tax prices respectively. This is the distance AF in Figure 7.1. The first term, $E(P_1, U_1)$, is the individual's budget, m_1, which in this case is assumed to be fixed, so that $m_1 = m_0 = E(P_0, U_0)$.

7.1.3 The Excess Burden

It is useful to concentrate on the area in Figure 7.1 around the two points E_2 and E_3, which lie on indifference curve U_1. This expanded area is shown in Figure 7.2. Since point B represents the position actually reached by the individual after the imposition of the tax on X, the vertical distance AB shows the tax paid, expressed in terms of good Y. This is less than the equivalent variation in income that also places the individual on U_1 at pre-tax prices. The difference between the equivalent variation and the tax paid, T, represents the excess burden, EB_{EV}, of the tax. This is the distance BC in Figure 7.2.

The tax revenue can be used to finance government projects or for re-distribution to other individuals. However, the excess burden $EV - T$ is not available for anyone to spend. It represents a pure efficiency loss arising from

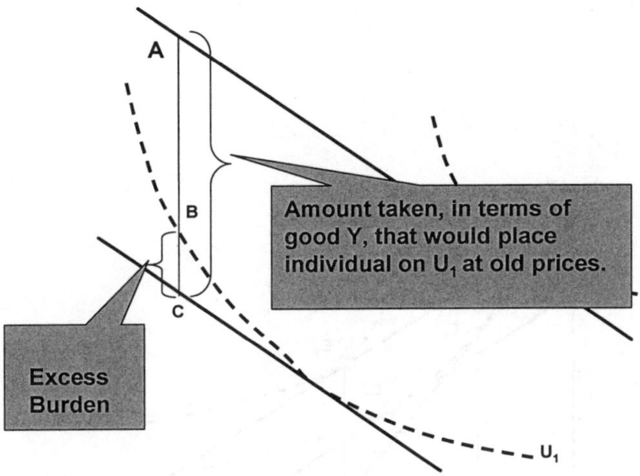

Figure 7.2: Welfare Change and Excess Burden

the tax. The size of this excess burden depends partly on the degree of convexity of the indifference curve, which reflects the degree of substitutability between the two goods.

7.1.4 The Excess Burden Expressed as an Area

As shown in the previous subsection, the excess burden is the vertical distance traced out by moving along the post-tax indifference curve from E_2 to E_3 as the relative price changes from the post-tax to the pre-tax ratio. This movement actually traces out part of a demand curve, in this case a Hicksian demand curve for good X: demand changes as the price varies, while utility is constant.[1] This contrasts with the Marshallian demand curve for X, which relates to the movement between E_1 and E_2. These two demand curves are shown in the lower part of Figure 7.3, for variations between P_0 and P_1.

For a small change in the price, the area to the left of the Hicksian de-

[1] Another Hicksian demand curve could be traced, relating to movements along U_0; this is examined in the following subsection.

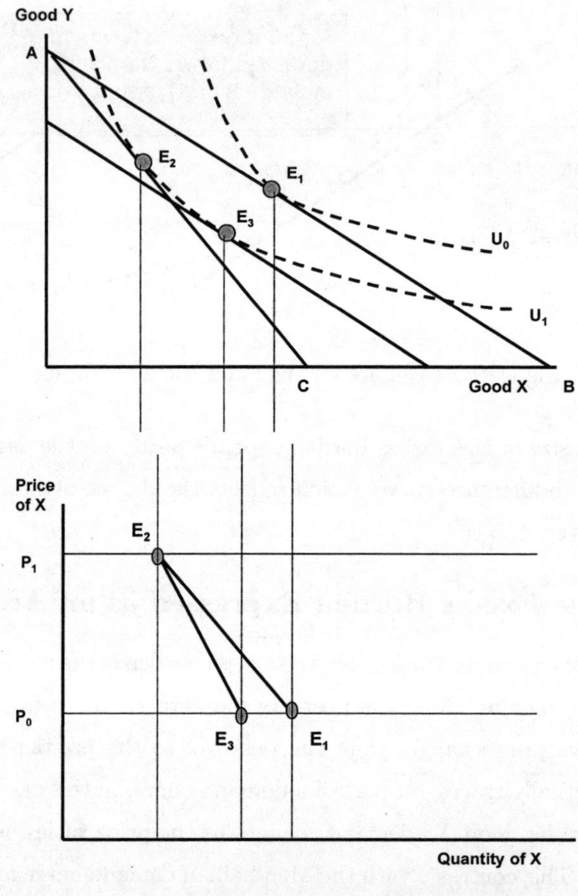

Figure 7.3: Demand Curves for Good X

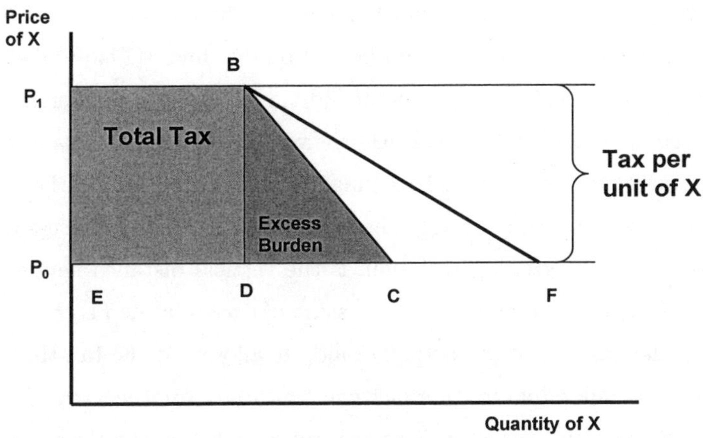

Figure 7.4: The Excess Burden as an Area

mand curve between the prices represents an expenditure level (since it is a money price per unit multiplied by a quantity). In just the same way that the Hicksian demand is produced by gradually moving along U_1 as the relative price varies, it is necessary to add up all the areas for each small price change. The total area – obtained by adding all horizontal strips – gives the expenditure required to obtain the equivalent variation. Hence EV is the area $P_1E_2E_3P_0$ in Figure 7.3.

The distance between the two price lines, $P_1 - P_0$, represents the tax per unit imposed on the good, so that multiplying this by the quantity of the good purchased after the imposition of the tax gives the tax revenue. Hence revenue is represented by the area indicated in Figure 7.4. The difference between these two areas is the excess burden, BDC in Figure 7.4.

7.1.5 The Compensating Variation

It is also possible to consider the amount of money that, if given to the individual, would allow the initial indifference curve, U_0, to be reached at the new prices. This is the compensating variation. The comparisons are illustrated in Figure 7.5. The hypothetical budget line FG is parallel to the post-tax budget line AC but places the individual at E_3 on indifference curve U_0. The compensating variation is AF, the vertical difference between the two budget lines at the new prices. Dropping a vertical line from E_3, the tax paid is the distance between the budget lines AB and AC, and the excess burden, based on the compensating variation, is the vertical distance between lines AB and FG at E_3. A feature of this measure of excess burden is that it is not based on the amount of tax actually paid. It allows for the tax that would be paid if the individual were in fact compensated. Another way of looking at the compensating variation is to recognise that it is the negative of the equivalent variation arising from a price change in the opposite direction. As with the equivalent variation, the concepts can also be illustrated in a diagram containing demand curves. In this case, the Hicksian demand curve relates to movements along U_0, so it starts from point F in Figure 7.4. The excess burden based on the compensating variation is shown in Figure 7.6. The tax deducted from the compensating variation (the area to the left of CF) is the rectangle ACGE.

7.1.6 Marginal Excess Burdens

The above analysis relates to the burden of the tax compared with the no-tax situation. It is often useful to measure the marginal excess burden, MEB, which relates to changes in the tax rate. In terms of the equivalent variation, this simply involves changes in EV and T, so that $MEB = \Delta EV - \Delta T$. This gives rise to two related concepts. First, the marginal welfare cost is given by $MWC = MEB/\Delta T = \Delta EV/\Delta T - 1$ and the marginal cost of funds, $MCF = \Delta EV/\Delta T$. Combining the two measures gives $MCF = MWC + 1$. When considering a policy of increasing a tax rate in order to finance a public project, it is the MCF that is relevant.

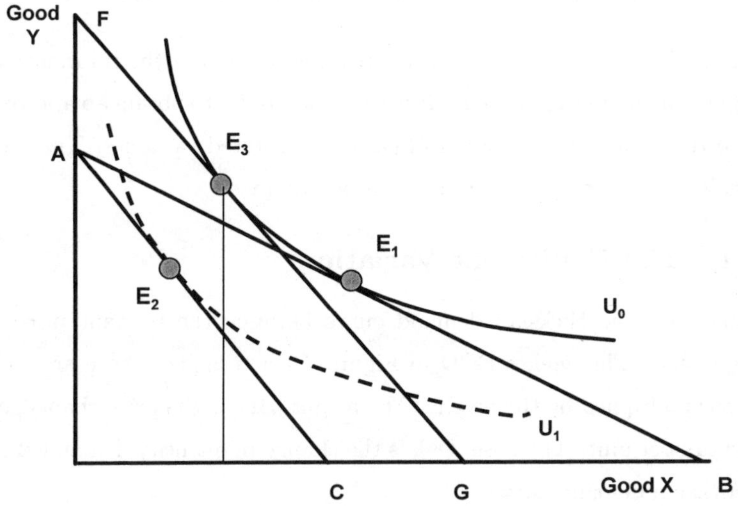

Figure 7.5: The Compensating Variation

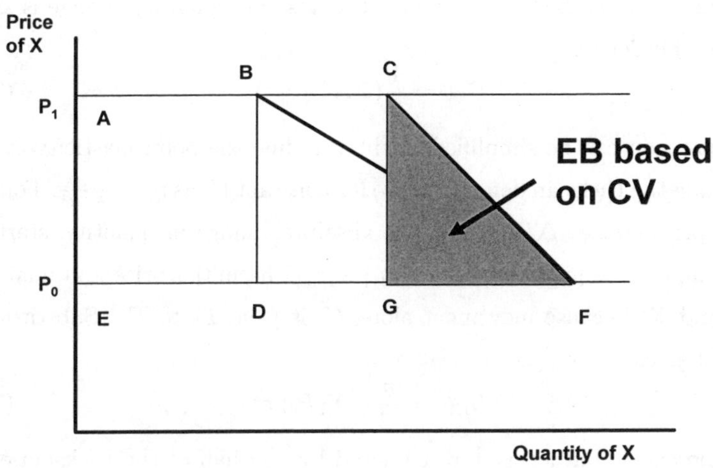

Figure 7.6: Excess Burden Based on Compensating Variation

7.2 Approximating the Excess Burden

In tax policy debates it is often not possible to obtain the information required to calculate tax burdens. It is therefore useful to obtain an approximation in terms of a small number of easily interpreted variables. This section shows how such an approximation can be obtained.

7.2.1 The Equivalent Variation

Assume that the Hicksian demand curve between the relevant prices is a straight line. This makes BCD in Figure 7.4 a triangle, whose area is half the base multiplied by the height. The height, BD, is the price change, equal to the tax per unit. The base, DC, is the change in quantity demanded along the Hicksian demand curve.

Let τ denote the proportional tax rate imposed on good X, defined as a tax-inclusive rate. This means that the tax paid on each unit of the good is τP_1, a proportion of the post-tax price. Hence the price change can be expressed simply as $\Delta P = \tau P_1$, and if the absolute quantity change is ΔX, the excess burden is:

$$EB_{EV} = \frac{1}{2}(\Delta X)(P_1 \tau) \tag{7.2}$$

This expression can be simplified further. Define the point elasticity of demand along the Hicksian demand curve for constant U_1 as $\eta_1 = \frac{P}{X}\frac{dX}{dP}$. For the discrete price change $\Delta P = P_1 \tau$, the absolute change in quantity, starting from P_1 and X_1, is given by $\Delta X = |\eta_1| X_1 \tau$. The initial price and quantity are P_1 and X_1 because movement along U_1 is from E_2 to E_3. Substituting into (7.2) gives:

$$EB_{EV} = \frac{|\eta_1|}{2}(X_1 P_1)\tau^2 \tag{7.3}$$

Hence the excess burden is approximated by one half of the Hicksian elasticity, multiplied by the initial expenditure, multiplied by the square of the proportional tax-inclusive rate of tax. This means, for example, that a doubling of the tax rate quadruples the excess burden. The elasticity is of course likely to vary along the demand curve, unless it is a rectangular hyperbola. The use of the point elasticity to obtain a discrete change in quantity in this way itself involves an approximation, even where the elasticity is constant.

7.2.2 The Compensating Variation

For the excess burden based on compensating variations, it is useful to express the tax per unit as a proportion, t, of the tax-exclusive price, P_0, so that the tax per unit is $P_0 t$. If this is fully shifted to consumers, the absolute price change is $\Delta P = P_0 t$ and the excess burden is:

$$EB_{CV} = \frac{1}{2}(\Delta X)(P_0 t) \tag{7.4}$$

If the Hicksian point elasticity of demand along this curve, for constant U_0, is $\eta_0 = \frac{P}{X}\frac{dX}{dP}$, then for the discrete price change $\Delta P = P_0 t$, the absolute change in quantity, starting from P_0 and X_0, is given by $\Delta X = |\eta_0| X_0 t$. In this case, the starting point is P_0 and X_0 because movement is along U_0 from E_1. Substituting into (7.2) gives:

$$EB_{CV} = \frac{|\eta_0|}{2}(X_0 P_0) t^2 \tag{7.5}$$

In this case the excess burden is approximated by one half of the relevant Hicksian elasticity, multiplied by the initial expenditure, multiplied by the square of the proportional tax-exclusive rate of tax. The two tax rates are connected by the relationship, $\tau = t/(1+t)$, since a tax-inclusive rate of $t/(1+t)$ raises the same revenue per unit as the tax-exclusive rate of t.

7.2.3 Some Further Issues

Although the role of the square of the tax rate is widely known, it is often forgotten that the elasticity required is the Hicksian elasticity, not the standard Marshallian demand elasticity. A completely inelastic Marshallian demand does not imply that the excess burden is zero. In using the approximation, it is also usually implicitly assumed that the elasticity is constant.

While the approximation is valuable, particularly in indicating the disproportionality of excess burdens with the tax rate, the question arises of the extent to which reliance should be placed on it. A common justification is that the formal definition appears to suggest that the measurement of excess burdens requires a substantial amount of information about preferences, enabling the precise form of the expenditure function to be known, and that in practice, observations are available only about Marshallian demands. However, the exact measures can be obtained from estimated Marshallian demand functions using a process of integration. While this may not be possible analytically for many demand function specifications, numerical integration methods can be used.

An alternative measure is the famous Marshallian concept of consumer's surplus, CS. This is based on the area to the left of the Marshallian demand curve between the relevant prices, so that $EV < CS < CV$, as can be seen from Figure 7.4 The CS effectively ignores any income effect of the price change. An approximation to the excess burden based on CS simply substitutes the Marshallian elasticity for the Hicksian elasticity in equation (7.3). While the CS is conveniently bounded by the two exact welfare measures, the excess burden obtained in this way may depart substantially from EB_{EV} and EB_{CV}. For a broad non-technical discussion of such welfare triangles in a historical context, see Hines (1999).

Another important issue is that the above discussion all relates to a tax on a single good. Nevertheless, the concepts of the equivalent variation and excess burden can be applied with little modification to taxes on several goods, although simple approximations based on diagrams are not available. With more than one good and if tax rates are initially unequal, it is possible that the equivalent variation from an increase in one tax rate can be negative, implying in turn a negative marginal excess burden and an improvement in efficiency.

All the above analysis relates to a single individual. In some contexts, for example when using a tax microsimulation model, it is indeed possible to obtain a measure of welfare change for each individual or household. Such money measures can then be used along with a specified social welfare function in order to provide an overall evaluation of the policy change. The welfare function may allow for inequality aversion. One particularly useful approach involves comparing the distributions of m (initial total expenditure) and $m - EV$. For further discussion of these aspects, see King (1983).

7.3 The Welfare Cost of an Income Tax

This section considers the welfare cost of an income tax, using a simple model in which the individual maximises a utility function that includes non-work time, or leisure time, as well as consumption (which is assumed to be equivalent to net income). Here the term 'income tax' is used rather than 'wage tax'. The context is a static one in which only a single period is considered and income from employment is, except for a government transfer payment, the only source of income. This case involves no new principles, but the application of the welfare measures introduces a number of complexities. It is therefore worth considering the details. But before turning to the income tax, it is useful to extend the earlier analysis of a tax on a single good to a policy which simultaneously imposes a tax on good X and changes the budget of the individual.

7.3.1 Changes in Price and Budget

Suppose that a tax is imposed on good X and at the same time the individual's budget is increased. This is shown in Figure 7.7, where the budget line shifts from FG to CH. The treatment of welfare changes in terms of the equivalent variation is the same as before. The optimal position shifts from

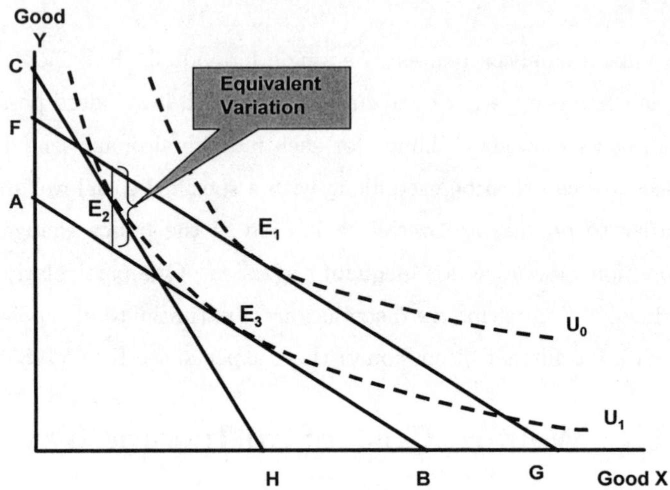

Figure 7.7: Changes in Price and Budget

E_1 to E_2. The policy change is equivalent, in terms of its effect on welfare, to a budget change equal to the vertical distance between budget lines AB and FG.

In terms of expenditure functions, point F is associated with the initial budget of $E(P_0, U_0)$, while A is associated with $E(P_0, U_1)$. Hence the equivalent variation is:

$$EV = E(P_0, U_0) - E(P_0, U_1) \tag{7.6}$$

Although the basic concept of the equivalent variation is unchanged, this expression differs from (7.1), which has $E(P_1, U_1)$, equal to m_1, as the first term: indeed, in the earlier context the budget was fixed so that $E(P_0, U_0) = E(P_1, U_1)$ by assumption.

Equation (7.6) can be divided into two separate components, associated with the two aspects of the policy change. The change in the budget is equal to $E(P_0, U_0) - E(P_1, U_1) = m_0 - m_1$, the distance FC, while the welfare change arising purely from the price change is, from equation (7.1), equal to

$E(P_1, U_1) - E(P_0, U_1) = m_1 - E(P_0, U_1)$, the distance CA. By adding and subtracting m_1 from equation (7.6), it becomes:

$$EV = \{m_1 - E(P_0, U_1)\} + \{m_0 - m_1\} \tag{7.7}$$

This is the distance FA. Using this form, the separate price and budget effects of the policy change are evident.

7.3.2 A Linear Income Tax

All that is needed to apply the result of the previous subsection to an income tax is a redefinition of some of the terms to allow for the different context. With an income tax, the budget (net income) is endogenous, since labour supply depends on the tax system. Let T be the total time available and let h denote the time devoted to working at a gross wage of w.[2] The wage is fixed in this partial equilibrium framework. In a general equilibrium context, factor prices would be expected to adjust. Net income is y, and utility can be written as $U(y, T-h)$, with $T-h$ measuring leisure time. Utility is maximised subject to a budget constraint that depends on the tax system. Consider a proportional tax applied to income from employment, so that the net wage is $w(1-t)$. If net non-wage income is μ, the budget constraint is:

$$y = w(1-t)h + \mu \tag{7.8}$$

By adding $Tw(1-t)$ to each side and rearranging, this becomes:

$$w(1-t)(T-h) + y = Tw(1-t) + \mu \tag{7.9}$$

This brings out the difference between the present context and the earlier case of a commodity tax with a fixed budget. Here, $w(1-t)$ represents the price per unit of leisure, so the left hand side of (7.9) shows the total amount spent on leisure and other consumption (net income). The right

[2] In chapter 6 the symbol w was used to denote a sample weight. However, in this chapter and all subsequent chapters, w indicates a wage rate.

hand side shows the total resources available to the individual, consisting of the amount that could be obtained if all the endowment, T, of time were devoted to working. Hence the individual can be viewed as converting the endowment into money and using this, along with non-wage income, μ, to buy goods and leisure. Instead of having a fixed budget, the individual can be said to have a 'full income', M, which would be realised if all time available were spent working. M is equal to:

$$M = Tw\,(1 - t) + \mu \tag{7.10}$$

Similarly, the expenditure function must be defined in terms of the full income needed to reach a specified indifference curve, U, with a given net wage rate, $w' = w\,(1-t)$, and is thus written as $M\,(w', U)$. It is possible to define the expenditure function in terms of 'virtual' income, equal to the value of net income where the budget line (or the extension of a relevant segment of the budget line, in the case of piecewise-linear constraints) intercepts a vertical line at T hours of leisure. The form adopted is a matter only of convenience, since the results are identical.

The income tax thus has two simultaneous effects: it reduces both full income and the price of leisure. The first effect reduces welfare while the second effect increases welfare. The expression in (7.7) can be directly translated into the income tax framework using:

$$EV = \{M_1 - M\,(w_0', U_1)\} + \{M_0 - M_1\} \tag{7.11}$$

The excess burden is, as before, obtained by subtracting the tax paid from the equivalent variation.

7.3.3 Approximation of the Excess Burden

To obtain an approximation of the excess burden, it is again useful to turn to diagrams. The linear tax is illustrated in Figure 7.8, which shows an initial optimal position, E_1, along indifference curve U_0. Non-wage income is

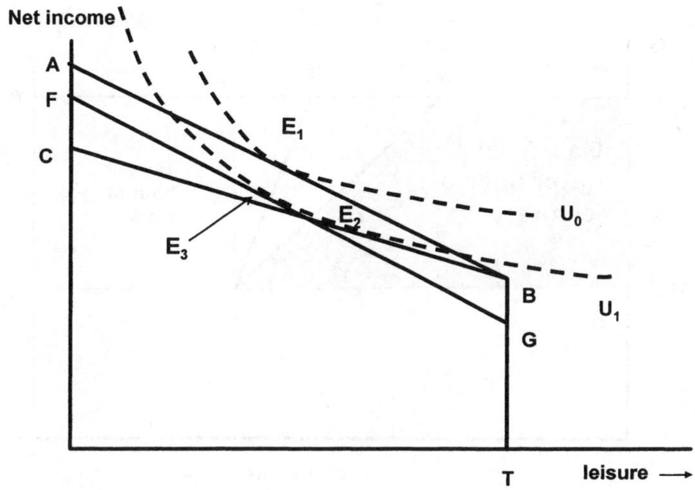

Figure 7.8: A Linear Income Tax

given by the height of BT, which represents the consumption available if the individual does not work. Point A indicates full income $M(w_0', U_0) = M_0$, the amount that could be consumed if all T were devoted to work. If the initial position is a 'no-tax' situation, then $w_0' = w$. Point C is associated with a full income of $M(w_1', U_1) = M_1$ and F with a full income of $M(w_0', U_1)$. The equivalent variation is thus the distance AF, or $M_0 - M(w_0', U_1)$, which is converted into the expression in (7.11) by the addition and subtraction of M_1.

Figure 7.9 converts the information in Figure 7.8 into a diagram showing the Hicksian demand curve for leisure between the two net wage rates of w_0' and w_1': this is the line E_3E_2. The Marshallian demand curve is E_1E_2. Since the price of leisure has fallen, the area DE_3E_2C, the area to the left of the Hicksian demand curve, is the gain from the price reduction. However, there is simultaneously a change in full income. The reduction in full income is measured by the change in net income when working T hours, so in Figure 7.9

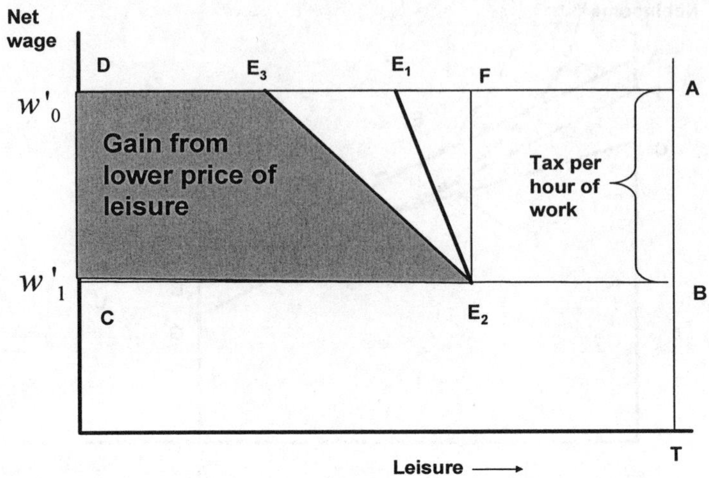

Figure 7.9: The Excess Burden of an Income Tax

it is the area ABCD. The equivalent variation is thus the area ABCD minus the area DE_3E_2C. This gives the area to the right of the demand curve for leisure, that is, ABE_2E_3. The tax paid, the tax per unit multiplied by the time worked, is equal to the area of the rectangle ABE_2F. Hence the excess burden is the area of the triangle E_2E_3F.

As before, the excess burden is approximated by the area of a triangle, equal to half the product of the base and the height. The base is the change in labour supply (associated with the Hicksian demand curve for leisure), Δh, and the height is the tax per unit of time, equal to tw. Hence:

$$EB_{EV} = \frac{1}{2} tw\left(\Delta h\right) \tag{7.12}$$

Following the previous derivations in section 7.2, the change in labour supply can be expressed in terms of the elasticity of the Hicksian supply curve (derived from the leisure demand curve), $\eta = \frac{w'}{h}\frac{dh}{dw'}$. Since the burden is based on the equivalent variation, movement is from the new position, with $h = h_1$

and $w_1' = w(1-t)$, so using the approximation $\eta = \frac{w(1-t)}{h_1}\frac{\Delta h}{wt}$:

$$\Delta h = |\eta|\, h_1 \left(\frac{t}{1-t}\right) \tag{7.13}$$

and substituting (7.13) into (7.12) gives:

$$\begin{aligned} EB_{EV} &= \frac{|\eta|}{2} w h_1 \left(\frac{t^2}{1-t}\right) \\ &= \frac{|\eta|}{2} w_1' h_1 \left(\frac{t}{1-t}\right)^2 \end{aligned} \tag{7.14}$$

This takes the same form as equation (7.3) although at first sight it looks different. This is because the tax rate, τ, in equation (7.3) is a tax-inclusive rate, whereas t in (7.14) is a tax-exclusive rate. In addition the price of leisure has fallen, so the equivalent tax-inclusive rate is $\tau = -t/(1-t)$.

In practice, tax systems are more complex than the linear tax considered here, as there are typically several tax thresholds and rates, giving rise to a piecewise-linear budget constraint. Also, means-testing of transfer payments often leads to non-convexities in the budget set. An approximation like (7.14) therefore needs to be treated with considerable caution. A more extensive analysis of welfare measures, paying careful attention to corner solutions, is given in the next chapter.

7.4 Conclusions

This chapter has defined money measures of welfare change and the associated concept of the excess burden of a tax. It was shown how an approximation to the excess burden can be obtained diagrammatically, involving indifference curves and associated Hicksian demand curves. An assumption that the demand curve is linear over the relevant range produces the result that the excess burden is proportional to the square of the tax rate.

This result provides a general warning that policies which erode the tax base, and therefore increase the tax rate, need special justification. Furthermore, tax-financed expenditure and redistribution policies must provide benefits that outweigh the efficiency costs of raising the required revenue.

The question arises of whether reliance can be placed on this result in practical policy analyses. One obvious point is that practical analyses often involve more than one tax change and these are seldom small changes, so that any approximation is unlikely to be reliable. Thus the use of approximations is not recommended, although an appreciation of the basic nature of the excess burden and the arguments leading to the approximation can be valuable in informing policy analyses.

Chapter 8

Welfare Measures and Labour Supply

The aim of this chapter is to examine the computation of welfare measures in the special context of labour supply models, where individuals typically face highly nonlinear budget constraints and the appropriate price, the net wage rate, is endogenous as well as labour supply itself. Few of the studies which estimate utility or labour supply functions actually produce individual measures of the welfare effects of tax reforms. Recent developments in behavioural tax microsimulation modelling and their use in policy analyses not only make the production of such measures possible but also provide a strong motivation for developing convenient methods of obtaining accurate welfare measures.

In the context of commodity demands, including situations in which there may be quantity constraints, a general approach was suggested by Neary and Roberts (1980), exploiting the Hicksian concept of virtual price; see also Latham (1980) or Johansson (1987). In these cases it is usual to define a modified expenditure function conditional on the rationed levels of consumption. Quantity constraints arise for example in the context of rationing of standard commodities, or where there are constraints on the consumption of environmental resources. However, where welfare changes have been produced in the labour supply context, the approach has been to adopt a minor modifification of the well-known expressions used to obtain welfare changes: see, for example, Hausman (1981, p.672; 1985a, pp.243-245), Blomquist (1983, pp.187-190), Blundell, Preston and Walker (1994, pp.4-8) and Creedy (2000, 2001).

It is suggested here that this 'standard' approach does not sufficiently allow for the precise nonlinearity of the budget constraint facing an individual. A method of computing the welfare change, allowing for the full relevant detail of budget constraints, is proposed and illustrated using diagrams. In allowing for the nonlinearity it differs from Apps and Rees (1999) and in its simple and wide applicability it differs from Preston and Walker (1999). The method can be applied to a wide range of utility specifications, independent of whether the expenditure function can be written down explicitly. The approach is illustrated using numerical examples.

Section 8.1 examines welfare changes in models in which individuals are allowed to change hours of work over a continuous range. The modification required when only a discrete number of hours levels are allowed is presented in section 8.2.

The next two sections consider specific utility functions which have been used in empirical studies of labour supply. Section 8.3 uses the quadratic direct utility function, while section 8.4 examines the quadratic translog form. In both sections numerical examples are provided. Most applications of the discrete hours framework have used these forms, although Vlasblom, De Gijsel and Siegers (2001) used the CES form, for which the approach discussed here could easily be applied. The discussion of the method of measuring welfare changes and the numerical examples assume that an individual's utility function is known precisely. In practice, estimation is based on data for members of a particular demographic group in which some unobserved heterogeneity in preferences remains. The use of such estimates to obtain an individual's value for welfare changes in tax microsimulation modelling is discussed in section 8.5. Conclusions can be found in section 8.6.

8.1 Continuous Hours Labour Supply

This section examines the type of labour supply model where the time spent working can be varied continuously. After setting out the basic framework in subsection 8.1.1, the expression for the compensating variation for the simple linear budget constraint is given in section 8.1.2. Subsection 8.1.3 gives an example for a nonlinear constraint, while the general case for nonlinear constraints is set out in subsection 8.1.4.

8.1.1 The Basic Framework

Let h denote the number of hours devoted to labour supply, which may be varied continuously, and let c denote net income. In this static framework, with the price index normalised to unity, net income and consumption are equal. The direct utility function is written as $U(c, h)$. Leisure is $T - h$, where T is the total number of hours available for work and leisure. The tax and transfer system is characterised by a piecewise-linear budget constraint.

Any optimal position can be regarded as being generated by a linear constraint of the form:

$$c = wh + \mu \tag{8.1}$$

For tangency solutions, w and μ represent the appropriate net wage rate and virtual income respectively. Virtual income is distinct from actual non-wage income. With a corner solution, virtual income is defined as the value generated by a linear constraint having a net wage, the virtual wage, equal to the slope of the indifference curve at the kink. An important characteristic of the optimal position is that the net wage and virtual income, as well as the hours worked, are endogenous.

The evaluation of welfare changes requires an expression for the expenditure function, giving the minimum expenditure needed to reach a specified indifference curve at a given net wage rate. This can be written in terms of virtual income, using $\mu(w, U)$ or in terms of full income, using $M(w, U)$.

Virtual income, $\mu(w, U)$, is obtained by first obtaining the indirect utility function. Substitute $c = wh + \mu$ into $U(c, h)$, and substitute the solution for optimal h, from $\frac{dc}{dh}\big|_U = w$ and $c = wh + \mu$, into U. Then invert the indirect utility function by solving U for μ. Full income, M, is equal to $M = \mu + wT$, so the corresponding expenditure function is:

$$M(w, U) = \mu(w, U) + wT \tag{8.2}$$

The above expenditure function is used in the following subsections to calculate the compensating and equivalent variations.

8.1.2 The Simple Case of a Linear Budget Constraint

Suppose there is a change in taxes and transfers from system 0 to system 1. Values in each system are indicated by 0 and 1 subscripts. In terms of virtual incomes, the standard expression for the compensating variation, which defines the amount of money necessary to keep an individual at the same utility level as in system 0 after the change to system 1, is:

$$CV = \mu(w_1, U_0) - \mu_1 \tag{8.3}$$

where w_i is either the virtual or actual net wage rate at the optimum position under policy i, U_i is the maximum utility that can be reached under tax system i, and $\mu_i = \mu(w_i, U_i)$. These changes are illustrated in Figure 8.1, where a tax change involves a movement from point A to point B. The payment of the compensating variation of $\mu(w_1, U_0) - \mu_1$ allows the individual to reach indifference curve U_0 at point C, while in receipt of the net wage w_1 and working fewer hours than at B.

The CV can be decomposed into separate price (of leisure) and income effects, using:

$$CV = \{M(w_1, U_0) - M_0\} + (M_0 - M_1) \tag{8.4}$$

where $M_i = M(w_i, U_i)$. The absolute value of the term in curly brackets corresponds to an area to the left of a compensated leisure demand curve

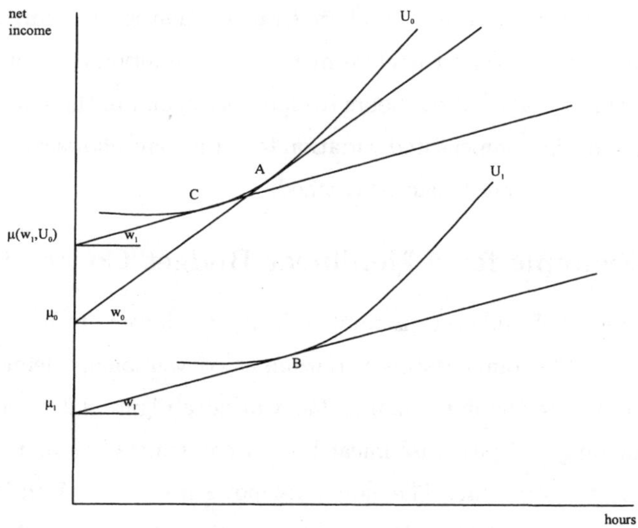

Figure 8.1: The Simple Case

between appropriate prices; see chapter 7. A fall in the wage rate reduces full income but lowers the price of leisure, so that the welfare change from the price effect, the term in curly brackets in (8.4), is negative. Hence the overall effect is ambiguous.

The equivalent variation is the amount that must be taken from an individual in order to keep utility constant at the new level, if the tax change were reversed. It is equal to the negative of the corresponding compensating variation for a change from tax system 1 to system 0, and is therefore $EV = \mu_0 - \mu(w_0, U_1)$. Since no different principles are involved, much of the following discussion concentrates on compensating variations. However, in later sections, illustrative examples are given for both the CV and EV.

The expressions given above are the standard welfare changes used in the literature. However, the approach implicitly assumes that the virtual budget line, given by the tangent to U_1 at point B, with associated virtual income of μ_1, does in fact apply over the relevant range. That is, the individual can move to the left of B (and therefore increase consumption of leisure) along the linear budget line until the hours worked correspond to those at point C. The addition of the compensated variation to net income allows consumption to increase so that point C can be reached.

8.1.3 Example for a Nonlinear Budget Constraint

The nonlinearity of budget constraints relating net income to hours worked can imply that the compensating variation, as conventionally defined, is insufficient to restore the individual to U_0. Consider Figure 8.2, which shows the relevant ranges of piecewise linear budget constraints before and after a change in the tax structure. The individual moves from point A on U_0, a tangency solution, to point B on U_1, a corner solution. The standard approach gives a compensating variation of $\mu(w_1, U_0) - \mu_1$, where μ_1 is the intercept (at $h = 0$) of a virtual budget constraint with a slope of w_1.

The ability to vary hours of work continuously means that labour supply can be reduced to correspond to point C, but in this case the increase in leisure involves a fall in net income below that implied by the virtual budget constraint. The vertical distance between D and C is required to bring the individual to point C on indifference curve U_0. This is greater than the standard compensating variation as given above.

It is required to find the minimum compensation necessary to move from budget constraint BC_1 to indifference curve U_0. Assume that the budget set is convex over the relevant range; allowance for further complexities is discussed in the following subsection. Let w_c denote the virtual wage, the slope of the indifference curve U_0, at point E and let $\mu(w_c, U_0)$ represent the associated virtual income. As long as w_c lies between the slope of BD and the slope of the budget constraint to the right of B, the distance between B and E represents the minimum compensation. That is, the compensation

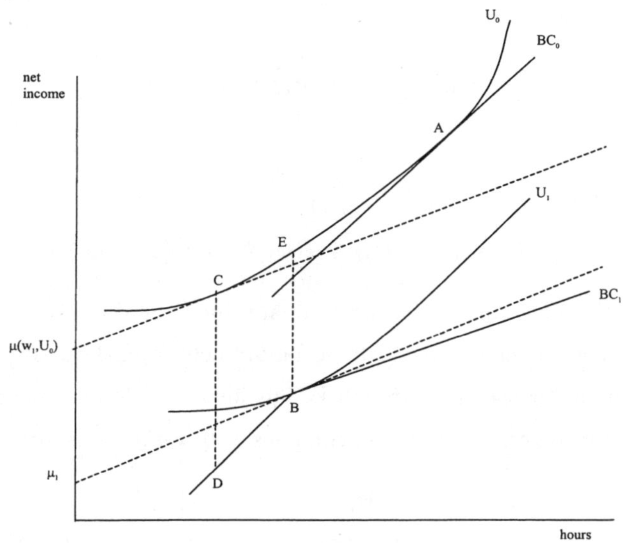

Figure 8.2: A Nonlinear Constraint

required is given by the difference between net income at B and net income at E, where the individual remains at the hours associated with B. Given that U_0 lies above U_1, the slope of the tangent to E, w_c, is always higher than the slope of the tangent at B, w_1. Therefore, the segment of the budget constraint to the right of B can never provide a tangency solution in this example. However, if the slope of BD is lower than w_c, there is a tangency solution on BD when shifted upwards in the direction of U_0. In this case, the distance between the point of this tangency solution and the point on BC_1 at the same hours would be the minimum compensation required. This is discussed further in the next subsection.

In the case where the distance between B and E represents the minimum compensation, h_1 is the number of hours worked at B and E:

$$CV = \{\mu(w_c, U_0) + w_c h_1\} - \{\mu_1 + w_1 h_1\} \tag{8.5}$$

which can be rewritten as;

$$CV = \{\mu(w_c, U_0) - \mu_1\} + (w_c - w_1) h_1 \tag{8.6}$$

or:

$$\begin{aligned} CV &= \{\mu(w_1, U_0) - \mu_1\} \\ &\quad + \{\mu(w_c, U_0) - \mu(w_1, U_0)\} + (w_c - w_1) h_1 \end{aligned} \tag{8.7}$$

This shows the addition to the conventional value (contained in the first line) needed to allow for the fact that leftward movement from B cannot take place along the virtual constraint through B, but involves a lower net income. In terms of full incomes, the adjusted compensating variation is given by:

$$\begin{aligned} CV &= \{M(w_1, U_0) - M_1\} + \{M_0 - M_1\} \\ &\quad + \{M(w_c, U_0) - M(w_1, U_0)\} + (w_1 - w_c)(T - h_1) \end{aligned} \tag{8.8}$$

where again the first line gives the standard expression. In this example, the standard expression for the equivalent variation is not affected so long as the kinks are far enough from the tangency point.

8.1.4 The General Case for Nonlinear Constraints

In the previous subsection, the relevant range of the budget constraint has one kink. In general, allowance must be made for more complex types of constraint. For example, the constraint to the left of point B in Figure 8.2 may have a number of convex and concave ranges over a relatively small range of hours of work. A convex range occurs if the marginal tax rate falls as hours of work increase. This may happen when entitlement to a means-tested benefit is exhausted. It is possible, even if B were a tangency solution, to have a level of hours, say h_c, where the net income is associated with an indifference curve, say $U_{c,1}$, that is lower than indifference curve U_1, but the increase in net income required to bring utility up to U_0 is a minimum. This is shown in Figure 8.3 by the length DC.

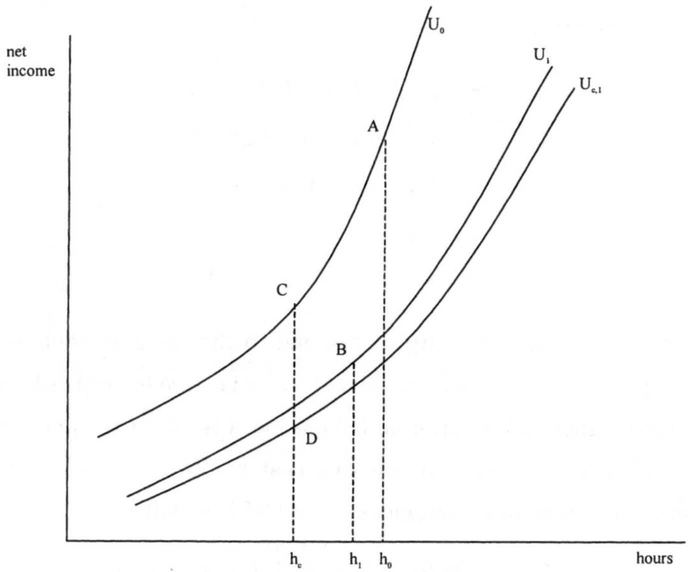

Figure 8.3: The General Case

Let the virtual wage associated with the hours level h_c, at point C on indifference curve U_0 in Figure 8.3 be denoted w_c. Similarly, let the virtual wage for hours h_c on $U_{c,1}$ at point D be $w_{c,1}$. The virtual incomes associated with these two points are $\mu(w_c, U_0)$ and $\mu(w_{c,1}, U_{c,1})$. Hence the compensating variation is:

$$CV = \{\mu(w_c, U_0) + w_c h_c\} - \{\mu(w_{c,1}, U_{c,1}) + w_{c,1} h_c\} \tag{8.9}$$

This can be rewritten as:

$$\begin{aligned} CV &= \{\mu(w_1, U_0) - \mu_1\} \\ &+ \{\mu(w_c, U_0) - \mu(w_1, U_0)\} \\ &+ \{w_c - w_1\} h_c \\ &+ \{w_1 - w_{c,1}\} h_c \\ &+ \{\mu_1 - \mu(w_{c,1}, U_{c,1})\} \end{aligned} \tag{8.10}$$

The first three lines of (8.10) correspond to the terms in equation (8.7). Hence the previous subsection considered a special case for which $h_c = h_1$. If $h_c < h_1$ the compensating variation is lower, as a result of the final two lines in (8.10). If $U_0 > U_1$, it must be the case that $h_c \leq h_1$.

In terms of full income components the CV is as follows:

$$\begin{aligned} CV &= \{M(w_1, U_0) - M_0\} + \{M_0 - M_1\} \\ &+ \{M(w_c, U_0) - M(w_1, U_0)\} \\ &+ \{w_1 - w_c\}(T - h_c) \\ &+ \{w_{c,1} - w_1\}(T - h_c) \\ &+ \{M_1 - M(w_{c,1}, U_{c,1})\} \end{aligned} \tag{8.11}$$

which can be compared with (8.8).

The same kind of argument can be applied to the equivalent variation, where it is required to maximise the change in income necessary to reach U_1 from the initial budget constraint under tax system 0. The general result for the equivalent variation is:

$$\begin{aligned} EV &= \{M_1 - M(w_0, U_1)\} + \{M_0 - M_1\} \\ &+ \{M(w_0, U_1) - M(w_e, U_1)\} \\ &+ \{w_e - w_0\}(T - h_e) \\ &+ \{w_0 - w_{e,0}\}(T - h_e) \\ &+ \{M(w_{e,0}, U_{e,0}) - M_0\} \end{aligned} \tag{8.12}$$

where $h_e, w_e, w_{e,0}$ and $U_{e,0}$ are the equivalents of $h_c, w_c, w_{c,1}$ and $U_{c,1}$.

Determining the location of h_c and h_e requires a systematic search over the corners and linear sections of the budget constraint, ignoring any non-convex ranges. The distances from the possible corners of the new budget constraint (the hours levels where the changes in marginal tax rates apply) to the indifference curve U_0 are compared. Furthermore, possible tangency solutions for linear sections of the new budget constraint, shifted vertically upwards to touch U_0, must be investigated. This is done for each segment by comparing the range of marginal rates of substitution, over the hours interval, with the net wage for the segment.

If a tangency is found to exist, the precise hours and net income are obtained by simultaneously solving the two relevant equations. Determine the tangencies to U_0 by solving c and h from $\left.\frac{dc}{dh}\right|_U = w_1$ and $U(c, h) = U_0$, for each linear segment of the budget constraint for which w_1 lies between the virtual wage rates at the surrounding corners of the segment. Depending on the form of the utility function, an iterative numerical procedure may be needed to solve these equations. In the case of the compensating variation, the compensation needed is obtained by minimising the distance in selecting h_c. For the equivalent variation, the corresponding vertical distance is maximised in obtaining h_e.

8.2 Discrete Hours Choices

This section examines a discrete hours model in which individuals are restricted to a limited number of hours levels, $h_1, ..., h_H$. The utility function and net incomes at each of the specified hours points are known. Evaluation of the optimal number of hours is therefore easily carried out by calculating utilities at a relatively small number of points, each of which is treated as a corner solution. The discussion of piecewise-linear constraints where there is a corner solution, as in the previous section, suggests that in the case of

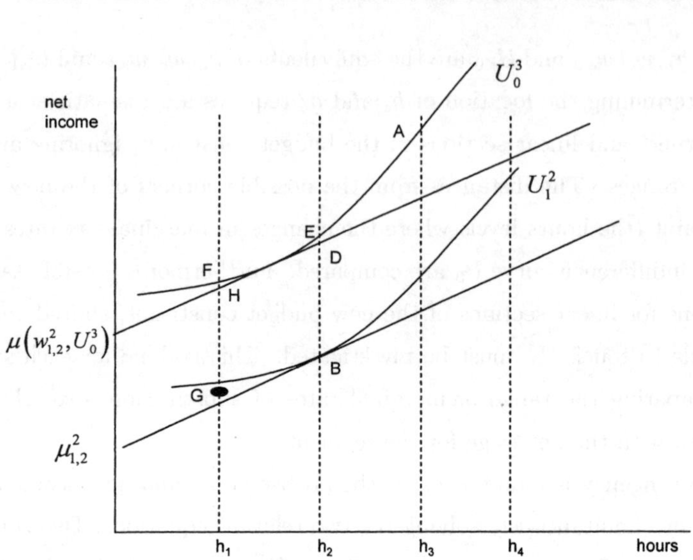

Figure 8.4: Discrete Hours

discrete hours it is again no longer appropriate to use the standard formulae for the welfare changes.

8.2.1 The Framework of Analysis

Consider Figure 8.4, where it is assumed that there are just four discrete hours levels available. Here it is useful to introduce a new notation system, in view of the use of $h_1, ..., h_H$ to refer to fixed discrete hours levels and the possible need to consider more than two indifference curves. In addition to the subscript denoting the tax system, each indifference curve is given a superscript which refers to the hours level; that is, U_j^k is the utility obtained from combination of the discrete hours level h_k and the associated consumption determined by tax and transfer system j.

A similar convention is used when referring to virtual incomes and virtual wages, defined as the tangent to a given indifference curve at a specified hours level. A superscript indicates the hours index which defines the utility level, while a second subscript refers to the discrete hours level to which the virtual values relate. Hence the virtual wage $w_{0,j}^{k}$ is the slope of indifference curve U_0^k at the discrete hours point h_j. Similarly, $\mu_{0,j}^{k}$ is the corresponding virtual income, the intercept on the net income axis of the tangent to the indifference curve U_0^k at the discrete hours level h_j.

8.2.2 Exact Welfare Changes

The original optimal position in Figure 8.4 is at point A on indifference curve U_0^3, corresponding to h_3 hours of work. A tax reform causes the optimal position to shift to point B on indifference curve U_1^2, involving h_2 hours of work. Hence the virtual linear budget constraints associated with A and B are defined by the pairs $(\mu_{0,3}^3, w_{0,3}^3)$ and $(\mu_{1,2}^2, w_{1,2}^2)$ respectively.[1] Given the limited hours choices available, calculation of the compensating variation using the standard approach understates the true amount needed to restore the individual to U_0^3. The approach used when discussing continuous hours variations can be directly applied here. The compensation is the difference between the net incomes at points E and B.

Using the notation described above, $w_{0,2}^3$ denotes the virtual wage corresponding to hours level h_2 at point E on U_0^3 and $\mu_{0,2}^3$ represents the associated virtual income.[2] Assuming that the individual remains at discrete hours level h_2, the compensation required, length EB, is given by:

$$CV = \left\{\mu_{0,2}^3 + w_{0,2}^3 h_2\right\} - \left\{\mu_{1,2}^2 + w_{1,2}^2 h_2\right\} \tag{8.13}$$

or equivalently:

$$CV = \left\{\mu_{0,2}^3 - \mu_{1,2}^2\right\} + \left(w_{0,2}^3 - w_{1,2}^2\right) h_2 \tag{8.14}$$

[1] For each discrete hours point, h_j, net income under the two alternative tax systems, c_j^0 and c_j^1, can be determined, after which $U\left(c_j^0, h_j\right)$ can be calculated. Then $w_{0,i}^i$ is the virtual wage in the optimal point U_0^i and $\mu_{0,i}^i = c_i^0 - w_{0,i}^i h_i$.

[2] Determine net income $c_{0,2}^3$ necessary to reach U_0^3 in h_2 by solving for c in $U(c, h_2) = U_0^3$ and then use $\mu_{0,2}^3 = c_{0,2}^3 - w_{0,2}^3 h_2$.

In terms of associated full incomes, this can be written as:

$$CV = \left(\mu_{0,2}^3 + w_{0,2}^3 T\right) - \left(\mu_{1,2}^2 + w_{1,2}^2 T\right) + \left(w_{1,2}^2 - w_{0,2}^3\right)(T - h_2) \tag{8.15}$$

However, the possibility must be considered that the individual could work h_1 hours and reach indifference curve U_0^3 with a smaller increase to net income than the value given in (8.13). If net income at h_1 in system 1 is at point G (which is above the virtual budget constraint associated with B), it is possible that the distance between G and F is smaller than that between B and E. Even if G were slightly below the virtual budget line through B, it is possible for the compensating variation to be lower than if hours were fixed at h_2, depending on the distance FH compared with ED.

Point G is the combination of net income on the actual budget constraint under the post-reform tax system and the hours level h_1, so the indifference curve through this point is labelled U_1^1. If the individual is at G, the compensation required to reach U_0^3 is the length GF and is given by:

$$CV = \left\{\mu_{0,1}^3 + w_{0,1}^3 h_1\right\} - \left\{\mu_{1,1}^1 + w_{1,1}^1 h_1\right\} \tag{8.16}$$

or equivalently:

$$CV = \left\{\mu_{0,1}^3 - \mu_{1,1}^1\right\} + \left(w_{0,1}^3 - w_{1,1}^1\right) h_1 \tag{8.17}$$

The appropriate compensation is the minimum of this type of difference, over all discrete hours points. The search for the appropriate hours level which produces a minimum compensation is therefore simpler in the discrete hours context, where all possible hours levels are specified *a priori*, compared with the continuous hours framework, where an alternative tangency may apply. In the examples given below, the appropriate hours levels for compensating and equivalent variations are referred to as h_c and h_e, by analogy with their use in the continuous hours context.

If a utility function is used for which the labour supply and expenditure functions cannot be derived explicitly, it is not possible to obtain an analytical expression for the virtual income $\mu\left(w_{1,2}^{2}, U_{0}^{3}\right)$, shown in Figure 8.4, or the associated expenditure function expressed in terms of full income. But this does not matter as it is not actually required in the discrete hours context.

8.2.3 Computational Requirements

The use of a discrete hours framework has substantial advantages from the point of view of econometric estimation of preferences. In addition to avoiding the need to deal with the endogeneity of net wage rates (compared with estimation of a continuous labour supply function where hours worked are expressed as a continuous function of net wage and virtual income), and the need to compute net incomes over the complete hours range for each individual, it is not necessary to solve the first-order conditions for maximising utility subject to a linear budget constraint. Hence an explicit form for the labour supply function is not needed. This means that a wider range of direct utility functions can be used. In the continuous case, even if estimation is based on an explicit labour supply function (expressed in terms of μ and w), it is necessary, for welfare measurement, to integrate from the labour supply to the expenditure function. This integration may need to be carried out numerically.

The same advantage applies to the calculation of welfare changes. The procedure outlined above requires only the calculation of virtual wage rates, virtual incomes and the net income corresponding to a specified hours level and indifference curve. These are obtained as follows.

First, the virtual wage, w, at any point (defined by a combination of c and h) is given by the slope of the indifference curve at that point. Hence:

$$w = \left.\frac{dc}{dh}\right|_{U(c,h)} \tag{8.18}$$

and this can usually be calculated with little difficulty, since first derivatives of U are usually easy to obtain. Second, the corresponding virtual income,

$\mu(w, U)$, can be calculated using the equation of the virtual linear budget constraint. Using the combination of w, c and h in (8.18), the corresponding virtual income is:

$$\mu(w, U) = c - hw \tag{8.19}$$

Third, it is necessary to compute net income, c, corresponding to a specified hours level, h, along an indifference curve with known utility level, U, computed from a known different optimal combination of consumption and hours. Having outlined the general procedure, the following two sections provide detailed discussions of two important direct utility functions.

8.3 The Quadratic Direct Utility Function

This section describes the main properties of the quadratic direct utility function and presents numerical examples of welfare changes in both continuous and discrete hours contexts. The quadratic utility function has been used frequently in empirical analyses of labour supply in the context of discrete hours models. Examples include Keane and Moffitt (1998), Duncan and Weeks (1997, 1998) and Duncan and Giles (1998).

8.3.1 The Main Properties

The quadratic direct utility function is:

$$U = \alpha c^2 + \beta h^2 + \gamma ch + \delta c + \varepsilon h \tag{8.20}$$

and:

$$\left.\frac{dc}{dh}\right|_{U(c,h)} = -\frac{2\beta h + \gamma c + \varepsilon}{2\alpha c + \gamma h + \delta} \tag{8.21}$$

It is required to compute net income, c, corresponding to a specified hours level, h, along an indifference curve with known utility level, U (computed from net income and hours at the optimal position). This is obtained as the appropriate root of the quadratic:

$$ac^2 + bc + d = 0 \tag{8.22}$$

with:

$$\begin{aligned} a &= \alpha \\ b &= \gamma h + \delta \\ d &= \beta h^2 + \varepsilon h - U \end{aligned} \tag{8.23}$$

In practice the appropriate root is obvious.

Explicit analytical expressions can be obtained for the labour supply and expenditure functions; see Appendix E for further details. Creedy (2001) showed that the expenditure function, in terms of virtual income, is given by the smallest root of the quadratic:

$$q_1\mu^2 + q_2\mu + q_3 = 0 \tag{8.24}$$

where:

$$q_1 = \alpha - \frac{(2\alpha w + \gamma)^2}{4(\alpha w^2 + \gamma w + \beta)} \tag{8.25}$$

$$q_2 = \delta - \frac{(2\alpha w + \gamma)(\delta w + \varepsilon)}{2(\alpha w^2 + \gamma w + \beta)} \tag{8.26}$$

$$q_3 = -\left(U + \frac{(\delta w + \varepsilon)^2}{4(\alpha w^2 + \gamma w + \beta)}\right) \tag{8.27}$$

This expenditure function facilitates comparison with the standard approach in the continuous hours case.

8.3.2 Numerical Examples

In order to demonstrate the above procedures, this subsection presents numerical examples based on the utility function:

$$U(h, c) = -0.007c^2 - 0.005h^2 + 5.5c - 2.5h \tag{8.28}$$

with $T = 80$. Setting $\gamma = 0$ makes selection of hypothetical values for the other parameters easier but does not greatly affect the computation of welfare measures. Three hypothetical tax schedules are used, as shown in Table 8.1. The following examples relate to two policy changes, from structure 1 to 2, and from 1 to 3. There are five effective marginal tax rates, t_i, and

Table 8.1: Hypothetical Tax Structures

		Structure 1		Structure 2		Structure 3	
Segment	y_i	t_i	μ_i	t_i	μ_i	t_i	μ_i
1	0	0.0	100	0.0	**75**	0.0	100
2	30	0.5	115	0.5	**90**	0.5	115
3	70	0.3	101	0.3	**76**	0.3	101
4	200	0.4	121	0.4	**96**	**0.5**	**141**
5	350	0.5	156	0.5	**131**	**0.6**	**196**

corresponding income thresholds, y_i, above which these rates apply; these thresholds are the same for all structures. For example, structure 1 has a range where the marginal effective tax rate is zero, but after the threshold of $y_2 = 30$ the rate becomes 0.5; this is regarded as arising from a taper rate applying to a means-tested transfer payment. At an earnings threshold of $y_3 = 70$, the effective marginal rate drops to 0.3, when entitlement to the means-tested benefit is exhausted. This produces a range where the budget set is non-convex. Beyond this range, the marginal tax rate increases. The transfer payment received by non-workers, μ_1, is set equal to 100. Given these values, the remaining virtual incomes, μ_i, can be calculated, and are shown in Table 8.1.

In structure 2, non-wage income for non-workers, μ_1, is reduced from 100 to 75, while all income thresholds and marginal tax rates remain constant. The new virtual incomes are shown in bold in the table. The third tax structure is the same as the first but has higher marginal rates in the 4th and 5th segments, leading to higher associated virtual incomes; the new values are also shown in bold. Continuous and discrete hours frameworks are examined in turn.

Continuous Hours

Suppose, first, that the individual has a gross wage of $w_g = 8$. With the tax structure of Table 8.1, the hours levels at which the effective marginal tax rates change are 0, 3.75, 8.75, 25.00 and 43.75. The gross wage of 8 gives rise to an optimal labour supply given by a tangency solution on section 5 of the constraint, corresponding to $h = 46$. The reduction in μ_1 to 75 means that the optimal position involves a tangency position on section 5 of the new constraint, where h rises to 51.98. The fact that the same section is relevant means that the net wage is unchanged, so there is only an income effect. Thus $h_c = h_0$ and $h_e = h_1$. Both compensating and equivalent variations are equal to the change in virtual and full income, which is 25. Hence, for this particular case, the standard method of calculating welfare changes gives the same results as in the general case discussed in section 8.1.

The second policy change involves an increase in labour supply to 47.05 hours, which is also on section 5 of the budget constraint. The standard method of computing the welfare change gives $CV = 15.549$, as shown in the second column of Table 8.2. However, the associated hours would take the individual beyond the 5th segment and into the 4th segment of the new budget constraint. Hence the method proposed above gives values associated with the corner at $h_c = 43.75$ hours. The various components of the welfare change are given in Table 8.2, which shows that the corrected CV is 15.687. However, in considering the equivalent variation, an hours level of $h_e = 50.60$ is calculated, which is still on the 5th linear segment. Hence the standard method gives the correct value, as seen by the fact that the other components in Table 8.2 are zero.

Suppose next that the gross wage rate is $w_g = 5$. This implies that, for the tax system in Table 8.1, the hours levels at which the five marginal rates start to apply are 0, 6, 14, 40 and 70. The optimal position is found to be a tangency solution along section 4 of the budget constraint, with $h = 65.57$. For the first policy change, where there is only a reduction in μ_1, the new optimal position involves a shift from the tangency position on segment 4 to a corner solution at the start of segment 5, with $h = 70$. The shift to a corner solution means that both the endogenous virtual wage and income change.

Table 8.2: Welfare Changes for Continuous Hours

	Policy 2 Increase in t_4 and t_5 $w_g = 8$	Policy 1 Reduction in μ_1 $w_g = 5$
Compensating variation		
$\{M(w_1, U_0) - M_0\} + \{M_0 - M_1\}$	15.549	22.777
$\{M(w_c, U_0) - M(w_1, U_0)\}$	8.482	5.907
$\{w_1 - w_c\}(T - h_c)$	–8.344	–5.315
$\{w_{c,1} - w_1\}(T - h_c)$	–17.037	5.315
$\{M_1 - M(w_{c,1}, U_{c,1})\}$	17.037	–3.684
CV	15.687	25
Equivalent variation		
$\{M_1 - M(w_0, U_1)\} + \{M_0 - M_1\}$	19.207	25.685
$\{M(w_0, U_1) - M(w_e, U_1)\}$	0	3.000
$\{w_0 - w_{e,1}\}(T - h_e)$	0	–6.9525
$\{w_e - w_0\}(T - h_e)$	0	–3.684
$\{M(w_{e,1}, U_{e,0}) - M_0\}$	0	6.952
EV	19.207	25

The standard method of computing welfare changes gives $CV = 22.777$ and $EV = 25.685$, as shown in Table 8.2. However, using (8.11) the compensating variation, allowing for the precise nonlinearity of the budget constraint, is 25, equal to the reduction in μ_1. In this case, $h_c = h_0$ and $h_e = h_1$. Similarly, the equivalent variation is also equal to 25.

For the second policy change and a gross wage of $w_g = 5$, labour supply falls to 64.77, but this is also a tangency solution along the 4th segment. The fall in full income is 20 while, following the standard approach, the welfare gains associated with the fall in the price of leisure are 8.356 and 6.248, for compensating and equivalent variations respectively. Thus $CV = 11.64$ and $EV = 13.75$. For this case, $h_c = 60.58$ and $h_e = 69.82$. Given that all the relevant hours positions involve tangency solutions along the same segment, the standard measures are exactly the same as those produced by the general approach.

Table 8.3: Welfare Changes for Wage Rate of 8

Hours	Standard				Corrected				Optimal hours	
steps	CV	EV	h_c	h_e	CV	EV	h_c	h_e	Base	Reform
First tax change: reduction in μ_1										
5	22.32	23.53	45	50	25	25	45	50	45	50
10	21.85	25.00	40	50	25	25	50	50	50	50
20	-	15.27	40	40	25	25	40	60	40	60
Second tax change: increase in t_4 and t_5										
5	14.37	18.09	40	50	16.00	19.56	45	50	45	45
10	19.89	20.00	40	50	17.21	20.00	40	50	50	50
20	12.00	12.00	40	40	12.00	12.00	40	40	40	40

Discrete Hours

For the discrete hours case, results are reported for three situations where discrete hours are limited to intervals of 5, 10 and 20 over the range from 0 up to $T = 80$. Table 8.3 shows alternative welfare measures obtained for the tax policy changes considered above, where the gross wage is 8. For the first policy change there is, as with the continuous hours context, an income effect only, whereby equivalent and compensating variations are 25. Since the restriction to discrete hours causes a deviation of the hours level from the level that would be optimal under continuous hours models, the standard approach can lead to values that deviate substantially when the discrete interval is large. Indeed, the CV when hours intervals of 20 are imposed is meaningless because it involves a range of the utility function where indifference curves slope in the wrong direction.

Table 8.4 shows results for a gross wage rate of 5. Again the approach proposed here gives results for the first policy that are different from those obtained using the standard approach. For the second policy, involving changes in two of the marginal tax rates, the alternative approaches are closer together because the values of h_c and h_e are the same for both methods.

For both gross wage rates and the second policy, the case where the

Table 8.4: Welfare Measures for Wage Rate of 5

Hours	Standard				Corrected				Optimal hours	
steps	CV	EV	h_c	h_e	CV	EV	h_c	h_e	Base	Reform
First tax change: reduction in μ_1										
5	22.95	24.81	60	75	25	25	65	70	65	70
10	21.92	28.95	60	80	25	25	70	70	70	70
20	46.21	22.03	60	80	25	25	60	60	60	80
Second tax change: increase in t_4 and t_5										
5	11.73	13.39	60	70	11.64	13.75	60	70	65	65
10	10.61	14.79	60	70	10.61	14.79	60	70	70	60
20	10.00	10.00	60	60	10.00	10.00	60	60	60	60

discrete hours interval is 20 hours gives rise to equal values for both the EV and the CV for both methods. Here, $h_0 = h_1 = h_c = h_e$ for each measure. This is not surprising in view of the fact that there are so few hours positions available.

8.4 The Quadratic Translog Utility Function

A popular alternative to the quadratic function used in the previous section is the quadratic translog function, although the logarithmic transformation can be awkward where fixed costs of working are included, since circumstances exist where consumption can be negative. Several econometric studies, using a discrete set of hours, have estimated this form of utility function in which utility is expressed as a function of the square of the logarithms of consumption and other variables; see Van Soest (1995), Callan and Van Soest (1996), Van Soest and Das (2000) and Kalb (1999, 2000).

8.4.1 The Main Properties

These studies do not report welfare changes arising from tax reforms. The main results needed to apply the present approach are given in this section.

The direct utility function $U = U(c, h)$ must in the translog case be written in terms of leisure, $T - h$, in order to avoid taking the logarithm of zero for non-workers. Hence:

$$U = \alpha (\log c)^2 + \beta (\log (T - h))^2 + \gamma (\log c) (\log (T - h)) + \delta \log c + \varepsilon \log (T - h) \tag{8.29}$$

The virtual wage, w, at any point is given by the slope of the indifference curve at that point. Thus:

$$w = \left.\frac{dc}{dh}\right|_{U(c,h)} = \left(\frac{c}{T - h}\right) \left(\frac{2\beta \log (T - h) + \gamma \log c + \varepsilon}{2\alpha \log c + \gamma \log (T - h) + \delta}\right) \tag{8.30}$$

Analytical expressions cannot be obtained for optimal c and h, given the budget constraint $c = wh + \mu$, so indirect utility and expenditure functions cannot be derived.[3] Comparisons with the standard approach in the continuous hours case are therefore complicated by the need to solve the simultaneous equations $c = wh + \mu$ and $w = \left.\frac{dc}{dh}\right|_{U(c,h)}$ numerically. Using the combination of w, c and h used in (8.30), the corresponding virtual income is, as mentioned earlier, $\mu(w, U) = c - hw$.

To compute the value of net income, c, corresponding to a specified hours level, h, along an indifference curve with given utility level, U, let $x = \log c$. The required value of x is given by obtaining the appropriate root of the quadratic:

$$ax^2 + bx + d = 0 \tag{8.31}$$

with:

$$\begin{aligned} a &= \alpha \\ b &= \gamma \log (T - h) + \delta \\ d &= \beta (\log (T - h))^2 + \varepsilon \log (T - h) - U \end{aligned} \tag{8.32}$$

whence the required consumption is given by $c = \exp x$. It is found from numerical analyses that the largest root is without ambiguity the appropriate one to take.

[3]Stern (1986, p.184) devoted only one line to this case, saying that it 'gives intractable supply functions'.

8.4.2 Numerical Examples

Consider an individual with a translog quadratic utility function of the form:

$$U = 0.427\,(\log c)^2 + 0.828\,(\log (T - h))^2 - 0.340 \log c - 3.183 \log (T - h) \tag{8.33}$$

In this case T is set at 100 hours, which avoids any chance of having $T-h < 0$.

Continuous Hours

Using the same tax structures as for the previous examples, results for the context of continuous hours are shown in Table 8.5 for both the standard method and the exact method, for each wage rate. The computation of welfare changes for the continuous case requires, as mentioned earlier, the use of numerical solution procedures in view of the fact that the labour supply and expenditure functions cannot be derived analytically. The optimal hours under both the initial tax structure and structure 2 for $w_g = 5$ is at the corner solution where $h = 40$, at the end of segment 3 and the start of segment 4. Hence the exact method involves only an income effect, with $h_c = h_e = 40$. This differs from the value obtained using the standard approach. The second policy change for this wage rate has no effect since the new marginal rates are irrelevant.

For $w_g = 8$, the first two tax structures both give rise to an optimal solution at the corner given by the start of segment 5, where $h_0 = h_1 = 43.75$. The standard and exact solutions therefore differ, since the latter involves only an income effect, again equal to the change in μ_1 of 25. The second policy change for $w_g = 8$ involves a movement from the corner solution to a tangency solution along segment 4, with $h_1 = 40.25$. Calculation of the compensating variation in the standard case involves an hours level of 38.37, which is on the same segment: hence the standard and exact methods give the same result, with $h_c = 38.37$. However, for the equivalent variation, the relevant hours level is beyond that at which the 5th segment begins, so the

Table 8.5: Continuous Hours: Quadratic Translog Utility

	$w_g = 5$				$w_g = 8$			
	Standard		Corrected		Standard		Corrected	
	CV	EV	CV	EV	CV	EV	CV	EV
Policy 1	24.39	25.60	25	25	24.57	25.43	25	25
Policy 2	0	0	0	0	13.82	14.64	13.82	14.50

two methods give different welfare change values. Here the exact method is associated with $h_e = 43.75$, that is at the kink.

Discrete Hours

Table 8.6 gives results of using the different methods in the discrete hours context, using three alternative discrete hours intervals, for a gross wage rate of 8. Here there are several cases where the welfare changes involve only an income effect, whereby all measures are equal. This is true even where, as in the second policy change, a marginal tax rate changes; the discrete hours context means that, with fewer hours levels available, the associated hours levels are all equal.

Table 8.7 gives results for the discrete hours context with a wage of $w_g = 5$. Here results are shown only for the first policy change, since all welfare changes for the second policy change are (as in the continuous hours context) zero. With the first policy change and hours intervals of 10 and 20, all welfare changes are again equal because all the relevant hours levels are the same, at 40 hours.

8.5 Using Estimates of Utility Functions

The previous sections of this chapter have assumed that an individual's utility function is known precisely. In practice, estimation uses data for members of a particular demographic group in which some unobserved heterogeneity in preferences remains. This is despite the fact that parameters can depend

Table 8.6: Welfare Measures for Wage Rate of 8

Hours	Standard				Corrected				Optimal hours	
steps	CV	EV	h_c	h_e	CV	EV	h_c	h_e	Base	Reform
First tax change: reduction in μ_1										
5	24.72	25.23	40	50	25	25	45	45	45	45
10	27.54	24.64	50	40	25	25	40	50	40	50
20	25	25	40	40	25	25	40	40	40	40
Second tax change										
5	13.32	14.07	40	45	13.32	14.07	40	45	45	40
10	12.00	12.00	40	40	12.00	12.00	40	40	40	40
20	12.00	12.00	40	40	12.00	12.00	40	40	40	40

Table 8.7: Welfare Measures for Wage Rate of 5

Hours	Standard				Corrected				Optimal hours	
steps	CV	EV	h_c	h_e	CV	EV	h_c	h_e	Base	Reform
First tax change: reduction in μ_1										
5	24.40	25.59	35	45	25	25	40	40	40	40
10	25.00	25.00	40	40	25	25	40	40	40	40
20	25.00	25.00	40	40	25	25	40	40	40	40

on a wide range of observed characteristics of individuals which are typically recorded in large cross-sectional surveys. Therefore, it is necessary to decide on an appropriate method of dealing with individuals, based on an estimated form of the stochastic term's distribution. Preston and Walker (1999) used an analytical approach to derive the expressions for expected welfare.[4] Here a simulation approach is suggested to calculate expected welfare. Two approaches may be used.

One approach is to compute expected values of a welfare change for the individual, in a simulation in which random values for the error terms are drawn and assumed to remain the same before and after a policy change.[5] Conditional on a random draw from the error term, the utility function is deterministic, as in the examples given in the previous section. Therefore, for each random draw, optimal pre-reform and post-reform hours, along with the welfare change, can be computed as described in the previous sections. Using this method, the expected labour supply before the policy change is of course likely to differ to some extent from the actual value reported by the individual in the survey data.

An alternative approach involves calibrating the simulation so that only the random draws of error terms are used which result in the implied optimal hours being equal to the observed labour supply in the pre-reform tax system. For each accepted draw, the welfare change is computed following the procedure outlined in the previous sections. Pre-reform hours are thus always equal to observed hours but there is a distribution of post-reform hours and a distribution of welfare changes for each individual. The expected value of the resulting distribution of welfare changes is used.

Both approaches are considerably easier to implement in the discrete

[4]Dagsvik and Karlström (2005) examined in detail the concept of the random expenditure function, deriving the distribution of expenditure conditional on the utility being equal to the initial utility level.

[5]Small and Rosen (1981) described an approach using calculated expected values for discrete choice models.

hours framework than in the continuous hours framework. In either case, given that, conditional on each random draw, the computation of the welfare change is carried out as described in this chapter, no special additional issues arise in the practical implementation of the proposed method. Similarly, no special issues arise in dealing with overall evaluations of policy changes using money metric utility measures and a social evaluation function.

In the context of microsimulation using a large cross-sectional survey of individuals, there is the possibility of using the calculated equivalent variations for each individual to produce a money metric welfare measure that can be inserted into a specified social evaluation (or social welfare) function. If this approach is followed, it must be borne in mind that there is a potential difficulty arising from the fact that the money metric welfare measure is not guaranteed to be concave, leading to the problem that its use in a social welfare function could lead the latter to favour inequality-increasing transfers. This chapter does not deal with this issue, but it was investigated in detail by Blackorby and Donaldson (1988), who showed that concavity requires quasi-homotheticity. Homothetic utility functions are positive monotonic transformations of linear homogeneous utility functions for which $U(\theta x) = \theta U(x)$. Blackorby, Laisney and Schmachtenberg (1994) showed that welfare prescriptions using this approach are not necessarily independent of the reference prices used.

8.6 Conclusions

This chapter extended the treatment of the previous chapter by examining the calculation of compensating and equivalent variations in the context of labour supply modelling, where highly nonlinear, typically piecewise-linear, budget constraints are common. It was shown that the standard method of computing welfare changes may not give appropriate values. This arises if the computation involves hours levels for which the linearised virtual budget constraint indicates a different net income from the exact nonlinear budget constraint, or when corner solutions are involved. Methods of calculating exact welfare changes, allowing for the full detail of the budget constraint, were proposed in the context of both continuous and discrete hours models.

It was shown that the computation of welfare changes involves the use of a search procedure in which comparisons are made, for all appropriate corner and tangency solutions, of the vertical distance between net income on the relevant budget constraint and that on the relevant indifference curve. In the continuous hours context, this method may require the use of numerical solution procedures to examine the tangency positions, depending on the choice of utility function.

Numerical examples were given using the quadratic direct utility function and the quadratic translog utility function, for continuous and discrete hours frameworks. The use of the standard method in the discrete case may result in unrealistic outcomes, particularly when the hours intervals are large. In such cases the general approach presented here provides more sensible results. It is suggested that the procedures outlined in this chapter offer considerable scope for extending the range of analyses and measures generally used to judge the effects of proposed reforms to include non-financial aspects of a reform.

Chapter 9

Distributional Analyses in Discrete Models

Microsimulation modelling using a discrete hours approach is essentially probabilistic, as discussed in chapters 3 and 5. It does not identify a particular level of hours worked for each individual after the policy change, but generates a probability distribution over the discrete hours levels used. As a result, individuals do not have a single income level to which the usual formulae for poverty and inequality measures can be applied. This chapter proposes a method of approximating the inequality and poverty measures when using discrete hours labour supply modelling in tax policy microsimulation studies. It examines the performance of this approximation against alternative approaches and against a benchmark which is known to be close to the true value but is impractical to use with real-life data.

Section 9.1 introduces the outcomes available after simulating policy reforms using a discrete hours labour supply model, and discusses three alternative approaches to poverty and inequality measurement. Special attention is given to the case of the variance. The formulae for the other measures are far less tractable analytically and are discussed briefly in Appendix F. Section 9.2 presents a Monte Carlo study for these other more complex measures. In Section 9.3, as an illustration, the method is applied to a hypothetical reform of the Australian tax and transfer system using the Melbourne Institute Tax and Transfer Simulator (MITTS).

9.1 Analytical Results for Three Approaches

This section derives analytical results to compare the performance of three alternative approaches to estimating summary measures of the income distribution after simulating changes in labour supply resulting from a policy reform. The three measures are described in subsection 9.1.1. In subsection 9.1.2, some properties of the methods are discussed and compared. These analytical results are for the variance; other inequality measures are too intractable to examine in this way. Formulae for the other measures are presented for the three alternative approaches in Appendix F.

9.1.1 The Alternative Approaches

For convenience the following discussion is in terms of single individuals, but it can easily be extended to couple households. Suppose there are n individuals and k possible outcomes of labour supply (hours levels) for each individual. This would result in k^n possible combinations of labour supply, and thus income distributions. Each outcome results in a different value for poverty and inequality measures.

Under the reasonable assumption that individuals' distributions of hours are independent, the probability of each income distribution or outcome (P_q) is given by the product of the relevant probabilities. Hence if $p_{i,j}$ is the probability that individual j is at hours level i, the joint probability P_q is equal to $p_{i,1}p_{j,2}...p_{r,n}$, where q runs from 1 to k^n; and i, j, r can attain values between 1 and k (indicating the labour supply points chosen in combination q for each individual). In principle, each inequality or poverty measure can be calculated as the weighted sum of the measures over all possible outcomes with weights equal to the probabilities P_q, where the sum over all P_q is equal to one. However, for any realistic sample size, even for few discrete labour supply points, the large number of possible combinations makes it computationally impractical to calculate all k^n distributions and associated probabilities P_q. It would be impossible to store all the information needed, although this would not be necessary as the appropriate weighted average could be obtained cumulatively using an algorithm for systematically working through all the k^n combinations. However, the computing time needed would be extremely long.

Instead of examining all combinations of income levels, it would be possible to adopt a sampling approach. A large number of possible income distributions could be obtained by taking random draws from each individual's hours distribution. This can be achieved by using a random number generator which produces random uniform variates between 0 and 1, which are then compared with the cumulative distribution at the hours points for each individual in order to select the relevant income for each sample drawn. Each choice of discrete hours is drawn with the probability of it occurring for the relevant individual, so no weighting is required in averaging inequality measures over the samples. With a sufficiently large number of randomly selected samples, the proportion of each hours combination would replicate the precise probabilities discussed above. This approach still requires a large computational effort, depending on the number of draws needed to obtain a good approximation. However, it provides a valuable way of examining the performance of alternative less computer-intensive approaches against this benchmark in a Monte Carlo experiment.

In considering alternatives which offer more practical solutions, the most obvious is perhaps a simple approach where the expected income is calculated for each individual and is used as if it were a single 'representative' level of income for that individual; see for example, Gerfin and Leu (2003). In addition, we explore an approach where all possible outcomes for every individual are used as if they were separate observations. The outcomes are weighted by the individual probabilities of labour supply to produce a pseudo distribution.

To illustrate the alternative approaches by a simple example, imagine a two-person population with two hours choices available. Person 1 has a wage of 2 and a probability 0.8 of working 10 hours and 0.2 of working 20 hours. Person 2 has a wage of 3 and a probability 0.3 of working 10 hours and 0.7 of working 20 hours. The exact approach has four possible outcomes {(20,30),(40,30),(20,60),(40,60)}, with probabilities 0.24, 0.06, 0.56 and 0.14 of occurring. The Lorenz curve would have an income proportion of 0.4, 0.43, 0.25 and 0.4 at the 0.5 fraction of the population for the respective outcomes. The average Lorenz curve (using the above probabilities) would have an income proportion of 0.3178 at 0.5.

Using the expected income approach, person 1 is expected to earn 24 $(2 \times 10 \times 0.8 + 2 \times 20 \times 0.2)$ and person 2 is expected to earn 51 $(3 \times 10 \times 0.3 + 3 \times 20 \times 0.7)$. At a fraction 0.5 of the population, there would be an income proportion of 0.32. Using the pseudo approach described here and constructing a pseudo income distribution, there are outcomes 20, 30, 40 and 60 with probabilities 0.4, 0.15, 0.1 and 0.35. Thus at fraction 0.4 there is an income proportion of 0.13; at fraction 0.55 there is an income proportion 0.33; and at fraction 0.65 there is an income proportion of 0.6.

9.1.2 The Variance of the Income Distribution

Suppose there are n individuals and k discrete hours levels, $h_1, ..., h_k$. Let $y_{j,i}$ and $p_{j,i}$ denote respectively the ith person's income at hours level j, and the probability of hours level j. On the assumption that the probability distributions for different individuals are independent, the joint probabilities of the k^n possible alternative combinations are as shown in Table 9.1. An arbitrary combination m from the set of all possible combinations consists of the set of hours points $h_{1m}, h_{2m}, ..., h_{nm}$ for persons 1 to n respectively, where h_{im} has a value between 1 and k, indicating one of the k possible hours points

Table 9.1: Alternative Possible Income Distributions

Comb	Incomes of persons:				Measure	Probability
q	1	2	...	n	g_q	P_q
1	$y_{1,1}$	$y_{1,2}$	...	$y_{1,n}$	g_1	$p_{1,1}p_{1,2}...p_{1,n}$
m	$y_{h_{1m},1}$	$y_{h_{2m},2}$	...	$y_{h_{nm},n}$	g_m	$p_{h_{1m},1}...p_{h_{nm},n}$
k^n	$y_{k,1}$	$y_{k,2}$	...	$y_{k,n}$	g_{k^n}	$p_{k,1}p_{k,2}...p_{k,n}$
Exact expected distributional measure:					$\sum_{q=1}^{k^n} P_q g_q$	

for each person.

Consider the arithmetic means of each possible combination, denoted $\overline{Y}_i$. The arithmetic mean of all these means, $\overline{Y}$, is given by:

$$\overline{Y} = p_{1,1}p_{1,2}...p_{1,n}\overline{Y}_1 + ... + p_{h_{1m},1}p_{h_{2m},2}...p_{h_{nm},n}\overline{Y}_m + ... + p_{k,1}p_{k,2}...p_{k,n}\overline{Y}_{k^n} \tag{9.1}$$

Substituting for $\overline{Y}_m = \frac{1}{n}\sum_{i=1}^{n} y_{h_{im},i}$, gives:

$$\overline{Y} = \frac{1}{n}\sum_{i=1}^{n}\sum_{h=1}^{k} p_{h,i}y_{h,i} \tag{9.2}$$

The arithmetic mean, $\overline{S}^2$, of the variances for each possible combination, S_i^2, is:

$$\overline{S}^2 = p_{1,1}p_{1,2}...p_{1,n}S_1^2 + ... + p_{h_{1m},1}p_{h_{2m},2}...p_{h_{nm},n}S_m^2 + ... + p_{k,1}p_{k,2}...p_{k,n}S_{k^n}^2 \tag{9.3}$$

where $S_m^2 = \frac{1}{n}\sum_{i=1}^{n} y_{h_{im},i}^2 - \overline{Y}_m^2$. Hence:

$$\begin{aligned}
\overline{S}^2 &= \sum_{m=1}^{k^n} p_{h_{1m},1}p_{h_{2m},2}\cdots p_{h_{nm},n}\frac{1}{n}\sum_{i=1}^{n} y_{h_{im},i}^2 \\
&\quad -\sum_{m=1}^{k^n} p_{h_{1m},1}p_{h_{2m},2}\cdots p_{h_{nm},n}\left(\frac{1}{n}\sum_{i=1}^{n} y_{h_{im},i}\right)^2 \\
&= \frac{1}{n}\sum_{h=1}^{k}\sum_{i=1}^{n} p_{h,i}y_{h,i}^2 - \frac{1}{n^2}\sum_{h=1}^{k}\sum_{i=1}^{n} p_{h,i}y_{h,i}^2 \\
&\quad -\frac{1}{n^2}\sum_{m=1}^{k^n} p_{h_{1m},1}p_{h_{2m},2}\cdots p_{h_{nm},n}\left(2\sum_{i=1}^{n}\sum_{j=1}^{i-1} y_{h_{im},i}y_{h_{jm},j}\right) \\
&= \frac{1}{n}\sum_{h=1}^{k}\sum_{i=1}^{n} p_{h,i}y_{h,i}^2 - \frac{1}{n^2}\sum_{h=1}^{k}\sum_{i=1}^{n} p_{h,i}y_{h,i}^2 \\
&\quad -\frac{1}{n^2}\left(2\sum_{i=1}^{n}\sum_{j=1}^{i-1}\sum_{h=1}^{k}\sum_{l=1}^{k} p_{h,i}y_{h,i}p_{l,j}y_{l,j}\right)
\end{aligned} \tag{9.4}$$

The Expected Income Method

Consider the use of the arithmetic mean income for each individual as a representative income. Other possible candidates are the median and the mode of the hours distribution for each individual. These are rejected here on the grounds that they ignore potentially important information, as they are based on just one value in the distribution, and the arithmetic means of resulting income distributions do not correspond to $\overline{Y}$. Using expected incomes, $\overline{y}_1 = \sum_{h=1}^{k} p_{h,1}y_{h,1}$ to $\overline{y}_n = \sum_{h=1}^{k} p_{h,n}y_{h,n}$, the overall mean of the n individual means, $\overline{Y}_m$, is identical to (9.2). The variance of the individual mean incomes, S_m^2 is:

$$
\begin{aligned}
\overline{S}_m^2 &= \frac{1}{n}\sum_{i=1}^{n}\overline{y}_i^2 - \overline{Y}_m^2 \\
&= \frac{1}{n}\sum_{i=1}^{n}\left(\sum_{h=1}^{k}p_{h,i}y_{h,i}\right)^2 - \left(\frac{1}{n}\sum_{i=1}^{n}\sum_{h=1}^{k}p_{h,i}y_{h,i}\right)^2 \\
&= \frac{1}{n}\sum_{i=1}^{n}\left(\sum_{h=1}^{k}p_{h,i}^2y_{h,i}^2 + 2\sum_{h=1}^{k}\sum_{l=1}^{h-1}p_{h,i}y_{h,i}p_{l,i}y_{l,i}\right) \\
&\quad -\frac{1}{n^2}\sum_{i=1}^{n}\sum_{h=1}^{k}p_{h,i}^2y_{h,i}^2 - \frac{2}{n^2}\sum_{i=1}^{n}\sum_{h=1}^{k}\sum_{l=1}^{h-1}p_{h,i}y_{h,i}p_{l,i}y_{l,i} \\
&\quad -\frac{2}{n^2}\left(\sum_{i=1}^{n}\sum_{j=1}^{i-1}\sum_{h=1}^{k}\sum_{l=1}^{k}p_{h,i}y_{h,i}p_{l,j}y_{l,j}\right) \qquad (9.5)
\end{aligned}
$$

The terms in (9.5) contain powers of the various probabilities. Hence $S_m^2 \neq \overline{S}^2$. The arithmetic means, as linear functions, are identical, but the variances, involving nonlinear functions of the various terms, are unequal. A similar feature is expected for any inequality measure that is expressed as a nonlinear function of incomes. The difference between the method using all combinations and the method using the expected income is:

$$
\begin{aligned}
\overline{S}_m^2 - \overline{S}^2 &= \left(\frac{1}{n} - \frac{1}{n^2}\right)\left[\sum_{i=1}^{n}\left(\sum_{h=1}^{k}p_{h,i}y_{h,i}\right)^2 - \sum_{i=1}^{n}\sum_{h=1}^{k}p_{h,i}y_{h,i}^2\right] \\
&= \left(\frac{n-1}{n^2}\right)\sum_{i=1}^{n}\left((\overline{y_i})^2 - \overline{y_i^2}\right) \leq 0 \qquad (9.6)
\end{aligned}
$$

This confirms the trivial case where the two approaches give identical results for the variance if either the hours distributions are concentrated on a single hours level for each individual or the incomes are the same irrespective of the hours worked. The method using the expected income always underestimates the true expected variance. The square of the expected value is always smaller than or equal to the expectation of the squared values. This is as expected given that the use of the expected income understates the variety in incomes in the population.

The Pseudo Income Distribution Method

Consider the pseudo income distribution with nk income levels, each associated with a corresponding probability. The incomes are $y_{h,i}$, where h ranges from 1 to k and i ranges from 1 to n, and associated probabilities are $p_{h,i}/n$. The division by n ensures that the sum of the probabilities adds to 1. The $y_{h,i}$ values are placed in a single vector, $z = \{y_{h,i}\}$ with nk elements, with the associated probabilities given by $p' = \{p_{h,i}/n\}$. Hence:

$$\sum_{j=1}^{nk} p'_j = \sum_{i=1}^{n} \sum_{h=1}^{k} p_{h,i}/n = 1 \tag{9.7}$$

The arithmetic mean of this pseudo distribution, $\overline{Y}_p$, is equal to $\overline{Y}$ in (9.2) above. The variance of this pseudo distribution, S_p^2, is given by:

$$\begin{aligned}
\overline{S}_p^2 &= \frac{1}{n}\sum_{i=1}^{n}\sum_{h=1}^{k} p_{h,i}y_{h,i}^2 - \left[\frac{1}{n}\sum_{i=1}^{n}\sum_{h=1}^{k} p_{h,i}y_{h,i}\right]^2 \\
&= \frac{1}{n}\sum_{h=1}^{k}\sum_{i=1}^{n} p_{h,i}y_{h,i}^2 - \frac{1}{n^2}\sum_{h=1}^{k}\sum_{i=1}^{n} p_{h,i}^2 y_{h,i}^2 \\
&\quad -\frac{2}{n^2}\sum_{i=1}^{n}\sum_{h=1}^{k}\sum_{l=1}^{h-1} p_{h,i}y_{h,i}p_{l,i}y_{l,i} \\
&\quad -\frac{2}{n^2}\left(\sum_{i=1}^{n}\sum_{j=1}^{i-1}\sum_{h=1}^{k}\sum_{l=1}^{k} p_{h,i}y_{h,i}p_{l,j}y_{l,j}\right)
\end{aligned} \tag{9.8}$$

Again, this expression depends on the powers of the various probabilities, which appear in the term in square brackets, so it cannot be expected to equal the arithmetic mean of the individual sample variances given in (9.4). The difference between the method using all combinations and that using the pseudo method is:

$$\begin{aligned}
\overline{S}_p^2 - \overline{S}^2 &= -\frac{1}{n^2}\left(\sum_{h=1}^{k}\sum_{i=1}^{n}(p_{h,i}^2 y_{h,i}^2 - p_{h,i}y_{h,i}^2) + 2\sum_{i=1}^{n}\sum_{h=1}^{k}\sum_{l=1}^{h-1} p_{h,i}y_{h,i}p_{l,i}y_{l,i}\right) \\
&= -\frac{1}{n^2}\left(\sum_{h=1}^{k}\sum_{i=1}^{n}\left(p_{h,i}^2 y_{h,i}^2 + 2\sum_{l=1}^{h-1} p_{h,i}y_{h,i}p_{l,i}y_{l,i}\right) - \sum_{h=1}^{k}\sum_{i=1}^{n} p_{h,i}y_{h,i}^2\right) \\
&= -\frac{1}{n^2}\left(\sum_{i=1}^{n}\left(\sum_{h=1}^{k} p_{h,i}y_{h,i}\right)^2 - \sum_{h=1}^{k}\sum_{i=1}^{n} p_{h,i}y_{h,i}^2\right) \\
&= -\frac{1}{n^2}\sum_{i=1}^{n}\left((\overline{y}_i)^2 - \overline{y_i^2}\right) \geq 0 \qquad (9.9)
\end{aligned}$$

The pseudo method overestimates the true expected variance because it exaggerates the true variety of incomes by treating all individual hours points as separate observations with weights relative to the probability of occurring. Comparing this difference with the difference for the method using expected income demonstrates that, for samples of more than two persons, estimates of the variance using the pseudo method are closer to the variance calculated in the method using all combinations, compared with estimates using the expected income method. Furthermore, the true outcome lies in between the pseudo method and the expected income method. The difference is expected to become smaller for the pseudo method as the sample size increases, indicating that the exaggeration of the income variability becomes less important when the number of individuals in the sample increases.

9.2 Monte Carlo Experiments

The previous section compares differences in average income and the variance using three approaches. As mentioned earlier, comparing other summary measures is intractable. Thus this section uses Monte Carlo simulation methods to examine the relative performance of the alternative approaches discussed in the previous section.

9.2.1 The Experimental Approach

To ensure that the simulations were based on realistic distributions, a base sample of 10,293 individuals was produced using the Melbourne Institute Tax and Transfer Simulator (MITTS); see Appendix C for a brief description. This sample was generated from the confidentialised unit record files from the 1996/97 and 1997/98 Surveys of Income and Housing Costs made available by the Australian Bureau of Statistics. A sample of single persons was selected to avoid the additional run time and complexity that would be introduced by examining the hours distribution of couples jointly, thus keeping the number of hours points to a minimum for the experiment. Extension of the method to apply to couples is however straightforward and only involves an increase in the number of possible combinations. The sample provides, for each individual, the incomes and probabilities associated with $k = 11$ discrete hours levels ranging from 0 to 50 hours in five-hourly bands. Examples of three such hours distributions are shown in Figure 9.1.

It is of interest to consider the properties of poverty and inequality measures as the sample size n varies, so values of n of 50, 100, 250 and 500 were examined. The use of the smaller sizes is relevant where samples are divided into particular socio-economic or demographic groups. In each case, 1000 subsamples of size n were drawn from the basic data set of about $10,000$ individuals. Gini, G, and Atkinson inequality measures, A (with relative inequality aversion set to 0.4), were computed along with the variance, V. In addition, three poverty measures were computed from the Foster, Greer and Thorbecke (1984) family. The measures chosen are the headcount measure, P_0; one that depends on the extent to which individuals fall below the poverty line, P_1; and finally a measure that also depends on the coefficient of variation of incomes of those in poverty, P_2.[1] The poverty line was set in relative terms at half the median income; hence the poverty line varies across

[1] See Creedy (1996) or Deaton (1997) for an overview of these measures.

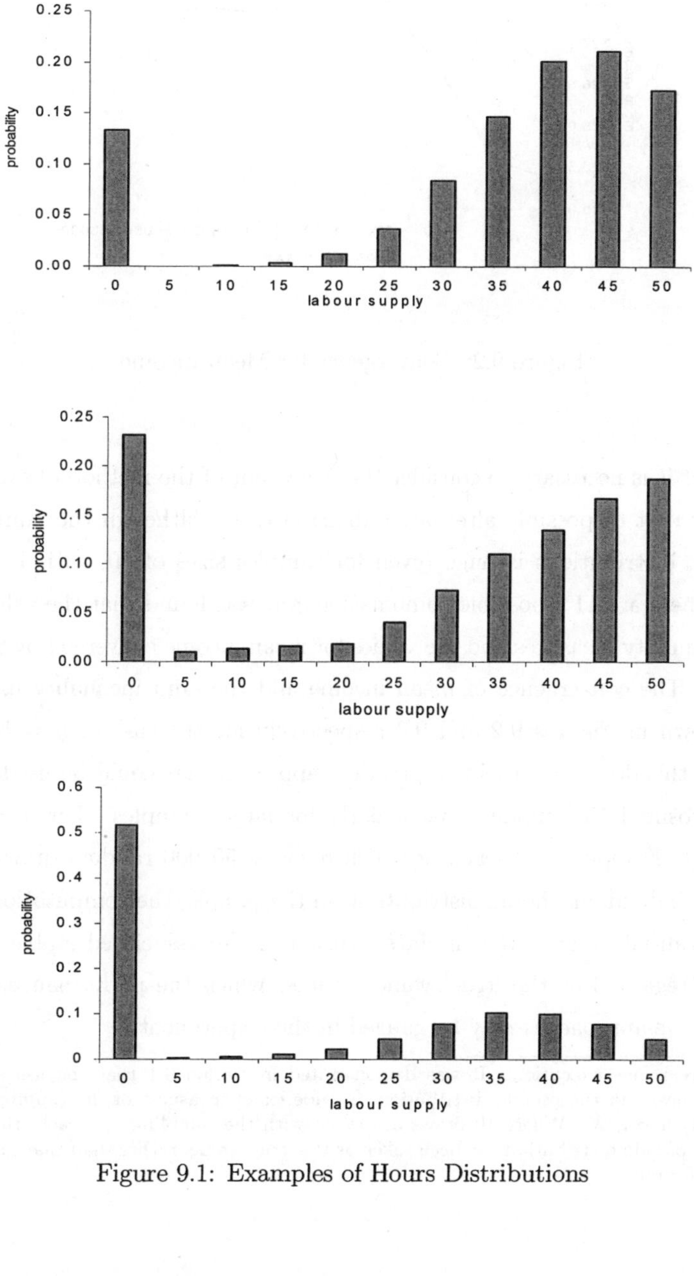

Figure 9.1: Examples of Hours Distributions

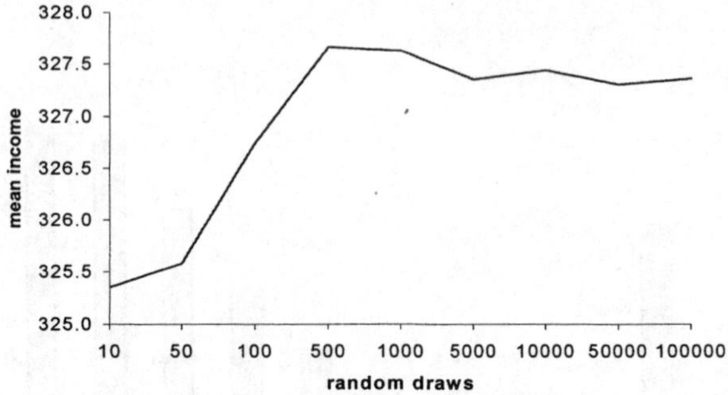

Figure 9.2: Convergence for Mean Income

samples.

First it is necessary to consider the behaviour of the method of sampling from the set of possible alternative distributions. Although the number of possible distributions is huge (even for samples sizes of 50, with 11 hours levels there are 11^{50} possible combinations), it was found that the values for the inequality measures and the values for mean income converged by 50,000 draws. The convergence of mean income and the Gini inequality measure are shown in Figures 9.2 and 9.3 respectively for the case of $n = 50$. Of course, this does not provide a practical approach that could be used easily in microsimulation models, particularly for larger samples. For $n = 500$, taking 1000 repetitions, each of which involves 50,000 random draws from the 500 individuals' hours distributions in the sample, the computation time is substantial at around four days. However, the associated stable values can be regarded as the 'true' values against which the performance of the alternative approaches may be gauged in this experiment.[2]

[2]There is one exception. It was demonstrated in section 9.1 that the use of average incomes, and the pseudo distribution, provide exact measures of the (appropriately weighted) mean, $\overline{X}$. Where 10 draws are taken with the sampling approach, the mean from the pseudo distribution has been taken as the 'true' value, rather than that produced by 50,000 draws.

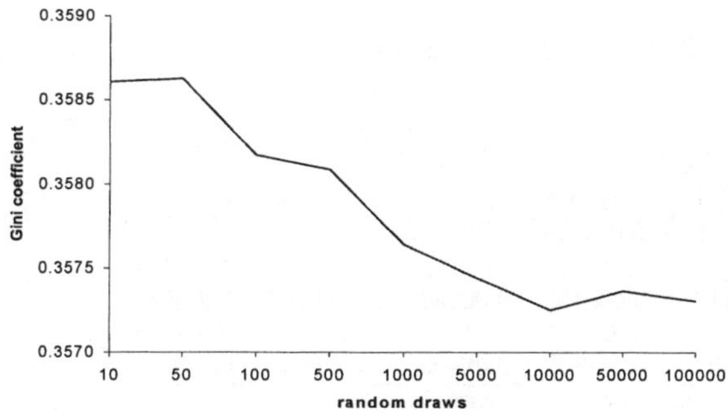

Figure 9.3: Convergence for Gini Measure

9.2.2 Monte Carlo Results

Tables 9.2 to 9.5 present the Monte Carlo results for three approaches comparing deviations of the various approaches from the 'true' values for 1000 replications of the experiments.[3] The first two methods are the expected income method and the pseudo method. To explore the quality of the sampling approach when few draws are used, results are also produced for the sampling approach with 10 draws. The use of 10 draws would be feasible in practice and this number has been shown to be sufficient in other situations, such as, for example, simulated maximum likelihood estimations. In Van Soest (1995), 5 draws seemed sufficient in one of the models estimated using the simulated maximum likelihood approach.

From all measures in the tables, it is clear that the pseudo method performs much better than the expected income method. As shown analytically for the variance, the two inequality measures are also always underestimated

[3]The experiment where a sample of 500 individuals is used took roughly four days to run. This involved drawing around 50,000,000 times (which is less than 10^8) from the 500 hours distributions and computing averages across the 50,000 draws in each of the 1000 replications. The exact measure for the same sample would involve 11^{500} different combinations which, compared with the above drawing of 50,000, would require an enormous amount of time and be infeasible to carry out.

Table 9.2: Distribution of Differences from 'True Value': n=50

	G	A	P_0	P_1	P_2	$\overline{X}$	V
Average 'true' values							
	0.33391	0.084995	0.115037	0.062394	0.047425	318.27	42674.11
Use of each individual's expected income							
Mean	-0.0336	-0.01199	-0.00526	9.18E-06	0.000372		-7303.94
mse[a]	0.00117	0.00015	0.00040	2.78E-05	1.26E-05		55194286
Min	-0.06056	-0.01993	-0.0821	-0.01785	-0.01328		-11498.1
Max	-0.01467	-0.00621	0.08906	0.025669	0.017747		-3531.46
Use of pseudo distribution of income							
Mean	0.004543	0.000275	0.001585	0.000748	0.000459		149.8281
mse[a]	0.000021	7.87E-08	0.000083	2.52E-06	8.82E-07		23739.04
Min	0.001503	0.000079	-0.0253	-0.00373	-0.00267		4.246241
Max	0.006876	0.000499	0.041592	0.006866	0.004414		314.5633
Use of 10 random draws from possible distributions							
Mean	-3.5E-05	-6.3E-06	0.000419	9.77E-05	7.14E-05	0.09391	-41.5227
mse[a]	0.000017	3.24E-06	0.000057	5.67E-06	3.1E-06	14.72302	2736878
Min	-0.01408	-0.0078	-0.02878	-0.01001	-0.00698	-11.542	-11104.1
Max	0.01126	0.00622	0.049411	0.013506	0.01219	13.13847	9338.877

Note a: mse stands for the mean squared error

Table 9.3: Distribution of Differences from 'True Value': n=100

	G	A	P_0	P_1	P_2	$\overline{X}$	V
Average 'true' values							
	0.337054	0.085744	0.112875	0.062622	0.047801	318.11	43145.16
Use of each individual's expected income							
Mean	-0.03405	-0.01218	-0.00248	4.47E-05	0.00030		-7369.36
mse[a]	0.00118	0.00015	0.00019	1.23E-05	5.97E-06		55064023
Min	-0.0494	-0.0167	-0.05305	-0.01051	-0.00849		-10896.5
Max	-0.0194	-0.00813	0.06267	0.014378	0.00851		-4648.41
Use of pseudo distribution of income							
Mean	0.00227	0.00014	0.00116	0.00036	0.00024		74.73766
mse[a]	5.23E-06	1.94E-08	0.00004	7.18E-07	2.51E-07		5944.869
Min	0.00124	0.00006	-0.02872	-0.00286	-0.00110		6.374102
Max	0.00312	0.00024	0.02576	0.00347	0.00217		155.9846
Use of 10 random draws from possible distributions							
Mean	1.91E-05	1.3E-05	0.00020	6.33E-05	3.97E-05	0.18520	31.26735
mse[a]	7.41E-06	1.55E-06	0.00002	2.54E-06	1.54E-06	7.81495	1479075
Min	-0.00835	-0.0045	-0.02395	-0.00516	-0.00408	-10.4604	-7314.95
Max	0.00968	0.00546	0.02222	0.00561	0.00470	10.86006	5933.581

Note a: mse stands for the mean squared error

Table 9.4: Distribution of Differences from 'True Value': n=250

	G	A	P_0	P_1	P_2	$\overline{X}$	V
Average 'true' values							
	0.338943	0.086112	0.114024	0.063022	0.048044	317.97	43322.27
Use of each individual's expected income							
Mean	-0.03437	-0.01227	-0.00156	0.00018	0.000301		-7417.44
mse[a]	0.00119	0.00015	0.00011	5.11E-06	2.53E-06		55352057
Min	-0.04348	-0.01506	-0.03549	-0.00592	-0.00429		-10211.7
Max	-0.02511	-0.01005	0.03473	0.00838	0.00562		-5802.55
Use of pseudo distribution of income							
Mean	0.00091	5.38E-05	0.00057	0.00012	8.41E-05		29.81149
mse[a]	8.35E-07	3.05E-09	2.05E-05	1.75E-07	5.52E-08		1006.12
Min	0.00068	0.00002	-0.01327	-0.00145	-0.00080		-10.9953
Max	0.00115	0.00010	0.01483	0.00147	0.00093		85.59714
Use of 10 random draws from possible distributions							
Mean	-8.5E-05	-3.4E-05	2.62E-05	8.59E-06	-7.9E-07	0.02956	-10.633
mse[a]	3.25E-06	6.53E-07	9.87E-06	9.77E-07	5.83E-07	2.99928	595096.4
Min	-0.00574	-0.00267	-0.01384	-0.00367	-0.00302	-5.36467	-3252.28
Max	0.00499	0.00234	0.01611	0.00325	0.00282	4.94511	2578.688

Note a: mse stands for the mean squared error

Table 9.5: Distribution of Differences from 'True Value': n=500

	G	A	P_0	P_1	P_2	$\overline{X}$	V
Average 'true' values							
	0.340422	0.086779	0.115116	0.063697	0.048700	317.89	43486.24
Use of each individual's expected income							
Mean	-0.03424	-0.01227	-0.00090	0.00043	0.00036		-7422.69
mse[a]	0.00118	0.00015	0.00008	2.96E-06	1.35E-06		55254183
Min	-0.04077	-0.01474	-0.02098	-0.00449	-0.00378		-8674.50
Max	-0.02718	-0.01000	0.02746	0.00615	0.00445		-6235.62
Use of pseudo distribution of income							
Mean	0.00045	0.00003	0.00021	0.00001	0.00002		14.33324
mse[a]	2.07E-07	7.68E-10	1.68E-05	5.30E-08	1.55E-08		260.649
Min	0.00037	-0.00000	-0.01341	-0.00082	-0.00047		-20.8162
Max	0.00054	0.00005	0.01273	0.00095	0.00059		42.10908
Use of 10 random draws from possible distributions							
Mean	0.00007	3.12E-05	-5.84E-05	-3.02E-05	-7.50E-06	-0.00164	24.1993
mse[a]	1.55E-06	3.05E-07	6.84E-06	5.18E-07	3.12E-07	1.52216	256246.7
Min	-0.00343	-0.00188	-0.01053	-0.00198	-0.00184	-4.19253	-1608.05
Max	0.00407	0.00189	0.01091	0.00237	0.00178	3.82340	1670.176

Note a: mse stands for the mean squared error

by the expected income method and overestimated by the pseudo method for samples with 50 or 100 individuals. This is as expected given that the expected income understates the true income variability and the pseudo income distribution overstates the income variability. However, for samples with 250 or 500 individuals, some negative differences between the 'true' variance and the variance from the pseudo method are found, as can be seen from the 'min' and 'max' rows in Tables 9.4 and 9.5. This does not happen very often and it can be explained by the fact that our 'true' values which are used as benchmarks in the experiment are approximations as well. As the pseudo method improves with sample size, for $n = 250$ or 500 the pseudo method may sometimes get closer to the true value than the approximation by $50,000$ draws, causing the difference to be negative rather than positive. This will happen more often for larger samples, making the pseudo method a computationally very efficient approach with an approximate value close to the true value.

The sampling method, using 10 draws, ranks between the two other methods. Only its mean is nearly always smaller (except for some measures when n equals 500), but that is because negative and positive values partly offset each other in this approach, whereas the other two approaches either tend to over- or underestimate the true values. The pseudo method clearly outperforms the sampling method with 10 draws except for the case of the headcount measure P_0. Nevertheless, on many occasions the accuracy of the sampling method using only 10 draws would be considered sufficient.

With an increase in sample size, the methods tend to perform better with the exception of the variance and inequality measures for the expected income method. Using the latter method, the mean distance from the true value does not change with sample size for G, A, P_2 and V, whereas for P_0 it falls and for P_1 it increases. The result for V makes sense when considering equations (9.6) and (9.9) above. Although the minimum and maximum values move towards each other in the expected income method, a bias remains. In the pseudo method and the sampling method with 10 draws, the minimum and maximum value both move towards the true value. The pseudo method improves faster with sample size than the sampling method with 10 draws.

9.3 An Application

To illustrate the use of the pseudo method, a hypothetical reform of the Australian tax and transfer system is examined. The Australian transfer system is complex, with many different types of benefit, each with its set of thresholds and taper (or withdrawal) rates, giving rise to highly nonlinear budget constraints. The simulation described in this section replaces all existing basic social security benefits and additional payments such as rent assistance, pharmaceutical allowance and family payments by a basic non-taxable level of income. The structure of the September 2001 tax and transfer system is used as the pre-reform system. In the reform system, the existing tax structure (which includes the Medicare levy and all tax rebates) is replaced with a constant marginal tax rate on all taxable income (all non-benefit forms of income).

Basic income rates are set at the benefit levels as they were at September 2001 with basic income levels varying for different groups in the population reflecting the current situation. Characteristics that currently entitle individuals to a pension are used to determine whether an individual is entitled to a higher rate of basic income, which is referred to as the pension rate. This group includes those of Age Pension age, those with a disability, carers, veterans and sole parents. This payment is then differentiated by marital status to reflect the economies of scale of larger households. The remaining subset of the population receives a basic income level set at the current allowance payment rates. These payments also differ by age, such that single persons aged 16 or 17 years receive a lower basic income than older individuals, with youths still living at home receiving a lower rate again, and those aged 60 years or over receive a higher level than 18 to 59 year olds. Members of a couple are entitled to a lower payment rate each than the single rate, reflecting economies of scale.

To ensure revenue neutrality of the new system compared with the 2001 system, the marginal tax rate required was found to be 55 per cent. The reform is simulated using the Melbourne Institute Tax and Transfer Simulator (MITTS). The method of simulating labour supply responses to tax reforms in MITTS is briefly described in Appendix C and more extensively in Chapter 5.

The removal of means testing reduces the disincentives to work for those on low incomes as it reduces the effective marginal tax rates significantly. Lowering the marginal tax rate has two opposing effects. A lower tax rate would induce substitution out of leisure and into work, as the price of leisure is higher. However, at the same time net incomes are higher at lower levels of labour supply, so some individuals/families may decide to reduce their hours of work. The net result depends on relative preferences for leisure and income. Higher taxes imposed at the high end of the income distribution may have an adverse effect on the labour supply of higher income earners.

A summary of the estimated labour supply responses across demographic groups is presented in Table 9.6, with the expected effect on net expenditure reported in Table 9.7. The responses differ greatly across the groups. Singles without children exhibit labour supply responses, expressed as an average hours change which is similar to those of sole parents. However, single persons seem less likely to decrease participation, but at the same time are also less likely to increase their work effort as a result of a heavier tax burden than sole parents. Married males are the least likely to decrease their labour supply overall. Married women and sole parents tend to have larger income effects, thus having a greater tendency to move out of the labour force with an increase in household income. In addition, the current payments to sole parents are withdrawn very gradually and thus a tax rate of over 50 per cent is higher than the effective marginal tax rate currently faced by them at low income levels, reducing their incentive to work after the reform compared with the 2001 system.

Table 9.6: Behavioural Responses

	Couples:		Single:		
	Men	Women	Men	Women	Parents
Workers (% base)	58.6	45.7	55.1	44.2	42.4
Workers (% reform)	58.5	41.2	53.6	43.3	37.2
Non-work to work (%)	1.2	0.4	0.3	0.5	0.4
Work to non-work (%)	1.3	4.8	1.8	1.4	5.6
Workers working more	1.3	0.3	0.0	0.1	2.0
Workers working less	2.4	1.9	1.4	2.3	1.1
Average hours change	-0.2	-1.9	-0.9	-0.8	-0.6

Table 9.7: Net Expenditure Summary (Millions of Dollars)

	Couples	Single:			Total
		Men	Women	Parents	
Fixed hours	-4,024.5	1,735.8	2,042.8	-282.5	-528.4
Variable hours	2,044.3	2,859.5	2,895.4	-172.0	7,627.2

The adverse labour supply responses associated with a relatively high marginal tax rate impose a large increase in net government expenditure. A large share of each individual's income is paid in tax, so a reduction in labour supply considerably reduces the revenue collected by the government. The large reduction in the labour supply of married females increases net government expenditure on couples. The higher tax rates on middle to high income earners are not enough to offset the decrease in revenue resulting from the decrease in participation and average working hours for this group. With a general reduction in labour supply across all groups, net government expenditure increases after the reform when labour supply responses are taken into account.

To examine the effects of this policy change on the distribution of income in the Australian population before and after labour supply changes, three summary measures are presented. First, two commonly used measures of inequality, the Gini coefficient and the Atkinson measure of inequality, are examined. As the reform system provides relatively generous basic income levels financed by heavily taxing the working population, it is not surprising that inequality is reduced quite significantly after the reform; see Tables 9.8 and 9.9. Adjusting for labour supply responses does not have a strong effect on the presented measures of inequality in this case, since those who move out of the labour force were on low wages.

Table 9.8: Gini Coefficient by Income Unit Type

	Fixed hours			Variable hours		
Group	Before	After	% change	Before	After	% change
Couple	0.3103	0.2758	-11.1	0.3030	0.2701	-10.9
Cple+dependants	0.2460	0.1963	-20.2	0.2333	0.1857	-20.4
Single females	0.2925	0.2616	-10.6	0.2950	0.2609	-11.6
Single males	0.3297	0.2825	-14.3	0.3343	0.2839	-15.1
Sole parents	0.2154	0.2067	-4.0	0.2101	0.2029	-3.4
all	0.3014	0.2654	-12.0	0.2980	0.2616	-12.2

For the analysis of poverty, values of the Foster, Greer and Thorbecke index of poverty are presented in Table 9.10. The inclusion of labour supply responses in the simulation clearly affects the headcount measure, resulting from the larger shift in median income. Taking into account labour supply responses results in more poverty than would otherwise be the case. This effect becomes less pronounced when the extent of the poverty is taken into account in the poverty gap and the Foster, Greer and Thorbecke measure of poverty with $\alpha = 2$. There is a clear difference between the fixed and variable labour supply approaches, due to the discretised hours worked in the variable labour supply approach. This discretisation affects individual income and the poverty line to a small extent. However, having the discretisation affect two

Table 9.9: Atkinson Inequality Measures by Income Units

	Fixed hours			Variable hours		
Group	Before	After	% change	Before	After	% change
$\varepsilon = 0.1$						
Couple	0.0155	0.0123	-20.6	0.0147	0.0117	-20.4
Cple+dependants	0.0106	0.007	-33.0	0.0095	0.0062	-34.7
Single females	0.0141	0.0112	-20.6	0.0145	0.0112	-22.1
Single males	0.0182	0.0136	-25.8	0.0188	0.0137	-27.1
Sole parents	0.0083	0.0077	-7.2	0.0080	0.0075	-7.5
all	0.0151	0.0117	-22.5	0.0148	0.0113	-23.0
$\varepsilon = 0.5$						
Couple	0.0749	0.0597	-20.3	0.0711	0.0568	-20.1
Cple+dependants	0.0498	0.0332	-33.3	0.0448	0.0294	-34.4
Single females	0.0680	0.0540	-20.6	0.0697	0.0539	-22.7
Single males	0.0879	0.0646	-26.5	0.0906	0.0652	-28.0
Sole parents	0.0387	0.0360	-7.0	0.0373	0.0348	-6.4
All	0.0724	0.0564	-22.1	0.0710	0.0546	-23.0
$\varepsilon = 1$						
Couple	0.1429	0.1145	-19.8	0.1355	0.1091	-19.5
Cple+dependants	0.0934	0.0627	-32.9	0.0843	0.0560	-33.6
Single females	0.1300	0.1028	-20.9	0.1332	0.1020	-23.4
Single males	0.1686	0.1222	-27.5	0.1740	0.1232	-29.3
Sole parents	0.0711	0.0661	-7.0	0.0684	0.0641	-6.3
All	0.1380	0.1078	-21.9	0.1355	0.1046	-22.8
$\varepsilon = 2$						
Couple	0.2563	0.208	-18.9	0.2429	0.1981	-18.4
Cple+dependants	0.1684	0.1151	-31.7	0.1524	0.1037	-32.0
Single females	0.2383	0.1840	-22.7	0.2451	0.1814	-26.0
Single males	0.3114	0.2191	-29.7	0.3221	0.2202	-31.6
Sole parents	0.1218	0.1127	-7.5	0.1170	0.1098	-6.2
All	0.2527	0.1968	-22.1	0.2501	0.1914	-23.5

components of the measure has resulted in a more notable difference than in Table 9.9.

Table 9.10: Alternative Poverty Measures

	Fixed hours			Variable hours		
	Before	After	% diff.	Before	After	% diff.
Poverty line						
50% median	$182.15	$198.28		$176.28	$221.20	
$\alpha = 0$						
Couple	0.0157	0.0000	-100	0.0150	0.0490	227
Cple+dependants	0.0151	0.0000	-100	0.0173	0.0027	-84
Single females	0.0685	0.1177	72	0.0768	0.3980	418
Single males	0.0710	0.1137	60	0.0784	0.2798	257
Sole parents	0.0111	0.0000	-100	0.0035	0.0161	363
All	0.0409	0.0547	34	0.0444	0.1724	288
$\alpha = 1$						
Couple	0.0054	0.0000	-100	0.0053	0.0017	-68
Cple+dependants	0.0031	0.0000	-100	0.0029	0.0001	-93
Single females	0.0224	0.0157	-30	0.0258	0.0420	63
Single males	0.0260	0.0103	-60	0.0299	0.0316	6
Sole parents	0.0005	0.0000	-100	0.0001	0.0002	100
All	0.0135	0.0061	-55	0.0151	0.0177	17
$\alpha = 2$						
Couple	0.0021	0.0000	-100	0.0020	0.0001	-100
Cple+dependents	0.0007	0.0000	-100	0.0006	0.0000	-100
Single females	0.0096	0.0034	-65	0.0115	0.0080	-30
Single males	0.0121	0.0015	-88	0.0140	0.0054	-61
Sole parents	0.0000	0.0000	0	0.0000	0.0000	0
All	0.0058	0.0012	-81	0.0067	0.0032	-52

9.4 Conclusions

This chapter has compared alternative approaches to the measurement of inequality and poverty indices in the context of behavioural microsimulation with discrete hours labour supply models. Special consideration is needed because microsimulation modelling using a discrete hours approach does not identify a particular level of hours worked for each individual after a policy change, but generates a probability distribution over the discrete hours levels used. This makes analysis of the distribution of income difficult because, even for a small sample with a modest range of hours points, the range of possible labour supply combinations becomes too large to handle.

The approaches examined include the use of an expected income level for each individual. Alternatively, a simulated approach could be used in which labour supply values are drawn from each individual's hours distribution and summary statistics of the distribution of income are calculated by taking the average over each set of draws. Finally, the construction of a pseudo income distribution was proposed. This uses the probability of a particular labour supply value occurring for an individual, standardised by the population size, to refer to a particular position in the pseudo income distribution.

It was shown that the outcomes of various distributional measures using the pseudo distribution method converge to their 'true' values as the sample size used in microsimulation increases. However, the method performs well for a sample as small as 50 individuals. The pseudo method performs better than the expected income method or the sampling approach with just 10 draws. The latter has a similar computational burden to the pseudo approach. The feasibility of the pseudo approach was demonstrated in an illustrative example where the labour supply responses and implications for the distribution of income were examined for a hypothetical reform of the Australian tax and transfer system.

Chapter 10

Choice of the Unit of Analysis in Distributional Measures

A major advantage of tax microsimulation models is that they deal with the considerable heterogeneity found in populations. They can be used to examine the effects of a policy reform on a wide variety of types of person distinguished, say, by household type, location, education, occupation or age. But this heterogeneity raises problems when making an overall evaluation of a policy change in terms of inequality or social welfare, since standard measures are designed for homogeneous populations. In making decisions about the two concepts of income and the unit of analysis, which are fundamental to the evaluation of inequality or social welfare, the difficulty is, as Ebert (1997, p.235) put it, that 'an (artificial) income distribution for a fictitious population has to be constructed'. Cowell (1984) discussed nine alternatives, arising from a distinction between three types of income recipient and three income measures. A third decision concerns the time period of analysis, but this is not considered here: attention is restricted to annual incomes.

Most studies regard the only relevant non-income difference as the household size and its composition. The first stage, involving the artificial income concept, is to convert total household income into a measure of the 'living standard' of each household member by dividing income by the adult equivalent household size. This method of constructing the 'money metric welfare measure' for individuals in a household has many well-known problems. However, it is taken as given here, where emphasis is placed instead on the choice of a fictitious population.

The aim of this chapter is to examine the implications for overall social welfare and inequality comparisons of using different definitions for the unit of analysis – the income recipient – in computing summary measures. Comparisons are made using the Melbourne Institute Tax and Transfer Simulator (MITTS). The model is used to simulate the effects of flattening the marginal tax rate structure. No suggestion is made that the comparisons reflect general properties. However, it is useful to provide some indication of potential orders of magnitude of differences between measures when using alternative definitions in a realistic context. The present study therefore supplements that of Decoster and Ooghe (2002), who made extensive comparisons for a policy reform in Belgium.

Three units of analysis are discussed, and summary measures for alternative definitions of the unit are described formally in section 10.1. The units considered are households, individuals and adult equivalent persons. Section 10.2 examines the relationship between inequality and adult equivalence scales, for net incomes before the reform. The hypothetical policy reform is described in section 10.3.

The reform is analysed using a microsimulation approach. The microsimulation model used here consists of a non-behavioural component, MITTS-A, and a behavioural component estimating the effect of changes in labour supply behaviour, MITTS-B. Non-behavioural results are reported in section 10.4. The effects of allowing for labour supply responses to tax changes are examined in section 10.5. Conclusions are in section 10.6.

10.1 Alternative Concepts and Measures

This section introduces the notation and describes the alternative summary measures of inequality and welfare used. First, equivalence scales are defined in subsection 10.1.1. The three types of unit of analysis are discussed in subsection 10.1.2, and the resulting welfare functions and inequality measures are defined in subsection 10.1.3.

10.1.1 The Concept of Income: Equivalence Scales

Let y_i denote the total income of the ith household, for $i = 1, ..., N$. The number of individuals in the household is n_i and the demographic structure is denoted by d_i. Here d_i can be regarded as a vector indicating the number of people of each of a number of types defined by age and gender. The adult equivalent size of the household, m_i, can be expressed as:

$$m_i = m(n_i, d_i) \tag{10.1}$$

This is normalised such that $m(n = 1, d = \text{adult}) = 1$. The adult-equivalent size of a household, m, is defined by the following: a household consisting of one adult with an income of y is regarded as having the same 'living standard' as an n-person household with y multiplied by $m(n, d)$.

The form of $m(n_i, d_i)$ needs to be specified. If there are $n_{k,i}$ individuals of demographic type $k = 1, ..., K$ in the ith household, the adult equivalent size may be written:

$$m_i = \left(\sum_{k=1}^{K} \phi_k n_{k,i}\right)^{\theta} \tag{10.2}$$

The term θ is regarded as a measure of economies of scale within the household, with $0 \leq \theta \leq 1$. This formulation is an extension of the simple form, n_i^{θ}, used by Buhmann *et al.* (1988) and Coulter, Cowell and Jenkins (1992) and modified by, for example, Cutler and Katz (1992), Banks and Johnson (1994) and Jenkins and Cowell (1994), who differentiated between adults and children.

The scales examined below are a special case of (10.2) which distinguishes the number of adults, $n_{a,i}$, and children, $n_{c,i}$, such that:

$$m_i = \{1 + \phi_1 (n_{a,i} - 1) + \phi_2 n_{c,i}\}^\theta \tag{10.3}$$

This makes a distinction between the 'head' of the unit, for whom the weight is unity, additional adults and children. No distinction is made between age and gender. In the following analyses, $\phi_1 = 0.56$ and $\phi_2 = 0.32$. This choice, with $\theta = 1$, corresponds to the Whiteford (1985) scales. With $\theta < 1$, this implies a smaller adult equivalent household size than in the Whiteford scales. This should be kept in mind when considering the results below.

10.1.2 The Concept of the Unit of Analysis: Three Types

A number of empirical studies have taken the household itself as the basic unit of analysis, usually with little discussion. This involves each household being assigned the living standard, defined as total income per adult equivalent (as outlined in section 10.1.1), and making no further allowance for the demographic structure of the unit. One way to describe this is to say that the living standard of each household is given a weight of $1/N$ in computing inequality and welfare summary measures. While this approach appears to have little rationale, it is included for comparative purposes here.

An alternative, which appears to treat the income concept and the unit of analysis consistently, is to define the basic unit of analysis as the adult equivalent person. This approach was recommended by Pyatt (1990) and Ebert (1997). The ith household contains m_i adult equivalent persons, each getting the living standard of y_i/m_i, where y_i is the household's total income. This approach means that an individual's contribution to inequality and social welfare depends on the composition of the household of which that person is a member. For example, an adult in a one-person household 'counts for one', but the same person in a household containing other adults and several children counts for 'less than one'. A feature of this approach is that it satisfies the basic equity principle, associated with the principle of transfers, that a transfer of income to those worse-off results in a reduction in inequality (and an increase in social welfare). As a result, Lorenz and generalised Lorenz curve analyses can be conducted using the resulting distribution. Despite explicitly not treating individuals as the unit, but instead using adult equivalents, this actually leads to a recommendation for equal standards of living; see Ebert (1997, p.242).

A third alternative is to treat the individual as the basic unit of analysis. In this case, each individual is assigned the living standard of the relevant household. Thus each individual effectively 'counts for one', irrespective both of the household to which he or she belongs and the person's age or gender. This approach therefore has the property of anonymity, such that welfare or inequality remain unchanged when one person (of whatever type) in the population is replaced by another person having the same living standard but belonging to any other type of household. This property was called the 'compensation principle' by Shorrocks (1997) and the 'Pareto indifference principle' by Decoster and Ooghe (2002). Jorgenson and Slesnick (1984) and Slesnick (1994) use this method, as does Glewwe (1991), who dismisses the use of adult equivalents in a footnote (1991, p.213). It was also preferred by Shorrocks (1997), Danziger and Taussig (1979) and Ringen (1991).

This approach does not in general satisfy the equity principle (of transfers). As shown by Glewwe (1991), an income transfer from a poor to a richer (and larger) household can reduce inequality and raise social welfare. Transfers of money do not correspond to transfers of 'living standard' units between individuals.[1] Despite being based on individuals, the application of anonymity can lead to a preference for inequality: with economies of scale,

[1] Glewwe (1991, p.213) used a simple numerical example with three households. Decoster and Ooghe (2002, pp.3-4) also construct some illustrative examples using three persons.

large households are regarded as being 'more efficient' at generating welfare.

An important implication is that in this context of heterogeneous populations, the basic equity principle inherent in the principle of transfers and the concept of Lorenz dominance (whereby one Lorenz curve lies unambiguously closer to the diagonal of equality) are no longer equivalent. This equivalence is a fundamental component of welfare analysis for homogeneous populations.

The choice between individuals and adult equivalents as the basic unit of analysis in inequality and social welfare calculations therefore involves a choice between two incompatible value judgements. They can in principle lead to opposite conclusions about the effects of a tax policy change on inequality. Shorrocks (1997) suggested that if concern is with equity, the use of adult equivalents is recommended, whereas if concern is primarily with social welfare, individuals should be the basic income unit. The disinterested economist is thus required to report results using both approaches. Before examining how they perform in a practical case, the approaches are described more formally in the following subsection.

10.1.3 Social Welfare Functions and Inequality

Social welfare is regarded as an additive function of income per equivalent adult, $z_i = y_i/m_i$, the living standard of each individual in the household. In the case where the unit of analysis is the individual, that is where the principle of anonymity (referred to alternatively in terms of compensation or Pareto indifference) is required, social welfare per individual is given by:

$$W_I = \frac{1}{\sum_{i=1}^{N} n_i} \sum_{i=1}^{N} n_i V(z_i) \tag{10.4}$$

where $V(z)$ is increasing and concave.

If the unit of analysis is the adult equivalent person, that is where the equity principle (of transfers) applies, social welfare is:

$$W_E = \frac{1}{\sum_{i=1}^{N} m_i} \sum_{i=1}^{N} m_i V(z_i) \tag{10.5}$$

Finally, if the household is treated as the unit of analysis, where each household is assigned its income per equivalent adult, the welfare function is:

$$W_H = \frac{1}{N} \sum_{i=1}^{N} V(z_i) \tag{10.6}$$

Each of the three welfare measures is a weighted sum, over all N households, of a function V of the income per equivalent adult, z. The only difference concerns the choice of the weights, which are respectively $n_i / \sum_{i=1}^{N} n_i$, $m_i / \sum_{i=1}^{N} m_i$ and $1/N$. In practice, microsimulation models assign a sample weight to each household so that appropriate population values can be obtained. The weights are often those provided by the statistical agency which collects the data, but they may also be modified for specific purposes (as described in chapter 6). The survey weights can easily be added to the above expressions. For example if the survey weight for the ith household is s_i, the weights for treating the individual as the unit of analysis become $n_i s_i / \sum_{i=1}^{N} n_i s_i$. The s's have been omitted from the above expressions for convenience only; they are used in the numerical examples reported below.

The type of additive welfare function discussed above is known to be consistent with the Atkinson inequality measure, A, of income. In the analysis below, concern is with net incomes, z. The Atkinson measure is defined as the proportional difference between the equally-distributed-equivalent (net) income, $\widetilde{z}$, and the arithmetic mean income, $\overline{z}$. Hence, $\widetilde{z}$ is the net income per equivalent adult which, if received by every unit of analysis, produces the same social welfare as the actual distribution, so $V(\widetilde{z}) = W$ and:

$$A = 1 - \frac{\widetilde{z}}{\overline{z}} \tag{10.7}$$

Although this may be used with any form of V, the most common form is:

$$V(z) = \frac{z^{1-\varepsilon}}{1-\varepsilon} \tag{10.8}$$

where $\varepsilon \neq 1$ is the degree of constant relative inequality aversion of the decision maker. For $\varepsilon = 1$, (10.8) becomes $V(z) = \log z$. In the case of the individual-based welfare function W_I (10.4), the use of (10.8) gives:

$$\widetilde{z} = \frac{1}{\sum_{i=1}^{N} n_i} \left\{ \sum_{i=1}^{N} n_i z_i^{1-\varepsilon} \right\}^{1/(1-\varepsilon)} \tag{10.9}$$

It is useful to express the welfare function in abbreviated form, that is in terms of the arithmetic mean and the measure of inequality, whereby in general, $W = \overline{z}(1-A)$. In this form W is the equally distributed equivalent income, though strictly abbreviated welfare per unit is $\widetilde{z}^{1-\varepsilon}/(1-\varepsilon)$. However, the trade-off between equity and mean income is the same in each case; on abbreviated welfare functions, see Lambert (2001).

10.2 Inequality and Equivalence Scales

Before examining the effects of any policy change, consider the variation in the Atkinson inequality measure as the economies of scale parameter θ varies. Pre-reform inequality measures, for two values of inequality aversion of $\varepsilon = 0.5$ and $\varepsilon = 2.0$, are shown in Figure 10.1, using the function given in (10.3). The data are from the Survey of Income and Housing Costs (SIHC) for 1997/98. When $\theta = 0$, all $m_i = 1$ so that the living standard is equal to total household income and the use of households and equivalent adults as income recipients give the same value of inequality.[2] As θ increases, inequality is seen to diverge, with household units giving higher inequality. The use of individuals gives lower measures of inequality. For the lower degree of inequality aversion, the values are in fact very close: the scales used for the vertical axes of the two parts of Figure 10.1 are different.

[2]The term 'household' is used in this practical example to refer to the concept of an income unit as defined by the ABS in the SIHC as units assumed to share income. This was undertaken to avoid confusion with the discussion on the three alternative units of analysis defined above.

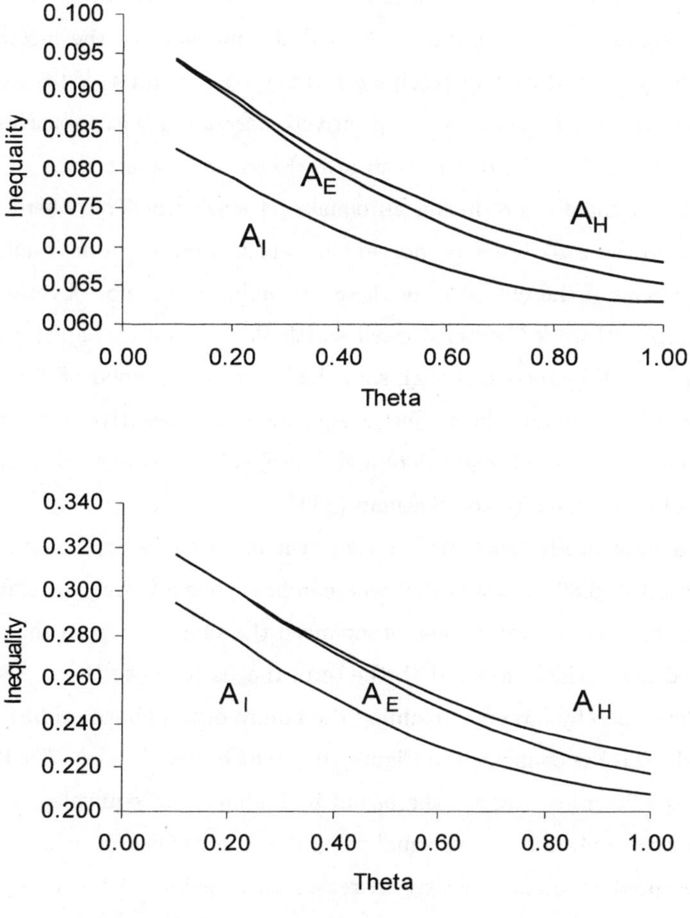

Figure 10.1: Pre-reform Inequality: $\varepsilon = 0.5$ and $\varepsilon = 2.0$

The systematic reduction in inequality as θ increases may be compared with the results of Coulter, Cowell and Jenkins (1992), who examined the effects on the generalised entropy class of inequality measures of varying θ, in the context of the simple scales $m = n^{\theta}$, using the individual as the basic unit of analysis and total income per adult equivalent as the income measure. They showed that increasing θ has two effects. First, if (as expected) unadjusted household income is positively correlated with household size, then for larger households the ratio y/m decreases by more than for smaller households, thereby producing an equalising effect. Second, there may be changes in the rank order of individuals, which produces a disequalising effect. In general the net effect of these two influences is not obvious, but in their empirical work Coulter, Cowell and Jenkins found U-shaped profiles of inequality as θ increases, though some had reverse J-shaped profiles. It can be shown that the reranking effect is equivalent to a negative correlation between income per adult equivalent and household size, which arises for larger values of θ: see Creedy and Sleeman (2005).

In a later study, allowing for the form $m = (n_a + \eta n_c)^{\theta}$, Jenkins and Cowell (1994, p.894) showed that where indices have a U-shaped relationship with θ, the U shape will be less pronounced the smaller is η. In the example reported here, which uses (10.3), the term that is taken to the power of θ is quite low, thereby largely explaining the failure of the above profiles to turn upwards. This is confirmed in Figure 10.2, which uses $m = n^{\theta}$. For this case the inequality measures for the use of individuals and equivalent adults as income recipients are always equal when $\theta = 1$, for which $m = n$.

Measured inequality clearly increases as aversion to inequality, ε, increases: an example is provided in Figure 10.3, for $\theta = 0.8$. Further unreported results show that the pre-reform inequality of net income is systematically lower when individuals are selected as the unit of analysis.[3] In

[3] However, results in Creedy and Sleeman (2005) show cases in which inequality is higher when the unit of analysis is the individual compared with the use of equivalent adults.

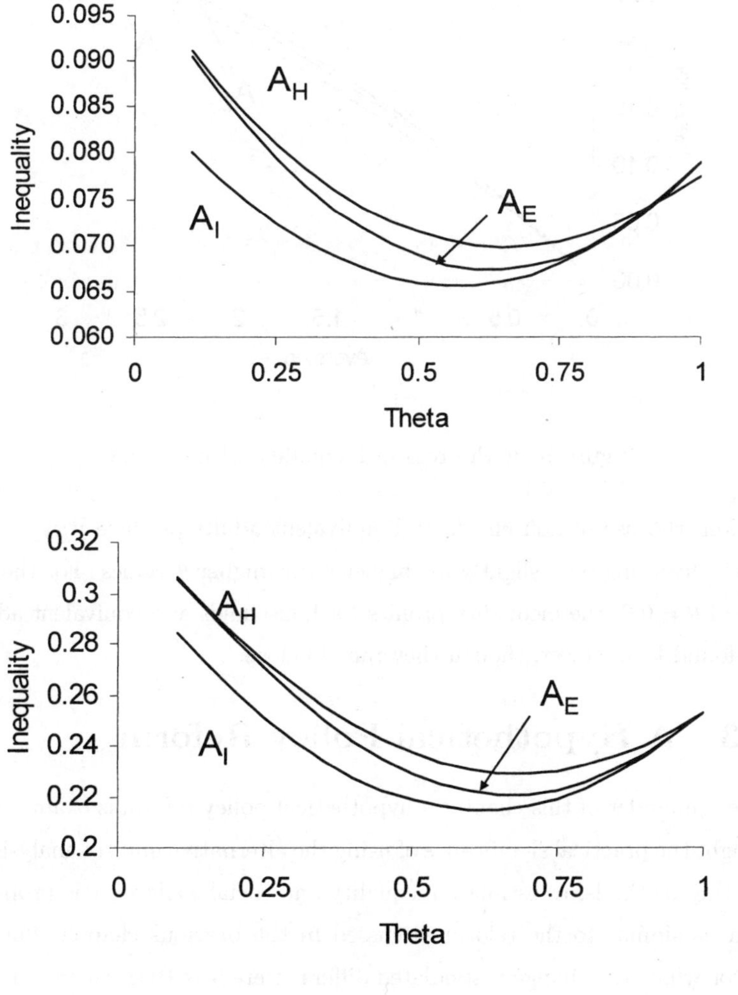

Figure 10.2: Pre-reform Inequality with $m = n^{\theta}$: $\varepsilon = 0.5$ and $\varepsilon = 2.0$

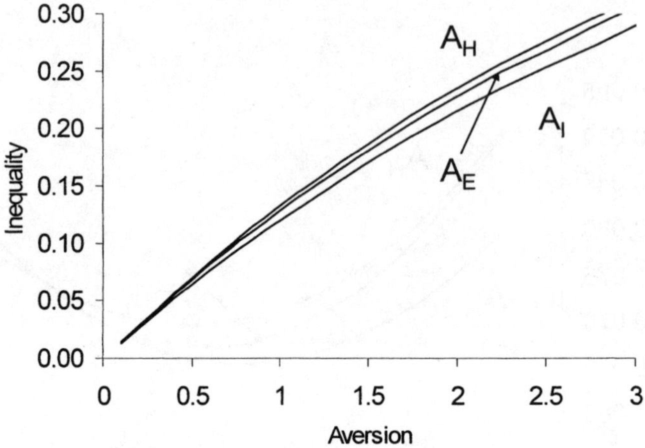

Figure 10.3: Pre-reform Inequality with $\theta = 0.8$

addition, the use of households and equivalent adults produce very similar results, diverging only slightly for higher ε, for higher θ values. For the low value of $\theta = 0.2$, the inequality profiles for households and equivalent adults were found to intersect, though they remain close.

10.3 A Hypothetical Policy Reform

In the remainder of this chapter a hypothetical policy reform is examined to highlight the practical significance of using the alternative units of analysis, or weighting methods, to estimate inequality and social welfare. The proposed reform is similar to the reform discussed in the previous chapter, but the year for which the change is simulated differs. Here it is 1998, whereas in the example in chapter 9 it was 2001.

The policy change considered involves a flattening of the marginal rate structure of the tax and benefit system in Australia. The system of means-tested benefits and increasing marginal income tax rates is replaced by a combination of a basic (non-taxable and non-means tested) income and a flat tax (BI/FT). The basic level of income replaces all existing basic social security benefits, and additional payments such as rent assistance, pharmaceutical allowance and family payments. The existing tax structure, which includes the Medicare levy and all tax rebates, is replaced by a constant marginal tax rate on all taxable income (that is, all non-benefit forms of income).

Details of the structure of the reform system are provided in Table 10.1. Basic income levels differ by individual characteristics. Characteristics that currently entitle individuals to a pension are used to determine whether an individual is entitled to a higher rate of basic income, which is here referred to as the pension rate. This group includes those of Age Pension age, those with a disability, carers, veterans and sole parents. This payment is then differentiated by marital status.

The remaining subset of the population receives a basic income level set at 1998 allowance payment rates. These payments differ by age. Singles aged 16–17 years receive a lower basic income than older individuals, with youths living at home receiving a lower rate again. Also, those 60 years and over receive a higher level than the 18–59 year olds. Each member of a couple is entitled to a lower payment rate than the single rate. The reform is approximately revenue neutral at the pre-reform levels of labour supply, with a relatively high marginal tax rate of 54 per cent.

The various basic income levels imply particular values of the degree of economies of scale, used by policy makers. For example, if the basic income for a single person is y_1 and that for each member of a couple is y_2, it can be shown that the implied scale parameter, θ, is given by:

$$\theta = 1 - \log\left(\frac{y_1}{y_2}\right) \tag{10.10}$$

This result is given by solving $2^\theta = 2y_2/y_1$. For the pensioner group, a value

Table 10.1: Details of Basic Income Levels in Reform System

	$ per fortnight
Pensioner group[1]	
Single	360.00
Couple (each)	298.50
Allowee group[2]	
Single: under 18 years, at home	145.40
Single: under 18 years, away from home	240.00
Single: 18–59 years	321.50
Single: 60 years plus	347.80
Couple (each): under 18 years	240.00
Couple (each): 18–20 years	265.50
Couple (each): 21 years plus	290.10
Maximum rate of rent assistance[3]	
Couple (combined), no children	70.60
Single, no children	74.80
Couple (combined), single: 1–2 children	87.40
Couple (combined), single: 3 children +	98.80
Single, in share accommodation	49.80
Additional payments for families with children	
Per child:	
Under 13 years	96.40
13–15 years	125.40

1) The pensioner group includes those who currently meet the eligibility requirements for a pension and consists of individuals over 65 years, individuals with a disability, carers and sole parents

2) The allowee group includes individuals who do not meet the eligibility requirements for any current pensions and thus cover the unemployed, individuals temporarily unable to work, partnered parents, jobless individuals not falling in any other category and (as this is a universal payment) those employed who are not in the pension group

3) The amount of rent assistance for which individuals are eligible is also determined by the amount of rent paid. The minimum levels of rent paid required to be eligible for rent assistance and the shade-in rates have been left at current levels

of $\theta = 0.730$ is implied, while the basic incomes for those aged 18–20 years imply $\theta = 0.724$. However, non-pensioners aged 21 years and over have an implied value of 0.852, and thus lower economies of scale are assumed.

10.4 Results Assuming Fixed Labour Supply

This section examines the impact of the hypothetical tax policy reform on inequality in the first subsection and on social welfare in the second subsection, prior to any labour supply adjustments.

10.4.1 Changes in Inequality

In considering the implications of using different types of unit of analysis, emphasis is placed on variations in the summary measures as the degree of inequality aversion is increased, for given values of θ. For all values of θ and ε, and for all three units of analysis, the reform was found to reduce inequality of net income. Figure 10.4 shows the absolute reductions in inequality as a result of the reform for the two cases of $\theta = 0.3$ and $\theta = 0.8$. The top section of the figure, for $\theta = 0.3$, shows that the change in inequality is greatest, for all units of analysis, when inequality aversion coefficients slightly above unity are chosen. While the use of households and equivalent adults produce similar changes, the choice of individuals as the income recipient produces larger absolute changes for most of the range of relative aversion shown. The upper value of $\varepsilon = 3$ used here is in fact extremely large, and reflects a substantial tolerance of a 'leaky bucket' in the mental experiment of making transfers. Surveys have produced values close to 0.2 for the majority of respondents; see Amiel, Creedy and Hurn (1999).

The larger value of $\theta = 0.8$, as shown in the lower section of Figure 10.4, shows a greater divergence between the different units of analysis, with the rankings remaining the same for all values of ε. The absolute inequality reductions are also larger for the larger θ value. Furthermore, the maximum absolute reduction in inequality occurs in each case for relative inequality aversion around $\varepsilon = 2$.

10.4.2 Changes in Social Welfare

Figure 10.5 shows absolute changes in social welfare, defined by the abbreviated social welfare function $W = \overline{z}(1 - A)$, for the two values of $\theta = 0.3$ and $\theta = 0.8$, as inequality aversion varies. For both values of θ, the increase in social welfare is highest when the unit of analysis is the individual. The lowest increase occurs when households are used: when θ is very low the use of equivalent adults and households give similar changes, not surprisingly since the adult equivalent size moves towards unity, independent of the household size. The inequality aversion for which the increase in social welfare is greatest varies positively with θ. For the case of $\theta = 0.8$, shown in the lower section of the figure, the increase in social welfare is largest for inequality aversion of around 2, whereas for $\theta = 0.3$, this occurs around 1.

For lower values of inequality aversion, the use of the household as the unit of analysis actually results in the policy reform reducing social welfare slightly. This is despite the reduction in inequality that occurs. It may be thought that, in the present context of fixed labour supply and a revenue-neutral tax policy change, social welfare would always move in the opposite direction from inequality, since aggregate net income is unchanged. However, the value of $\overline{z}$, in the abbreviated welfare function, depends significantly on the choice of the unit of analysis. Furthermore, the income concept itself is the 'living standard' rather than total net income.

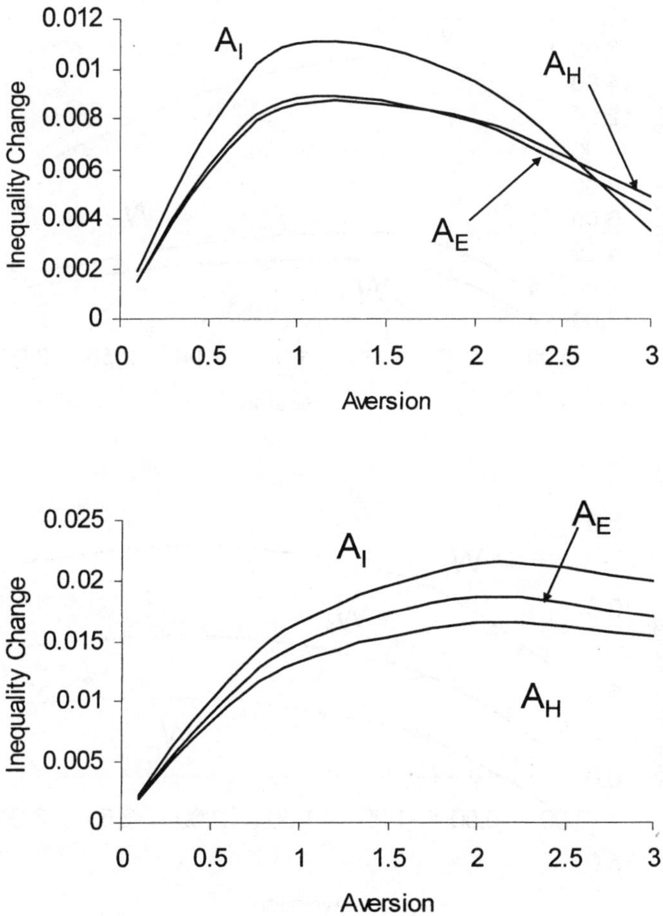

Figure 10.4: Reductions in Inequality: $\theta = 0.3$ and $\theta = 0.8$

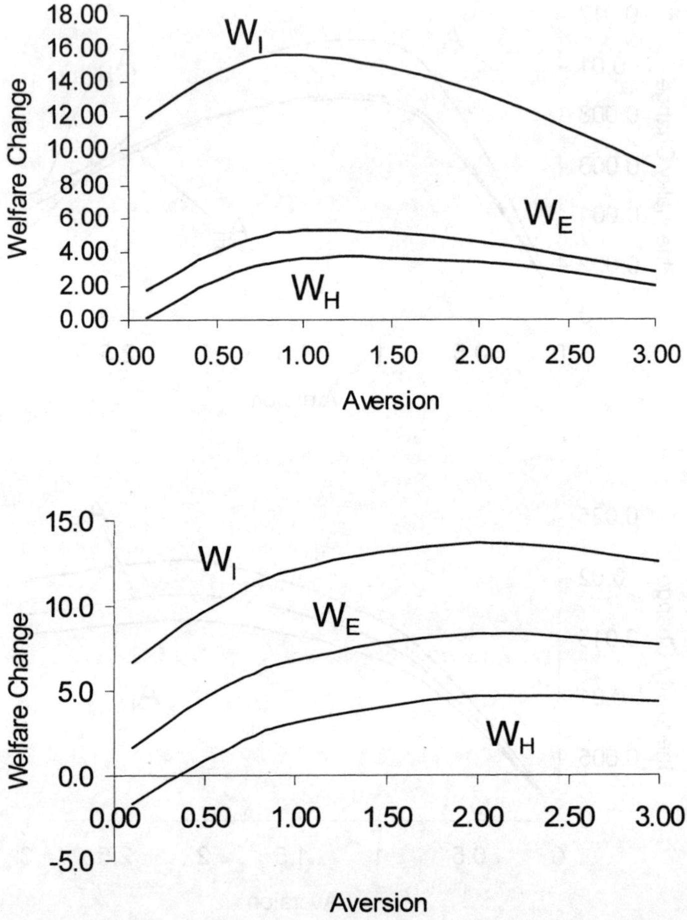

Figure 10.5: Absolute Changes in Social Welfare: $\theta = 0.3$ and $\theta = 0.8$

10.5 Results Allowing for Labour Supply Responses

This section uses MITTS-B to examine the alternative summary measures, allowing for the adjustment of labour supply behaviour.[4] Two qualifications must be made. First, the policy involves a substantial change in the tax structure, compared with that used to estimate the utility functions. Second, it can be argued that the living standard, net income per adult equivalent, may not be the appropriate welfare metric when labour supplies are variable. Although the labour supply modelling explicitly involves utility being attached to leisure, the benefits of any increases in leisure (or costs of reductions) are not captured by the living standard measure.[5] Nevertheless, many descriptive studies use this measure when examining data that have obviously been influenced by labour supply variations. In addition, it is of interest to provide a direct comparison with the non-behavioural results.

Subsection 10.5.1 reports the main changes in labour supply arising from the policy simulation and subsection 10.5.2 examines the inequality and social welfare changes for the different unit of analysis definitions.

10.5.1 Labour Supply Responses

Summary results for labour supply in the different demographic groups are provided in Table 10.2. The aggregate effect of the reform on labour supply is quite small, with many individuals increasing their labour force participation and hours of work while other individuals decrease their supply of labour. The increases are largely contributed by those who previously faced high marginal tax rates arising from the means-tested transfer payments, whereas

[4] A brief description of MITTS and the way in which labour supply is modelled is given in Appendix C.

[5] The calculation of money metric welfare measures based on the preference functions of households is beyond the scope of the present chapter, but is discussed in chapters 7 and 8.

Table 10.2: Summary of Labour Supply Responses: Percentages

Behavioural response	Couples		Single		Sole
	Men	Women	Men	Women	parents
Pre-reform workers	58.4	45.3	54.9	44.0	42.7
Post-reform workers	59.3	41.8	54.4	44.6	37.1
Non-work to work	2.0	0.9	0.8	1.3	0.5
Work to non-work	1.2	4.4	1.2	0.7	6.1
Workers working more	1.4	0.4	0.0	0.2	2.5
Workers working less	2.4	1.9	1.1	1.9	1.2
Average hours change	0.2	-1.7	-0.4	-0.2	-0.7

the reductions arise from the combination of the income effect, resulting in a decrease in hours worked due to the increase in household income, and the substitution effect, resulting in a decrease in hours worked due to the high marginal tax rate on all taxable income. Low-income households benefit whereas middle and higher income households have higher effective marginal tax rates.

The overall effect on labour supply – in terms of average hours worked – is negative, with most of the changes coming from a reduction in the labour supply of married women and sole parents. This is typical of studies of this kind as married women tend to have larger (negative) income elasticities and thus tend to decrease their hours of work with an increase in overall household income. In addition, sole parents actually face a higher effective marginal tax rate than under the 50 per cent taper rate.

The fact that there is also a significant probability of married women leaving the labour market is explained by the budget constraint changes. The post-reform budget constraints for all individuals are linear. The constraints for married women whose husbands are working reveal higher net incomes at zero hours of work and higher marginal tax rates over the whole range (a flatter budget line). This contributes towards the movements from work to non-work shown in the transition matrix. Those with husbands not working, and on a low wage, have an incentive to increase labour supply, except for a short range at low hours of work, where participation has become less attractive. However, the incentives are mixed for those with a higher wage and a non-working husband: those working fewer hours have an incentive to increase labour supply, while those working above about 25 hours per week face a higher marginal tax rate.

For sole parents, the tendency of some of those working lower part-time hours to move out of the labour market, along with a tendency to reduce labour supply for some of those working full-time, is also explained by the flattening of the budget constraint. Married men are the only group to experience an overall increase in hours worked, arising mainly from an increase in workforce participation. However, the overall effect on hours worked is negligible once the reduction in hours worked for those already in the workforce has been taken into account.

10.5.2 Changes in Inequality and Social Welfare

As explained in Part II, microsimulation modelling using a discrete hours approach is essentially probabilistic. That is, it does not identify a particular level of hours worked for each individual after the policy change, but generates a probability distribution over the discrete hours levels used. As a result, individuals have a set of probabilities of being at different income levels and the usual formulae for poverty and inequality measures cannot be applied. The following results were obtained using an approach in which all possible outcomes for every individual are used as if they were separate observations. The outcomes are weighted by the (suitably normalised) individual probabilities of labour supply to produce a pseudo distribution, as described in chapter 9.

As with the case of fixed labour supply, the reform has the effect of reducing overall inequality, whatever the type of unit of analysis chosen for the analysis, and whatever the degree of inequality aversion ε (or the value of

θ). Figure 10.6 shows the absolute changes for two values of θ, as inequality aversion varies. For the higher, and more realistic, value of θ, the absolute reduction in inequality increases systematically with ε throughout most of the range considered, decreasing only slightly at the upper end. The change in inequality is consistently higher when individuals are chosen as the basic unit of analysis, with households giving the smallest change. For the lower value of θ, shown in the upper section of the figure, the ranking in terms of the absolute change in inequality changes at the top end of the range of inequality aversion. Not surprisingly, the changes for equivalent adults and households are similar for this low value of θ, given that m is closer to unity as θ is closer to zero.

Changes in social welfare measures arising from the reform are shown in Figure 10.7, again for two values of θ, for variations in inequality aversion. For all values of ε, the use of individuals as the basic unit of analysis gives the largest increase in social welfare, with the smallest increase being for households. Indeed, for the higher and more realistic value of θ, social welfare is actually found to decrease for a substantial range of ε in the case of the household as the unit of analysis. Even for the case of equivalent adults, social welfare falls, again despite the reduction in inequality, for lower values of inequality aversion.

However, the overall patterns of changes in inequality and social welfare for varying inequality and social welfare parameters are similar for the fixed labour supply and endogenous labour supply cases. This perhaps reflects the finding that, overall, the policy reform is expected to have a small effect on average hours worked, despite substantial heterogeneity in the types of labour supply response. The larger negative effect on social welfare for some values of inequality aversion, and the lower increase across most values of aversion, arises because the value of leisure is not taken into account in measuring the living standard of individuals. In the simulation assuming fixed labour supply, leisure does not change and is therefore not relevant in the change in

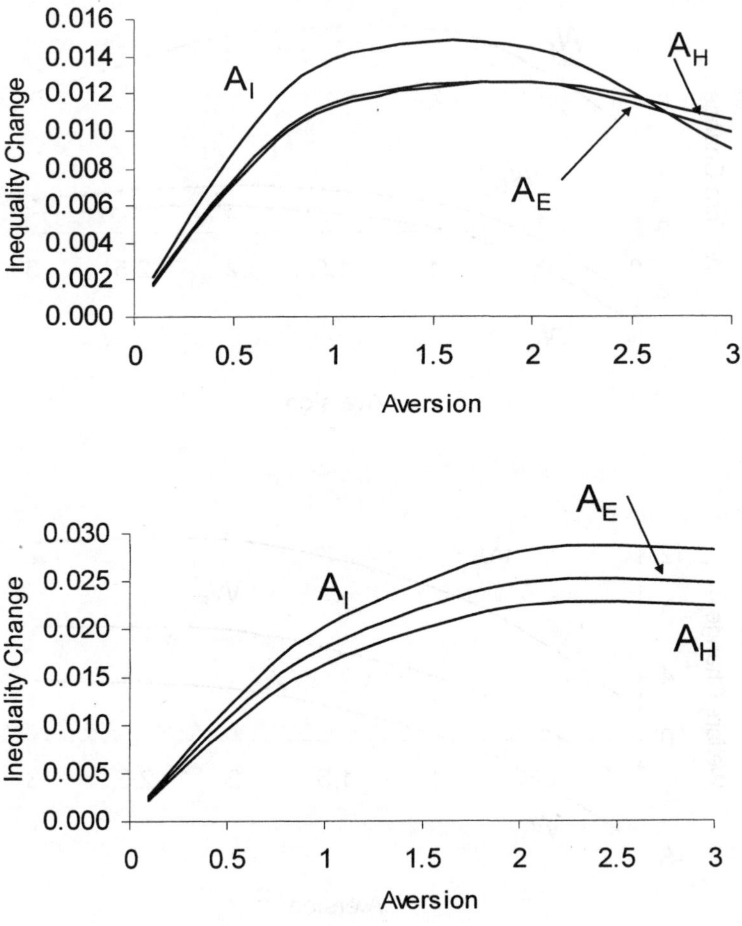

Figure 10.6: Reductions in Inequality: $\theta = 0.3$ and $\theta = 0.8$

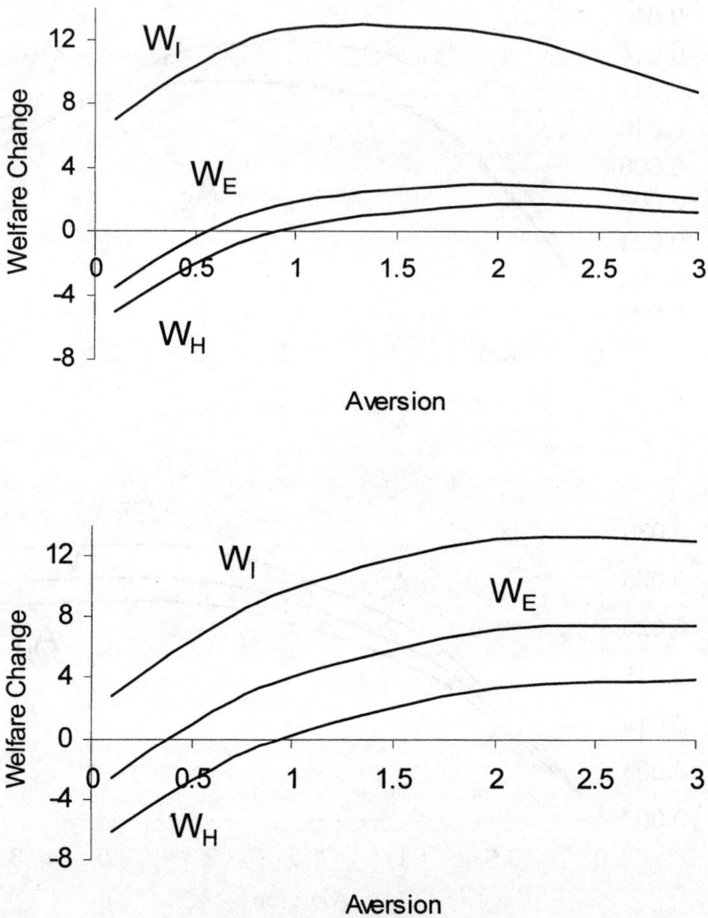

Figure 10.7: Absolute Changes in Social Welfare: $\theta = 0.3$ and $\theta = 0.8$

social welfare.

10.6 Conclusions

This chapter has investigated the implications for overall social welfare and inequality comparisons of using different definitions of the unit of analysis in computing summary measures. Comparisons were made using the Melbourne Institute Tax and Transfer Simulator. A tax reform involving a substantial flattening of the marginal effective tax rate structure in Australia, along with the use of a basic non-taxable level of income for all individuals, was examined. Standard summary measures are designed for homogeneous populations. Therefore decisions must be made about the concept of income and the unit of analysis to account for the heterogeneity of actual populations.

It was taken as given that adult equivalent income, obtained by dividing total household income by adult equivalent size, for a given set of scales, is a suitable measure of the living standard in a household. This view is often taken despite the fact that, in principle, it raises many complex issues. This chapter focused on the choice of the unit of analysis.

Using pre-reform incomes, it was found that the choice of individuals as the basic unit of analysis generally gave the lowest inequality values, with the use of households giving the largest values. However, as θ (the exponent in the equivalence scale function) became close to unity, the ranking was found to change: this cross-over point was higher for higher degrees of inequality aversion. For a given value of θ, the absolute differences between the inequality measures for different units of analysis were small, even for high degrees of inequality aversion. The higher inequality arising from the use of households occurs because the choice of this unit of analysis gives more weight to smaller households and there is a positive correlation between household size and income.

The policy reform was found to reduce inequality for all measures. The use of individuals as unit of analysis consistently gave the highest absolute changes, more clearly so as inequality aversion increased. The exception to this general result occurs when the value of θ is unrealistically low. The policy change was also found to increase social welfare when individuals were used as unit of analysis, and this consistently gave the highest increases. The increase in social welfare was found to rise as inequality aversion increased from a low value, eventually reaching a maximum and then falling again with higher levels of inequality aversion. The value of ε giving the maximum welfare change was found to increase with θ. When allowance was made for labour supply responses to the tax policy change, the use of equivalent adults and households was found to produce falls in social welfare, despite the reduction in inequality, for the lower ranges of inequality aversion.

The choice of different units of analysis was therefore found to lead to consistent rankings in inequality change resulting from the simulated policy change, for a wide range of inequality aversion coefficients and values of θ. However, while the policy change – the flattening of the rate structure – was found to reduce inequality in all cases, it was not always judged to improve social welfare, depending on the degree of inequality aversion and whether equivalent adults were chosen as the unit of analysis. The differences in simulated welfare changes could be substantial depending on the unit of analysis that was chosen.

The use of individuals as unit of analysis is known to satisfy the anonymity principle, while the use of equivalent adults satisfies the equity principle of transfers. With heterogeneous units these fundamental principles may well conflict. The choice is of course ultimately a value judgement, but Shorrocks (1997) conjectured that a main concern for inequality suggests the use of equivalent adults, while a major concern for social welfare leads to the use of individuals as the basic unit of analysis. On this reasoning all those judges with a primary concern for social welfare would conclude that the policy change is welfare enhancing, while all judges would view it as inequality reducing.

The potential sensitivity of policy conclusions to inequality aversion has long been established. The present analysis reinforces the additional argument that, in carrying out policy analyses, it is important to produce a range of summary measures, rather than relying on a single type of unit of analysis and set of equivalence scales.

Chapter 11

Confidence Intervals of Simulation Results

Behavioural tax microsimulation models can provide valuable policy advice about the likely labour supply, revenue and expenditure implications of a wide range of policy reforms. However, these implications are usually in the form of point estimates and microsimulation models typically provide no information about the sampling distribution of labour supply or expenditure changes. Such information would be of much interest to those involved in designing policy reforms with specific objectives and constraints in mind.

Uncertainty regarding a model's projections can arise for a variety of reasons; for a general discussion see Klevmarken (1998). These include, for example, the fact that estimates of wage rates are used (this is particularly true for non-workers in the dataset where wages are obtained from estimated wage functions) and preference parameters are estimated. In addition, sampling variations arise from the fact that the database is a sample of the population and household weights must be used for aggregation purposes. This is problematic for groups where only a small number of observations are available.[1] Errors can of course also arise from incorrect modelling of the

[1]This source of error was examined by Pudney and Sutherland (1994). They concentrated on the use of weights to deal with differential responses by different population strata, assuming that response rates are known. Sample weights are now often based on calibration methods, following Deville and Särndal (1992), where extraneous information

complex administrative rules governing taxes and benefits, reporting errors and problems relating to the (possibly endogenous) incomplete take-up of benefits. This chapter focuses on just one of these sources of error. Its aim is to investigate methods of obtaining confidence intervals where the appropriate distribution of values arises from the sampling distribution of parameter estimates of preference functions. Maximum likelihood estimation gives rise to a variance-covariance matrix for the estimated parameters, which forms the basis of the approaches discussed here. Analytical derivation of the sampling distribution of the various microsimulation outcomes is ruled out in view of the complexity of the transformations involved.[2] The decision to concentrate on uncertainties associated with preference functions does not arise from any judgement that the other sources are not important. Rather, those sources exist with both arithmetic and behavioural modelling, and interest here is in the additional uncertainty which results from the estimation requirements of behavioural models.

The method is discussed in the context of the Melbourne Institute Tax and Transfer Simulator (MITTS), which uses a discrete hours approach to labour supply, as discussed in Part II.[3] Section 11.1 briefly summarises the calibration approach to individual labour supply simulation, first discussed in chapter 5. This reminder is provided in view of its importance in appreciating the time involved in producing confidence intervals. A basic simulation method of constructing confidence intervals is described in section 11.2. This involves the numerical production of an approximate sampling distribution of the variable of interest. Numerical results for a simple policy reform,

about selected population totals is used.

[2]However, Pudney and Sutherland (1996) derived explicit results for the sampling variance of variables, such as total government expenditure, which are obtained by summing values over individuals in the sample. They estimated a three-state multinomial logit model for females, but did not consider hours variations (so that only earnings enter utility functions). Understandably, given the computation burden at the time, they rejected any kind of simulation approach.

[3]MITTS is briefly discussed in Appendix C.

using this approach in MITTS, are presented in section 11.3. This reform involves a flattening of budget constraints resulting from a reduction in benefit abatement, or taper, rates. The basic simulation method is highly computer intensive and can take several weeks or even months, depending on the number of households in the sample and the speed of the computer used. A much more time-efficient approximate method, assuming normality, is suggested in section 11.4, followed by conclusions in section 11.5.

11.1 Individual Calibration

Given estimated parameters of specified preference functions, and a set of net incomes for each individual or couple arising from every possible discrete hours level, the effects on labour supply of tax policy changes can be examined. The simulation method applied by MITTS and other microsimulation models is to use the labour supply observed in the data set to obtain a starting point for each individual. This ensures that the optimal labour supply of each individual corresponds precisely to the observed labour supply under the particular tax and benefit system at the time of the survey.

The first step is to discretise the observed hours, so that the individual's hours are set equal to the nearest discrete level available. Suppose there are n hours levels. In the calibration process, a set of n independent error terms is drawn from the relevant distribution, in this case the extreme value distribution. These are added to the deterministic utility levels at each of the hours points. If this results in the utility at the observed labour supply being the optimal choice for the individual, the set of random values is stored. It is useful to distinguish between 'draws' and 'tries': the former describes a set of values which are stored for further use, while the latter describes any set of random values from the extreme value distribution. If a 'try' does not result in optimal hours that correspond to observed hours, another set of error terms is obtained and another check is made. If, after say K attempts, no set of random values has been found that places the individual at actual pre-reform hours, instead of storing a 'draw', the individual's hours of work are assumed to be constant for this particular 'draw' when examining a policy reform.

This process is repeated a specified number of times, say k, each time using K tries if necessary. For most individuals, the draws are usually obtained with few tries. However, for some individuals, a proportion of attempts to produce a draw may not succeed after K tries. In a small number of cases, no successful draws may be obtained even after a total of K times k sets of n random values have been taken from the error distribution.

The sets of error terms that result in the observed labour supply, the k draws, are then used to compute a distribution of hours worked for each individual after a specified reform. Given the individual's characteristics and draws from the error term, utility at each hours level after the change can be determined using the new net incomes implied by the tax reform. The hours level at which utility is maximised after the reform is determined for each draw. In this way, a frequency distribution, based on k values, of post-reform hours worked can be obtained and the probability of being at each of the discrete hours points, conditional on the pre-reform labour supply, is calculated for each individual. As explained, some of the k draws, for a selection of individuals, fix labour supply at the pre-reform reported level.

11.2 Construction of Confidence Intervals

This section describes the simulation approach to generate an approximation to the sampling distribution of aggregate measures, allowing for the estimated joint sampling distribution of the parameter estimates for the quadratic preference functions. These parameters are augmented to allow for a range of individuals' characteristics, and are estimated separately for different demographic groups. Essentially, the distributions for the aggregate measures are assembled by repeatedly drawing from the estimated sampling distribution of parameters. For each set of parameters, the calibration process and policy reform exercise as described in the previous section are carried out.

In view of the discrete choice nature of the hours decision, revenue and expenditure items for each individual are based on expected values, using the computed probability distribution over hours for the post-reform tax structure. For the pre-reform structure the revenue and costs are based on the discretised value of observed hours worked. Population aggregates are then obtained using the household weights provided with the data.

The empirical confidence intervals are created using the point estimates of the parameters in the labour supply models (that is, the estimated parameters of the direct utility functions) and the estimated variance-covariance matrix. Suppose it is required to calculate the confidence intervals for the changes in expenditure and revenue resulting from a particular policy reform. These can be constructed through the use of the following simulation method. First, a vector of labour supply parameters is drawn randomly from a multivariate normal distribution with the mean and covariance matrix given by the point estimates of the labour supply parameters and the variance-covariance matrix for the parameters respectively. The method used to obtain random values from a multivariate normal distribution is described in Appendix G. This vector of labour supply parameters is used to carry out the calibration exercise described in the previous section. That is, the required number of sets of draws from the error distributions (the extreme value distributions) are generated such that optimal labour supply corresponds to actual discretised hours in the pre-reform situation. The process of these two steps taken together is described as a 'replication'. Thus each vector of preference parameters, drawn from the distribution of preference parameters, gives rise to a 'replication' of the preference function. This distinguishes it from the set of 'draws' from the error distribution for each discrete hours level, which gives optimal hours as observed hours in the pre-reform situation, and the 'tries' allowed in collecting the set of draws. The 'tries' resulting in successful 'draws' in the calibration exercise for one particular 'replication' may not place the individual at observed hours when a different replication is used. For this reason the calibration stage needs to be repeated for each replication.

Combining the randomly drawn vector of preference parameters with all the sets of draws from the error distributions obtained in the calibration stage, it is possible to predict the proportion at each of the discrete hours points after the reform. Given these proportions, the expected changes in expenditure and revenue after the reform can be computed for each individual and for the sample as a whole. This procedure is repeated a large number of times. After each replication, the corresponding estimate for the expected change in, say, expenditure is stored in a vector. After completing all replications, this vector, approximating the sampling distribution, is ranked in ascending order. A 90 per cent confidence interval can be constructed using this vector by taking the 5th percentile and the 95th percentile as the lower and upper bounds of the interval. In a similar fashion, confidence intervals can be constructed for other measures of interest, such as the probability of participation or changes in revenue.

These calculations are computationally intensive. Indeed, it could take weeks or even months – depending on the number of households, the number of specified draws from the error distribution, the number of tries allowed for each draw and the number of replications on which the intervals are based – before confidence intervals for the results from the behavioural component could be provided for a particular policy change.[4] It is clear that this is

[4]For example, on a Pentium-4 machine with 512 Mb of RAM and 1.90 GHz, it takes 200 minutes to run one behavioural simulation for 7170 households in the 1997/98 SIHC dataset if, for each household, the total number of draws is set to 100 and the maximum number of tries allowed to calibrate the observed hours for each draw is set to 1000. If the simulation is repeated 1000 times it would take approximately 200,000 minutes (around 4.5 months) in total to calculate the confidence intervals for this sample. The time required for each replication may not be the same, as different numbers of tries may be needed to obtain the requisite draws.

impractical.

An obvious influence on the computation time is the number of individuals or households examined. In order to keep the time to a minimum, it is therefore best where possible to calculate the confidence intervals for each demographic group (for which preference parameter estimates are obtained) separately rather than using all households in the dataset. This allows the user to use more than one computer to calculate the intervals, which will reduce the total amount of (calendar) time needed for calculations for the entire population.

11.3 Examples for a Taper Reduction

This section uses the approach described in section 11.2 to produce confidence intervals for the policy reform of reducing all taper rates in the March 1998 tax system, from 50 and 70 per cent to 30 per cent.[5] This simulation uses the 1997/98 Survey of Income and Housing Cost dataset, which is a cross-section of the Australian population providing detailed information on income, labour supply and individual and household characteristics. As mentioned in section 11.2, the number of draws as well as the maximum number of tries can be varied. Instead of taking an arbitrary number, it is useful to experiment to find the best combination; that is, the smallest set of draws and tries which produces stable results. This is discussed in subsection 11.3.1. Confidence intervals are then reported in subsection 11.3.2 for changes in labour supply and government revenue and expenditure.

11.3.1 Sampling from the Error Distributions

Computation of confidence intervals is complicated by the large number of random variables generated in the calibration process, and the associated

[5] This is the reform considered in Creedy, Kalb and Kew (2003) using point estimates of preference functions. However, the wage and preference functions used in MITTS have since been re-estimated.

utility maximisation analysis, which has to be repeated for each set of preference parameters. This subsection considers how this part of the process can be reduced to a minimum.

Table 11.1, for couples, single men and women, and sole parents, provides an idea of how sensitive the results of one replication are to different combinations of draws and tries. The first two columns of these tables give the specified combination of k, the number of draws, and K, the number of tries for each draw. The third column gives the time in minutes to do a single simulation for all households, using the point estimates of preference functions and using a Pentium-4 machine with 512 Mb of Ram and 1.90 GHz. In each case the variable r indicates the number of draws for which labour supply is held constant at the base discretised hours; that is, after K tries, it was not possible to find a set of random variables from the error distribution giving optimal hours equal to observed hours. For all groups, 11 hours points are used in the labour supply model, except for married men, who are less likely to work part time than the other groups. Therefore, only 6 hours points are distinguished to model labour supply for this group.

The first row of each segment of the table, where the number of draws and tries are both relatively large, may be used as a benchmark. The results concerning the average change in hours worked remain almost identical when the number of draws is increased from 100 to 150, suggesting that the results become stable as the number of draws and/or tries is increased above a certain number. Choosing a smaller number of draws means that substantially less time is needed to run one simulation. However, as the number of draws is decreased, the results become less accurate and more variable across simulations (depending more on the particular random draws that are taken from the error distribution). Decreasing the number of tries means labour supply is fixed at observed hours for more draws. That is, the average number of hours for the different subgroups are further from the benchmark results. The last row, which has only 10 draws and 100 tries, presents changes in the

Table 11.1: Average Hours Change (ΔH) by Number of Draws and Tries: All Couples

k	K	Time (min.)	Married men ΔH	r $< k$	r $= k$	Married women ΔH	r $< k$	r $= k$	ΔH	r $< k$	r $= k$
100	1000	200	0.46	164	37	-0.47	164	37			
150	1000	280	0.46	206	27	-0.47	206	27			
100	500	151	0.32	256	64	-0.50	256	64			
100	100	80	0.13	1002	99	-0.45	1002	99			
50	1000	115	0.46	93	64	-0.48	93	64			
40	1000	94	0.46	78	73	-0.50	78	73			
30	1000	80	0.45	57	81	-0.48	57	81			
20	1000	60	0.42	42	88	-0.48	42	88			
10	1000	40	0.38	21	99	-0.49	21	99			
10	700	38	0.35	21	125	-0.49	21	125			
10	500	35	0.26	37	155	-0.51	37	155			
10	100	30	0.01	286	289	-0.45	286	289			
			Single men			Single women			Sole parents		
100	1000	200	0.33	53	6	0.14	32	2	2.28	7	0
150	1000	280	0.33	63	6	0.13	43	1	2.26	9	0
100	500	151	0.28	134	7	0.08	80	5	2.27	27	0
100	100	80	0.13	214	18	-0.06	231	12	2.20	132	0
50	1000	115	0.30	32	7	0.13	22	5	2.40	3	0
40	1000	94	0.29	28	9	0.12	19	6	2.49	2	0
30	1000	80	0.28	24	11	0.13	18	6	2.55	1	0
20	1000	60	0.27	14	16	0.13	11	11	2.64	0	0
10	1000	40	0.29	10	18	0.13	6	12	2.71	0	0
10	700	38	0.26	17	33	0.06	10	23	2.71	1	0
10	500	35	0.24	23	52	0.01	9	31	2.71	2	2
10	100	30	0.10	63	104	-0.10	58	64	2.47	24	16

Note: The total number of couples with and without children is 2474.
The total number of single men, single women and sole parents is 1392, 1038 and 503.
k = number of draws; K = number of tries per draw;
r = number of draws which involve fixed labour supply at base discretised hours.
When r < k, at least one, but less than k, draws are fixed at base discretised hours.
When r = k, all k draws are fixed at the base discretised hours.

average numbers of hours worked that are very different from the benchmark figures.

The optimal number of draws and tries may be different for different subgroups and different policy simulations. Choosing 100 draws and 1000 tries is a safe choice for all groups, but it can most likely be reduced. It appears that married men, single men and single women are less sensitive to the number of draws, but more sensitive to the number of tries. Sole parents, on the other hand, are less sensitive to the number of tries, but the number of draws plays an important role in achieving a stable result. The results for married women are the least sensitive of all groups.

It was recommended in section 11.2 that the confidence intervals should be calculated for one demographic group at a time rather than for all households together, so that more than one computer could be used for the calculations. A further advantage of separating the groups is that one demographic group may require more draws to obtain a stable result than another demographic group. By calculating the intervals separately for each subgroup the minimum number of draws sufficient for that subgroup can be chosen.

These results show that it is impractical to set a large number of draws and tries when calculating confidence intervals, because the simulation needs to be repeated so many times that the time needed with many draws becomes problematic from a computational point of view. Table 11.1 showed that a large number of draws and tries may be unnecessary in many cases because the predicted values become stable for much lower numbers of draws and tries. In obtaining the results in the next subsections, in each case the decision was made to set the number of draws to 40 with 1000 tries per draw. The number of replications was set to 1000. The alternative choice of draws and tries more than halves the time required for one simulation. This shows that before starting repeated calculations to generate confidence intervals, it is useful to experiment with the number of draws and tries in a simulation, using the point estimates of the labour supply model, to find a combination that takes as little time to run as possible while providing stable results. Investing some time at this stage can reduce the time needed to compute the confidence intervals considerably.

11.3.2 Results for Labour Supply

Table 11.2 presents the simulation results regarding labour supply changes for couples. All values refer to percentages of the demographic group, with the exception of the last row of each segment which reports the change in average hours worked. Within each section of the table, the first item, 'all workers', refers to the percentage of the demographic group working, including the self-employed along with wage and salary earners. The second item, 'wage/sal. workers', refers to wage and salary earners, who are working and for whom hours of work are observed, as a percentage of the total number of people in the group. In the simulation, the behaviour of the self-employed is not modelled, so their gross income is assumed to remain constant. The final three columns of Table 11.2 show the 5th and 95th percentiles of the approximate sampling distribution, along with the median value.

The effect of the flattening of the budget constraints has an ambiguous effect on labour supply, since marginal tax rates are reduced at lower working hours while they are increased at higher levels of labour supply. The average hours for women is expected to fall as a result of the reform. Although the percentage of women who work fewer hours after the reform is actually lower than the corresponding value for men, more married women move from work to non-work. For men and women in couples, the confidence intervals are not particularly wide and it seems that these labour supply responses are obtained with a reasonable amount of precision.

The reform is expected to have a larger effect on the labour supply of sole parents; see Table 11.3. A much larger proportion moves from non-work to work than for couples, though this result is less precise than for married men

Table 11.2: Simulated Labour Supply Responses to a Reduction in Taper Rates: Couples

	Mean	Confidence intervals 5%	Median	95%
Married men with children:				
All workers: base (in %)	87.3			
Wage/sal. workers: base (in %)	72.57			
Wage/sal. workers: post (in %)	75.67	75.51	75.67	75.81
Non-work to work (in %-points)	3.53	3.40	3.53	3.65
Work to non-work (in %-points)	0.43	0.36	0.43	0.52
Workers working more (in %-points)	0.67	0.57	0.67	0.75
Workers working less (in %-points)	2.59	2.42	2.58	2.77
Average hours change (in hours)	0.99	0.91	0.99	1.06
Married women with children:				
All workers: base (in %)	59.94			
Wage/sal. workers: base (in %)	51.12			
Wage/sal. workers: post (in %)	50.74	50.52	50.74	50.97
Non-work to work (in %-points)	2.28	2.07	2.28	2.49
Work to non-work (in %-points)	2.67	2.50	2.67	2.83
Workers working more (in %-points)	0.20	0.16	0.20	0.23
Workers working less (in %-points)	1.02	0.89	1.02	1.15
Average hours change (in hours)	-0.63	-0.7	-0.63	-0.55
Married men without children:				
All workers: base (in %)	57.17			
Wage/sal. workers: base (in %)	45.24			
Wage/sal. workers: post (in %)	45.58	45.43	45.58	45.74
Non-work to work (in %-points)	1.11	0.99	1.11	1.22
Work to non-work (in %-points)	0.76	0.66	0.76	0.86
Workers working more (in %-points)	0.22	0.15	0.21	0.28
Workers working less (in %-points)	0.79	0.72	0.79	0.85
Average hours change (in hours)	0.03	-0.03	0.03	0.10
Married women without children:				
All workers: base (in %)	46.63			
Wage/sal. workers: base (in %)	39.79			
Wage/sal. workers: post (in %)	39.22	39.05	39.22	39.41
Non-work to work (in %-points)	0.57	0.46	0.56	0.68
Work to non-work (in %-points)	1.13	0.98	1.13	1.27
Workers working more (in %-points)	0.24	0.17	0.23	0.33
Workers working less (in %-points)	0.73	0.66	0.73	0.79
Average hours change (in hours)	-0.34	-0.40	-0.34	-0.27

and women, as indicated by the wider confidence interval. The increase in average hours is significantly larger than for people in couples, though again the confidence interval is wider. Smaller effects are found for singles and couples without children. The confidence intervals are again more narrow for couples but the confidence intervals for singles are not as wide as for sole parents. The table shows that in general the confidence intervals are quite narrow for singles without children as well.

Comparing the standard deviations for the point estimates of the labour supply parameters for sole parents and couples, not reported here, it is clear that those for couples are smaller, indicating more precise estimates; for details, see Kalb (2002). This has translated into more precise predictions for behavioural changes in the simulation for couples.

The comparisons show first that allowing for potential labour supply effects of tax reforms matters in the estimation of taxes and expenditures. Not allowing for such responses would, for example, lead to a significant overstatement of the income tax revenue change for couples. The assumption of fixed labour supply suggests that tax rebates for sole parents are expected to fall, yet the positive net labour supply responses imply that rebates increase. Furthermore, the increase in allowances for sole parents is substantially lower when labour supply is endogenous. The increase in net expenditure on this demographic group is significantly overstated when labour supply is held fixed.

In addition, Table 11.4 and Table 11.5 show that for couples and singles, the confidence intervals for most items are relatively small. However, some of the sole parent confidence intervals are relatively large. For example, changes in tax rebates, allowances and especially net expenditure are estimated with a relatively low precision. The width of the confidence interval for the change in net expenditure is about 200 million dollars for couples with children and about 160 million dollars for sole parents. Given the much lower number of sole parents in the population, this means that per individual the uncertainty

Table 11.3: Simulated Labour Supply Responses to a Reduction in Taper Rates: Singles

	Mean	Confidence intervals 5%	Median	95%
Single men				
All workers: base (in %)	67.30			
Wage/sal. workers: base (in %)	59.57			
Wage/sal. workers: post (in %)	61.31	60.89	61.30	61.78
Non-work to work (in %-points)	1.86	1.45	1.85	2.33
Work to non-work (in %-points)	0.11	0.06	0.12	0.16
Workers working more (in %-points)	0.08	0.00	0.07	0.17
Workers working less (in %-points)	1.24	1.04	1.21	1.57
Average hours change (in hours)	0.41	0.27	0.41	0.55
Single women				
All workers: base (in %)	48.01			
Wage/sal. workers: base (in %)	44.90			
Wage/sal. workers: post (in %)	46.92	46.59	46.91	47.28
non-work to work (in %-points)	2.16	1.83	2.14	2.52
Work to non-work (in %-points)	0.13	0.10	0.13	0.17
Workers working more (in %-points)	0.13	0.07	0.12	0.20
Workers working less (in %-points)	2.79	2.39	2.77	3.22
Average hours change (in hours)	0.17	0.07	0.17	0.26
Sole parents				
All workers: base (in %)	47.37			
Wage/sal. workers: base (in %)	42.71			
Wage/sal. workers: post (in %)	50.94	49.29	50.7	53.46
Non-work to work (in %-points)	8.45	6.81	8.20	10.96
Work to non-work (in %-points)	0.22	0.10	0.22	0.36
Workers working more (in %-points)	1.89	1.28	1.87	2.54
Workers working less (in %-points)	2.34	1.94	2.32	2.82
Average hours change (in hours)	2.63	1.98	2.56	3.49

associated with the expected change after the reform is substantially larger for sole parents.

11.4 An Alternative Approach

The previous section has demonstrated the value of examining confidence intervals using the proposed method of computing an approximate sampling distribution. It showed that all predicted changes were significantly different from zero. This indicates that there is some confidence in the direction of the predicted effects.

The main drawback of the method is the length of time needed, given the large computational burden. Even with fast modern computers, the time involved is too large to make it viable for regular use, particularly when attempting to design policy reforms. The design of policy changes, with a range of objectives in mind, including a government budget constraint, typically involves the examination of a large number of experiments. Hence the question arises of whether a faster method of constructing confidence intervals can be found. This question is addressed in the present section.

11.4.1 An Approximation

Examination of Tables 11.2 to 11.5 shows that the mean and median changes resulting from the tax change are in all cases close to each other, suggesting that the relevant distributions are close to being symmetric. Furthermore, inspection of the (unreported) results using only the point estimates of preference functions shows that these are also quite close to the mean and median values. The potential for reducing the number of replications was explored by plotting histograms of the various empirical sampling distributions. A range of distributions were obtained, such as distributions for various expenditure and revenue items, as well as total expenditure and revenue, based on 1000 replications. Examples for sole parents are shown in Figure 11.1. The left

Table 11.4: Change in Tax and Transfer Costs Resulting from a Reduction in Taper Rates: Couples

	Pre-reform	Changes from pre- to post-reform				
		Fixed labour	Variable labour supply			
			Mean	Confidence intervals		
	($m)	($m)	($m)	5%	Median	95%
Couples with children						
Income tax	28929.8	527.1	392.6	349.4	393.0	431.6
Medicare	1736.5	74.6	70.2	67.1	70.2	73.0
Total Revenue	*30666.3*	*601.7*	*462.8*	*417.1*	*463.0*	*504.0*
Tax rebates	1181	-363.4	-350.3	-353.5	-350.3	-346.9
Family payment	4078.3	1686.9	2035.6	2017.7	2035.3	2055.4
FTP/FTB	402.4	179.2	214.7	211.6	214.6	217.7
Allowances	4271.7	3620.8	3468.0	3426.9	3467.1	3509.2
Pensions	737.7	42.5	27.0	23.5	27.0	33.5
Pharmacy allow.	8.9	0.6	0.1	0.0	0.1	0.2
Rent allow.	359.8	119.9	156.7	153.3	156.7	160.0
Total Expenditure	*11039.9*	*5286.6*	*5551.6*	*5493.8*	*5551.9*	*5611.9*
Net expenditure	-19626.4	4684.8	5088.8	4992.6	5088.2	5191.5
Couples without children						
Income tax	21001.1	527.3	337.6	308.0	338.2	367.7
Medicare	1327.4	58.0	48.4	46.3	48.4	50.6
Total Revenue	*22328.5*	*585.3*	*386*	*354.2*	*386.7*	*418.2*
Tax rebates	1327.8	-194.0	-193.9	-196.3	-193.9	-191.7
Allowances	2612.2	2403.6	2495.5	2463.6	2496.4	2524.8
Pensions	10151.2	771.5	768.5	762.4	769.1	772.4
Pharmacy allow.	109.1	10.1	10.2	10.1	10.2	10.4
Rent allow.	170.8	127.0	141.7	139.7	141.8	143.4
Total Expenditure	*14371.0*	*3118.3*	*3222.0*	*3187.7*	*3222.5*	*3254.7*
Net expenditure	-7957.5	2533.0	2836.1	2770.8	2835.8	2897.9

Note: FTP/FTB stands for Family Tax Payments and Family Tax Benefits.

Table 11.5: Change in Tax and Transfer Costs Resulting from a Reduction in Taper Rates: Singles

		Changes from pre- to post-reform				
	Pre-	Fixed	Variable labour supply			
	reform	labour	Mean	Confidence intervals		
	($m)	($m)	($m)	5%	Median	95%
Single men						
Income tax	12667.8	352.2	389.7	353.8	390.9	421.1
Medicare	863.1	35.0	43.6	40.2	43.6	47.1
Total revenue	*13530.9*	*387.1*	*433.3*	*394.2*	*434.4*	*468.1*
Tax rebates	436.0	-8.7	-24.9	-29.9	-24.9	-20.5
Allowances	3564.5	1266.8	1108.2	1053.5	1107.8	1158.7
Pensions	3336.7	142.7	134.3	130.5	134.2	137.7
Pharmacy allow.	58.2	3.1	3.2	3.1	3.2	3.2
Rent allow.	356.3	333.2	344.0	342.0	343.7	346.9
Total expenditure	*7751.7*	*1737.1*	*1564.7*	*1506.1*	*1564.3*	*1619.7*
Net expenditure	-5779.2	1349.9	1131.3	1036.3	1130.5	1224.3
Single women						
Income tax	7192.9	329.3	267.4	242.3	267.5	291.8
Medicare	473.9	32.0	36.0	34.0	36.1	38.1
Total revenue	*7666.7*	*361.3*	*303.4*	*276.8*	*303.8*	*329.8*
Tax rebates	707.8	-23.4	-36.0	-38.5	-36.0	-33.3
Allowances	2264.8	1051.4	1023.7	995.3	1022.5	1053.6
Pensions	7456.4	236.6	203.9	196.4	204.5	209.5
Pharmacy allow.	117.2	4.6	4.6	4.6	4.6	4.6
Rent allow.	289.3	261.0	278.2	275.3	278.2	281.0
Total expenditure	*10835.4*	*1530.2*	*1474.5*	*1442.1*	*1473.8*	*1508.5*
Net expenditure	3168.7	1169.0	1171.1	1112.5	1168.3	1229.7
Sole parents						
Income tax	1900.4	75.6	158.7	123.9	156.4	199.7
Medicare	83.9	4.8	5.6	4.0	5.6	7.1
Total revenue	*1984.4*	*80.4*	*164.3*	*128.1*	*161.8*	*206.9*
Tax rebates	553.6	-12.5	18.7	12.6	17.9	28.0
Family payment	2139.7	90.2	132.5	124.6	132.2	141.1
FTP/FTB	229.9	0	0	0	0	0
Allowances	3025.2	264.2	93.7	35.6	97.8	136.6
Pensions	155.0	1.1	-4.1	-5.6	-4.0	-2.6
Pharmacy allow.	49.8	6.0	7.5	7.2	7.4	7.8
Rent allow.	405.7	5.8	14.8	12.6	14.8	17.2
Total expenditure	*6558.9*	*354.7*	*263.1*	*220.2*	*265.4*	*299.3*
Net expenditure	4574.5	274.3	98.8	11.3	102.4	171.0

Note: FTP/FTB stands for Family Tax Payments and Family Tax Benefits

hand set of distributions relate to labour supply changes and the right hand set is for total revenue and expenditure, and net expenditure. In each histogram, the smooth bell-shaped line shows the density function of a normal distribution having the same arithmetic mean and variance as the empirical frequencies.

While the distributions do not appear to be well described by the normal distribution, and in fact normality is rejected for some of the distributions, it is useful to consider an approach that is based on the properties of the normal distribution given the reasonably symmetric shape of many of the distributions. Thus, instead of taking a large number of replications and finding the 5th and 95th percentiles, consider using a smaller number of replications to estimate the mean μ and standard deviation σ for the outcomes of interest. Assuming normality, the appropriate percentiles of the standard normal $N(0,1)$ distribution can be used to find the required confidence interval based on $N(\mu, \sigma^2)$. For example, the 5th and 95th percentiles are obtained as $\mu \pm 1.645\sigma$.

11.4.2 Results

Results using the alternative approach are given in Figure 11.2, which shows, for each summary variable, the 90 per cent confidence limits obtained when using 1000 replications (represented by the solid horizontal lines in the graphs) and the limits produced when an assumption of normality is used, as the number of replications, N, is increased. It can be seen that the confidence limits produced by assuming normality are reasonably close to those obtained from 1000 replications, in some cases even for as few as 50 replications. However, the limits using 1000 replications take about 20 times longer to produce than those obtained using only 50 replications. This means that most results could be produced within one or two days with this more approximate approach.

Figures 11.3 and 11.4 show the histograms for the labour supply summary

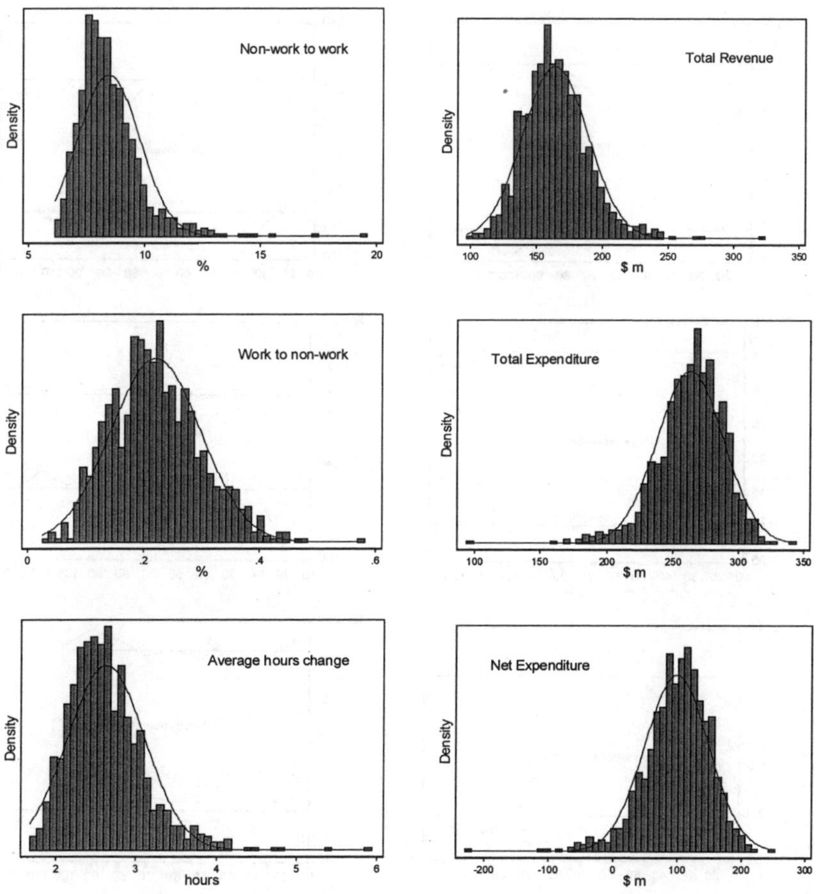

Figure 11.1: Sole Parents' Histograms of Labour Supply and Expenditure/Revenue Simulation Outcomes

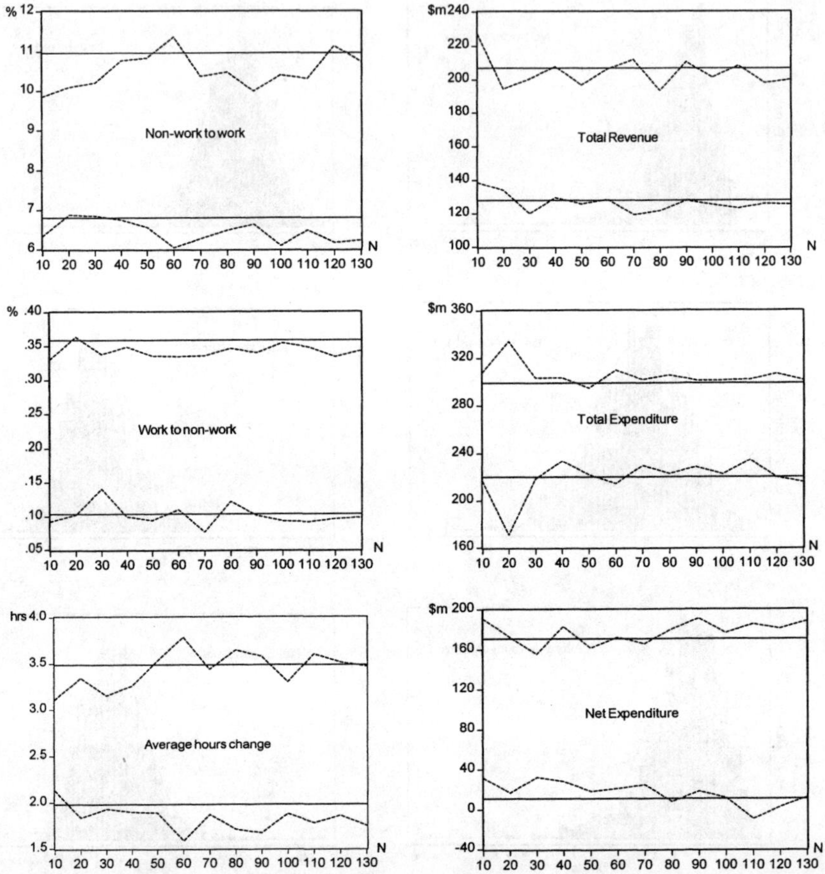

Figure 11.2: Confidence Intervals by the Number of Replications (N): Sole Parents

changes for married men and married women respectively. For this group, the empirical sampling distributions are closer to normality (as also shown by a range of distributions for other variables, not presented here). The right hand segments of these figures compare the confidence limits obtained from 1000 replications compared with the use of small samples and an assumption of normality. Again, good approximations are produced with as few as 50 replications. Similar results apply to tax and expenditure totals for couples, as shown in Figure 11.5.

Similar results were found to apply to a wide range of expenditure and revenue categories. The same is true for other demographic groups, as shown in Figures 11.6 to 11.12. Even where the plotted histograms are not particularly close to being normal, the use of a smaller number of replications combined with an assumption of normality provides a good guide to the confidence intervals that are produced using a large number of replications to generate an approximate sampling distribution. That is, the use of a small number of replications combined with an assumption of normality can provide reliable estimates of those intervals. Exceptions to this general rule were found to arise in the case of the pharmaceutical allowance for couples and sole parents. Where very few individuals in the sample are in receipt of a particular benefit, as in this case, caution must be exercised. However, the aggregate amount of this payment compared with those of other payments is negligible, so the uncertainty associated with it tends to have only a small effect on the total expenditure and revenue.

11.5 Conclusions

This chapter has examined one important source of uncertainty surrounding tax policy simulations of labour supply, taxation and revenue changes, when using a behavioural tax microsimulation model. This arises from the fact that the preference functions, on which predicted labour supply behaviour

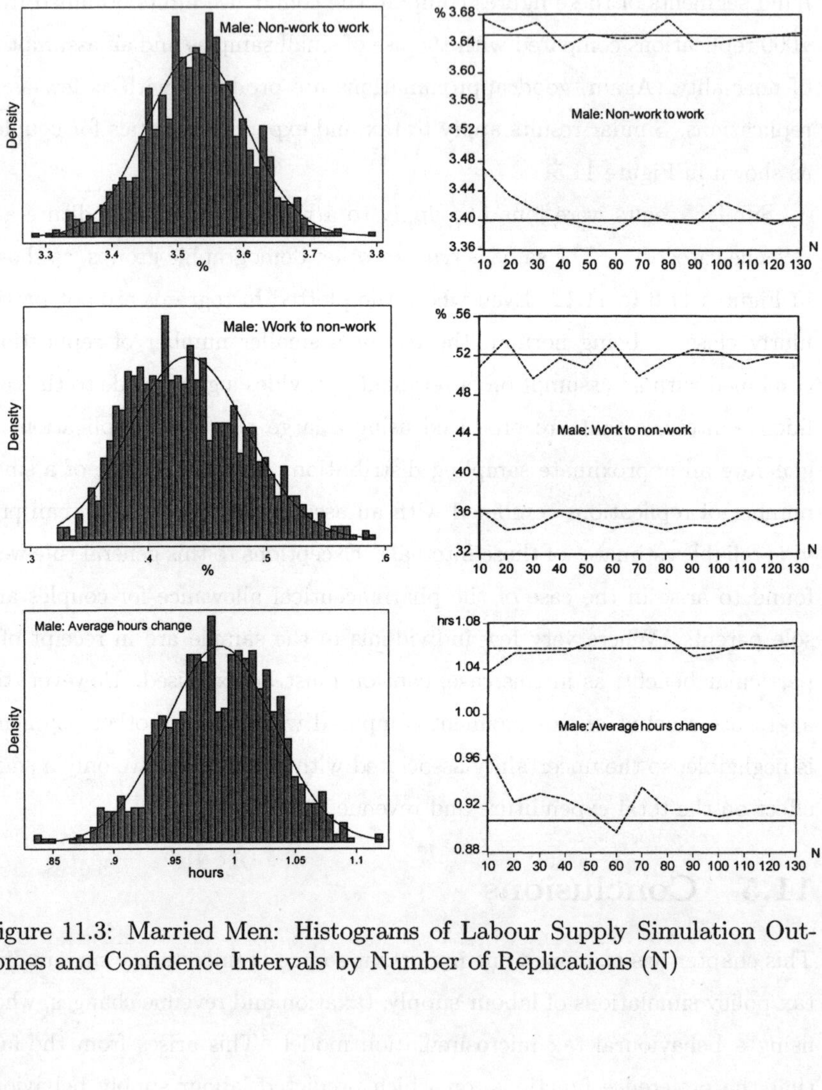

Figure 11.3: Married Men: Histograms of Labour Supply Simulation Outcomes and Confidence Intervals by Number of Replications (N)

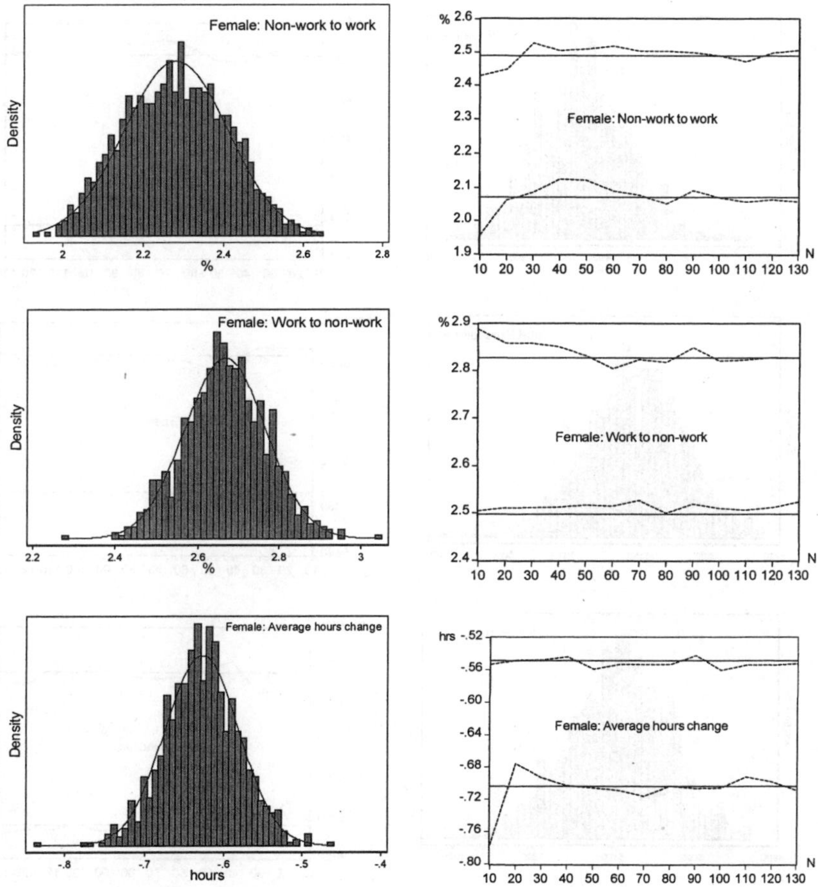

Figure 11.4: Married Women: Histograms of Labour Supply Simulation Outcomes and Confidence Intervals by Number of Replications (N)

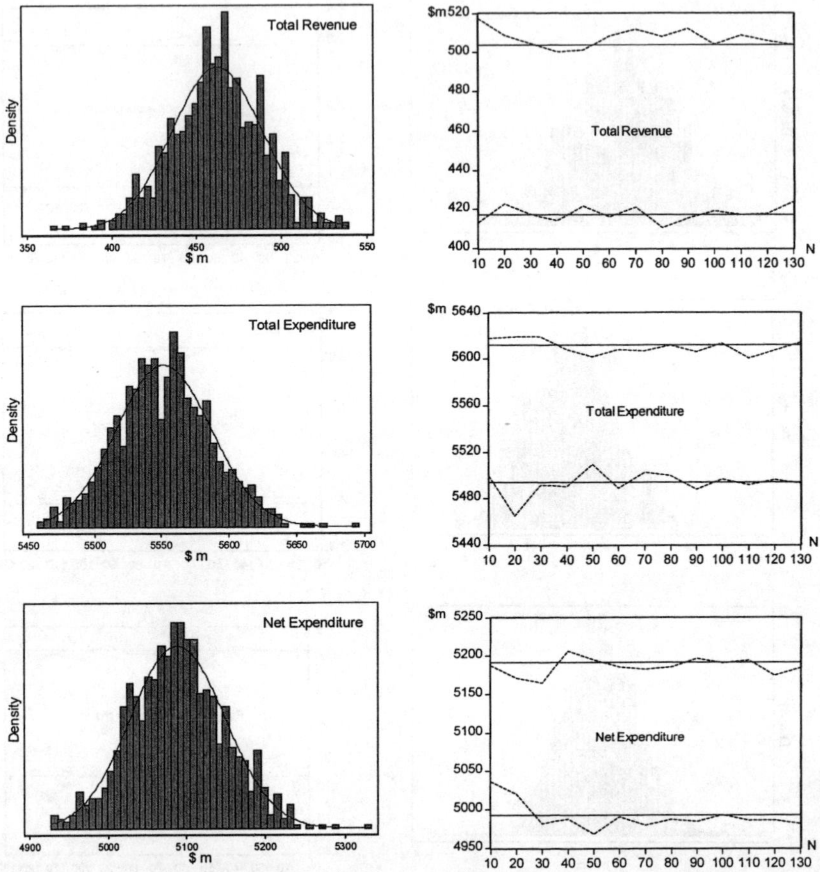

Figure 11.5: Couples: Histograms of Revenue and Expenditure Simulation Outcomes and Confidence Intervals by Number of Replications (N)

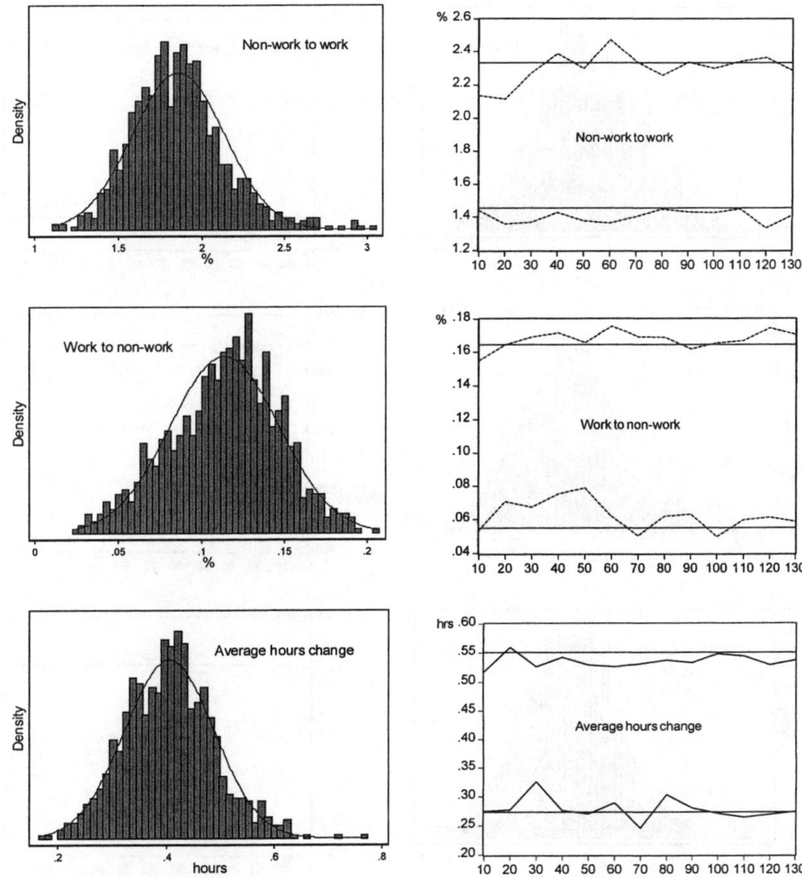

Figure 11.6: Single Men: Histograms of Labour Supply Simulation Outcomes and Confidence Intervals by Number of Replications (N)

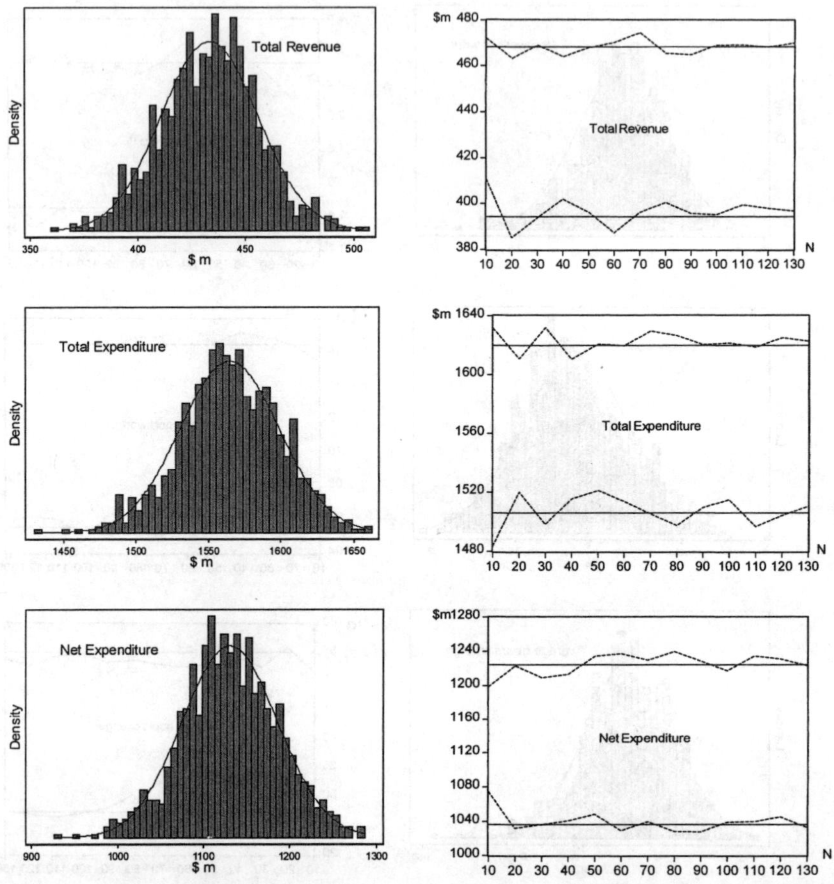

Figure 11.7: Single Men: Histograms of Revenue and Expenditure Simulation Outcomes and Confidence Intervals by Number of Replications (N)

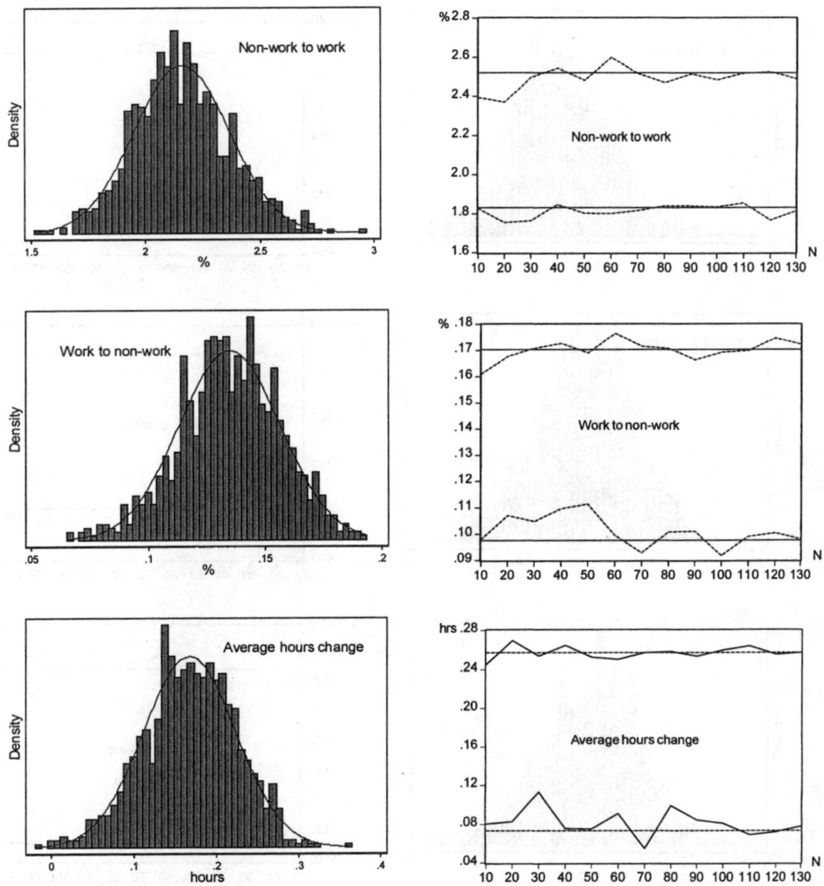

Figure 11.8: Single Women: Histograms of Labour Supply Simulation Outcomes and Confidence Intervals by Number of Replications (N)

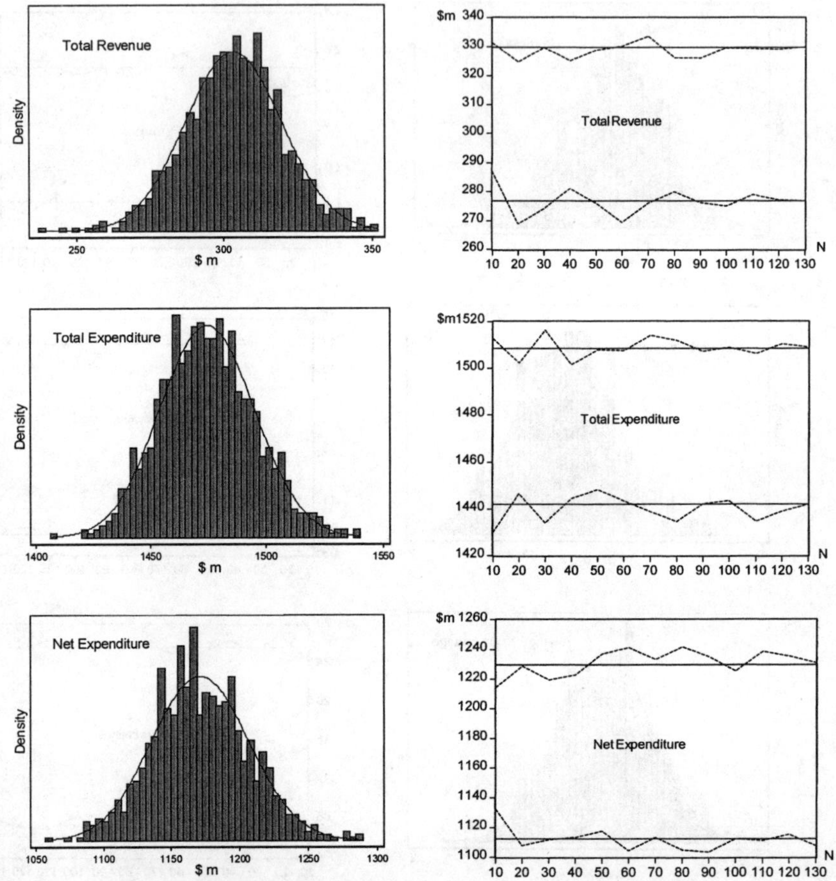

Figure 11.9: Single Women: Histograms of Revenue and Expenditure Simulation Outcomes and Confidence Intervals by Number of Replications (N)

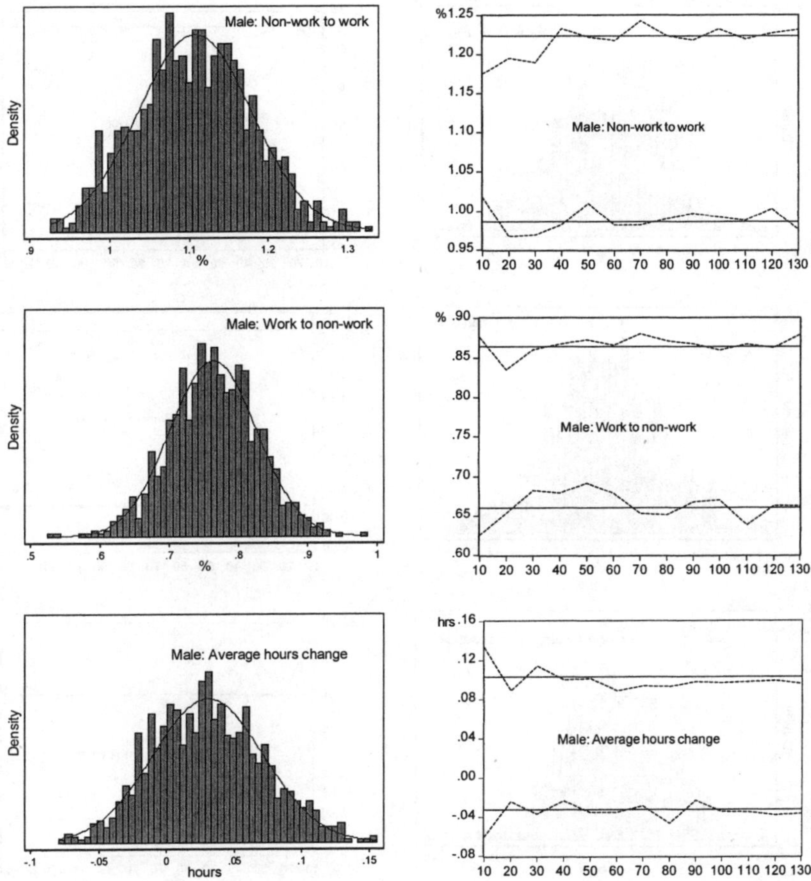

Figure 11.10: Couples without children: Histograms of Male Labour Supply Simulation Outcomes and Confidence Intervals by Number of Replications (N)

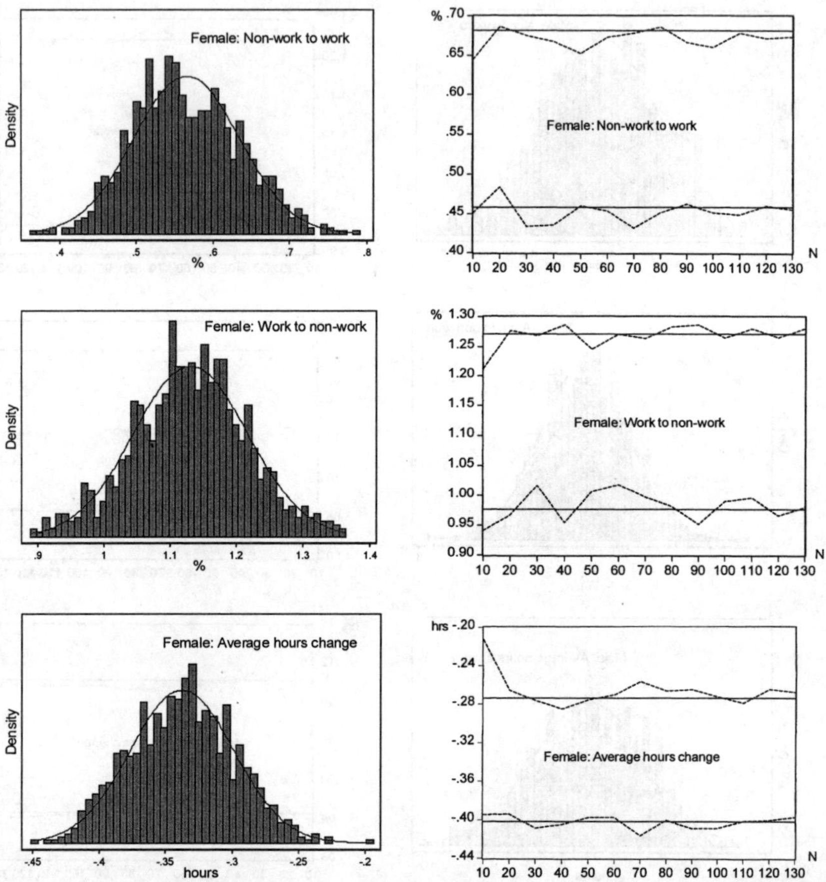

Figure 11.11: Couples without children: Histograms of Female Labour Supply Simulation Outcomes and Confidence Intervals by Number of Replications (N)

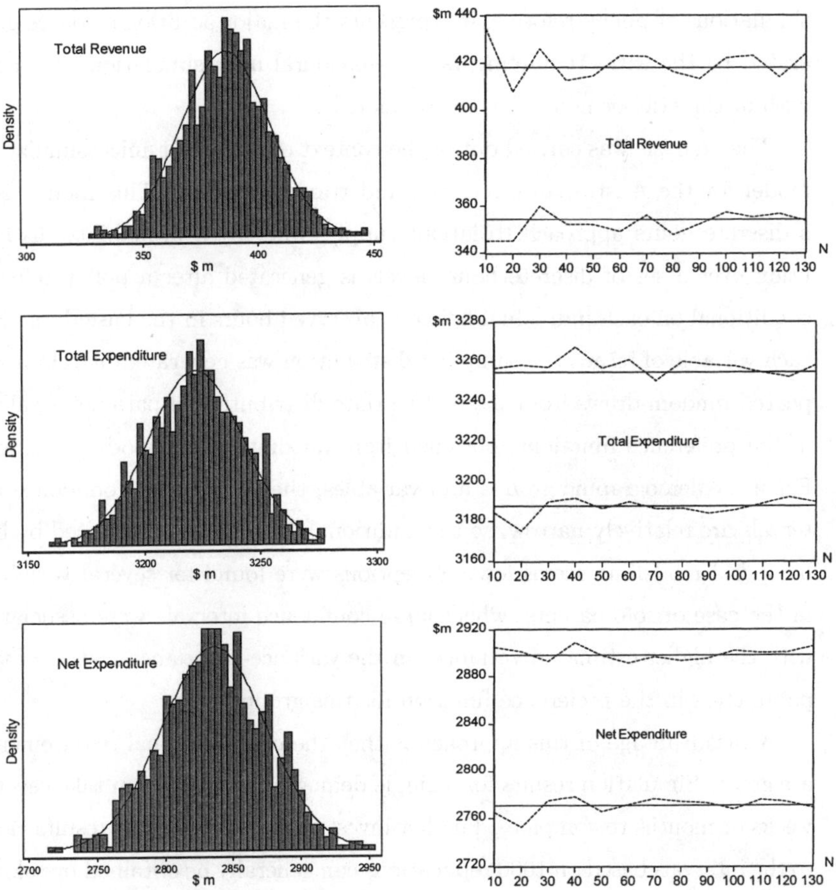

Figure 11.12: Couples Without Children: Histograms of Revenue and Expenditure Simulation Outcomes and Confidence Intervals by Number of Replications (N)

is based, are estimated using econometric methods, and typically only the point estimates are used in simulations. While the uncertainty associated with the estimated parameters is just one source of uncertainty regarding simulations of policy reforms, it represents the major additional source generated by the extra requirements of behavioural microsimulation compared with arithmetic, or non-behavioural, models.

The analysis was carried out in the context of MITTS, a microsimulation model for the Australian direct tax and transfer system. This model uses a discrete hours approach to labour supply, whereby a probability distribution over a set of discrete hours levels is generated after a policy reform, conditional on each individual being at observed hours in the base data. For each variable of interest, a sampling distribution was generated by taking repeated random draws from the multivariate distribution of parameter values in the preference functions, obtained from maximum likelihood estimation. For most demographic groups and variables, the 90 per cent confidence intervals are relatively narrow, so the additional uncertainty introduced by behavioural modelling seems low. Exceptions were found for several variables in the case of sole parents, where large confidence intervals were associated with the higher estimated variances in the variance-covariance matrix of the parameters in the preference function for this group.

A disadvantage of this approach is that the computational requirements are great. Simulation results for a single demographic group can take several weeks or months to complete. Further investigation showed that results close to the intervals based on 1000 replications can generally be obtained by taking a smaller number of replications, sometimes as low as 50 to 70, and using these to estimate the mean and variance of the outcome of interest. Under the assumption of the outcome being normally distributed, a confidence interval can then be constructed. This method was found to reduce the computational burden considerably without appearing to sacrifice much accuracy.

Chapter 12

Simulating Feedback Effects on Wages

This chapter explores an extension of behavioural microsimulation modelling so that third round effects of a policy change can be simulated. The first round effects relate to a simulation where fixed hours of work are assumed, while second round effects allow for changes in desired hours of work at unchanged wages. Third round effects allow for endogenous changes to the distribution of wage rates resulting from the labour supply responses to tax changes. This is achieved using the concept of an aggregate 'supply response schedule', which identifies the extent to which average labour supply responds to a proportional change in wage rates. The third round effect is obtained after re-running a microsimulation model with a suitable modification to individuals' wage rates.

Behavioural microsimulation models for the analysis of tax policy changes are designed to examine the effects on government expenditures, taxation and labour supply, allowing for the considerable complexity of individuals' budget constraints and taking into account the heterogeneity of individuals, their personal circumstances and preferences. These models are partial equilibrium supply-side models in which the wage rate distribution is fixed. However, substantial changes in labour supply as a result of a non-marginal tax policy change may give rise to changes in the wage rate distribution, depending on the demand for labour. It is therefore desirable to be able to allow for such wage changes, at least to some extent.[1]

The first round effects of a tax policy change refer to effects on government expenditure and revenue while holding labour supplies fixed. The second round effects allow for labour supply responses, with wage rates held constant. This chapter considers the question of how to take behavioural microsimulation analysis one stage further, by modelling possible aggregate effects of tax policy reform on wages. The analysis remains static in the sense that cross-sectional information only is used and individuals are not treated as forming expectations about future wages and prices, or optimising within a life-cycle framework. Given a method of producing changes to the wage rate distribution, such changes can be fed back into the microsimulation model in order to obtain adjusted labour supply responses and government expenditure estimates: this would give the so-called third round effects. The proposed method involves a multi-stage procedure in which the simulated labour supply effects of a policy change are aggregated and combined with extraneous information about the demand side of the labour market. The method allows for different degrees of aggregation to be used.

A preliminary problem involves labour supply aggregation, for generating an aggregate supply response schedule and combining with a demand schedule. A straightforward correspondence between the output from a microsimulation model and a conventionally defined aggregate supply curve is not possible, as discussed in section 12.1. The proposed procedure for simulating feedback effects is presented in section 12.2. A numerical example is provided in section 12.3 using the Melbourne Institute Tax and Transfer Simulator (MITTS). Section 12.4 concludes this chapter.

[1] Bergmann (1990) discussed microsimulation models in which aggregate unemployment is generated, resulting from job search behaviour in the presence of unemployment insurance. However, all considerations relating to wage levels (on either supply or demand sides of the market) were ignored.

12.1 Aggregate Labour Supply

This section discusses the problems of aggregating labour supply and explains why a synthetic aggregate supply function is not appropriate. First, the complexities for aggregation are discussed in section 12.1.1. Aggregate supply functions discussed in the macroeconomics literature cannot be used in the present context.[2] When estimating labour supply functions using aggregate time series data on variables such as average hours and real wage rates, it is extremely difficult to deal with the types of labour supply variation discussed in Part II above and with individual heterogeneity. Strong conditions are needed for aggregate labour supply and commodity demands, as functions of some index of prices and wages, to be consistent with individual optimisation. The use of a representative agent framework was examined by Deaton and Muellbauer (1980) and, in the context of labour supply by Muellbauer (1981), who abstracted from corner solutions which are crucial in the present context. The models typically involve no explicit treatment of aggregation issues.[3]

An approach is proposed in section 12.1.2 involving the concept of a 'supply response schedule'. The discussion below is, for convenience, in terms of continuous hours modelling with piecewise-linear budget constraints, although recent work on labour supply has often adopted a discrete choice approach where choices are made over a limited number of hours levels.[4] However, the approach to aggregation proposed here is easily adapted to the

[2]Some analyses of aggregate labour supply in macroecomic models are based on the intertemporal substitution model of Lucas and Rapping (1969); see also Altonji (1982, 1986) and Kennan (1988), who examines identification issues. The model is based on the argument that individuals form expectations about future real wages, in relation to current wages, based on movements in commodity prices. If real wages are considered to be high relative to expected future wages, current labour supply increases as a result of intertemporal substitution. The present approach excludes such dynamic considerations.

[3]Discussion of the extensive or intensive margin usually involves the use, in the econometric modelling, of either changes in average hours worked or changes over time in the number of individuals; see, for example, Alogoskoufis (1987).

[4]Examples include Bingley *et al.* (1995), Hagstrom (1996), Tummers and Woittiez (1991), Van Soest, Woittiez and Kapteyn (1990) and Van Soest (1995).

case of discrete hours models, and indeed the empirical application presented in section 12.3 uses estimates obtained from such a model.

12.1.1 Individual Labour Supply

A standard individual labour supply function cannot be used in the present context in view of its complexity; these aspects were discussed in Part II. Consider maximisation of a direct utility function $U(c_i, h_i; X_i)$, where h_i and c_i represent hours worked and consumption (or net income, where the price index is normalised to unity) for individual i with characteristics X_i, which include non-wage income, subject to a budget constraint. The individual's labour supply function, for variations in the gross wage, w, takes the general form:

$$h_i^* = h(w; X_i, T) \tag{12.1}$$

where T refers to the complete tax and transfer system.[5] At the observed wage of w_i for person i, the predicted labour supply when faced with tax system $T = T_0$ is:

$$h_i^*(w_i) = h(w_i; X_i, T = T_0) \tag{12.2}$$

One approach to aggregation might average labour supply predictions over a range of wage rates, with each individual being presented with the same wage rate. Using sample weights g_i, representing the number of individuals of type i in the population, this results in an aggregate supply of the form:[6]

$$H^*(w) = \left(\sum g_i\right)^{-1} \sum_{i=1}^{n} g_i h(w; X_i, T) \tag{12.3}$$

at some common wage w. However, the interpretation of a function representing the average of a set of individual labour supplies on the presumption

[5] In previous chapters the symbol T was used to denote the total time available for work per week. It is used throughout the present chapter to refer to the tax system.

[6] In chapter 6 the symbol w was instead used to refer to sample weights. However, all other chapters use w to denote a wage rate.

that all are given the same wage is unclear. In practice, it would involve predictions of individual labour supplies at wage rates far from their observed wage, which may be totally irrelevant to the person.

12.1.2 The Supply Response Schedule

The approach suggested here involves the concept of a 'supply response schedule', defined to measure how labour supply responds to shifts in the distribution of wage rates. This supply response schedule is a numerical construction, based on simulated labour supply responses to wage changes, conditional on a given tax and transfer structure. The individual supply responses are based on optimising behaviour, allowing for the full complexity of budget constraints and population heterogeneity.

A supply response schedule is generated by using a behavioural microsimulation model to obtain individuals' hours responses to a proportionate change in all observed wage rates. That is, the full wage distribution is perturbed, and the aggregate labour supply response to that perturbation is obtained. The perturbation is based on an index $\mathbf{i_w} \in (-1, \infty)$ which replaces each individual's wage w_i with an amount $w_i(1+\mathbf{i_w})$. The aggregate schedule $H_a^*(\mathbf{i_w})$ is constructed by summing (averaging) individuals' labour supply responses at a given index $\mathbf{i_w}$, giving a function, in per capita terms, of the form:

$$H_a^*(\mathbf{i_w}) = (\sum g_i)^{-1} \sum_{i=1}^{n} g_i h(w_i(1 + \mathbf{i_w}); X_i, T) \tag{12.4}$$

For $\mathbf{i_w} = 0$ this reduces to $H_a^*(\mathbf{0}) = (\sum g_i)^{-1}. \sum_{i=1}^{n} g_i.h(w_i; X_i, T)$, which should be close to the observed average $\overline{H} = (\sum g_i)^{-1}. \sum_{i=1}^{n} g_i h_i$.

The advantage of this type of supply response schedule is that each point on the schedule is consistent with a distribution of wages, together with the underlying tax and transfer scheme and population characteristics. Movement along the supply response schedule arises from a shift in the entire wage distribution. A schedule of this type is shown in Figure 12.1.

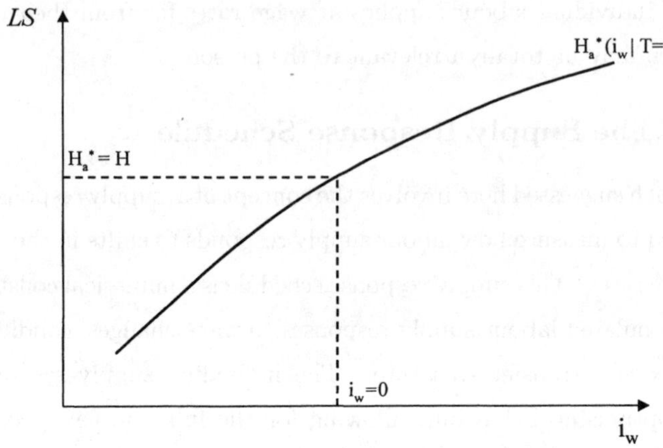

Figure 12.1: An Aggregate Supply Response Schedule

The supply response schedule is an entirely numerical concept, as it traces the aggregate labour supply resulting from equal proportionate changes in wage rates, conditional on the tax and transfer system and the nature of the population. It can be produced directly from a behavioural microsimulation model and generates the information needed to produce feedback effects of tax policy changes.

12.1.3 Shifts in the Supply Response Schedule

The approach can be used to simulate shifts in the supply response schedule resulting from a change in tax or welfare policy. Because the supply response schedule is built from the predictions of a behavioural microsimulation model, the effects of an enormous range of policy reforms could be simulated. Suppose there are two tax systems, T_0 and T_1, where T_0 represents some benchmark tax system corresponding to a given year's microdata, and T_1 represents the tax system following a hypothetical policy reform. Let the predicted labour supplies of the ith individual at wage rate $w_i(1+\mathbf{i_w})$ under systems T_0 and T_1, be denoted respectively by $h^*_{i0}(\mathbf{i_w}) = h(w_i(1+\mathbf{i_w}); X_i, T = T_0)$ and $h^*_{i1}(\mathbf{i_w}) = h(w_i(1+\mathbf{i_w}); X_i, T = T_1)$. By aggregating the difference between these predictions at any value of $\mathbf{i_w}$ in the manner of (12.4), a simulation of the shift in overall labour supply when moving from tax system T_0 to T_1 is obtained as

$$\begin{aligned} \Delta H^*_a(\mathbf{i_w}|T_0, T_1) &= \left(\sum g_i\right)^{-1} \sum\nolimits_{i=1}^{n} g_i \left[h^*_{i1}(\mathbf{i_w}) - h^*_{i0}(\mathbf{i_w})\right] \\ &= H^*_a(\mathbf{i_w}|T = T_1) - H^*_a(\mathbf{i_w}|T = T_0) \end{aligned} \tag{12.5}$$

12.2 A Multi-stage Procedure

This section describes a multi-stage procedure used to produce third round effects of a policy change to the tax and transfer system, allowing for the effects on the distribution of wages.

12.2.1 Modelling Feedback Effects

The first round effects of a policy change are based on the assumption that there are no labour supply responses. The second round effects allow for labour supply responses but keep the wage rate distribution fixed. This is illustrated in Figure 12.2: it is equivalent to the vertical movement from an initial supply response schedule (under T_0) to the revised schedule (for T_1) at $\mathbf{i_w} = 0$.

Section 12.1 described how a shift in the supply response schedule, as a result of a tax change, can be generated. This shift can be used, in combination with information about a corresponding aggregate demand response schedule for labour, to generate a suitable value of $\mathbf{i_w}$, which results in a new equilibrium of demand and supply. This value of $\mathbf{i_w}$ is given by the intersection between the new supply response schedule and the demand response

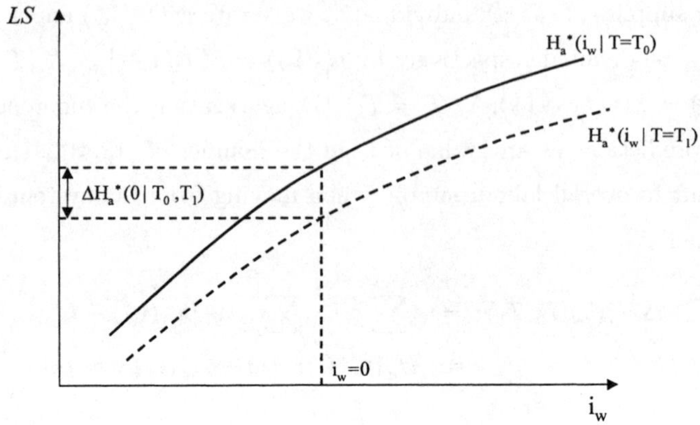

Figure 12.2: A Shift in the Aggregate Supply Response Schedule

schedule. The updated wage rates can then be fed into a revised behavioural simulation to generate a new set of labour supply responses and government expenditures for the same tax policy change, using the predicted shift in the wage rate distribution. These new responses give the third round simulation results.

12.2.2 Measuring Wage Effects in Microsimulation

The second round effect of a tax or welfare policy reform is equivalent to the interaction of the aggregate supply response schedule with an infinitely elastic labour demand response schedule; a change in labour supply is absorbed with no changes in the distribution of wage rates. Therefore, in the absence of further information, it is useful to consider the other extreme assumption of a completely inelastic demand response. That is, if aggregate supply increases, wages must fall proportionately in order to keep employment (aggregate hours) fixed at the initial level. This is illustrated in Figure

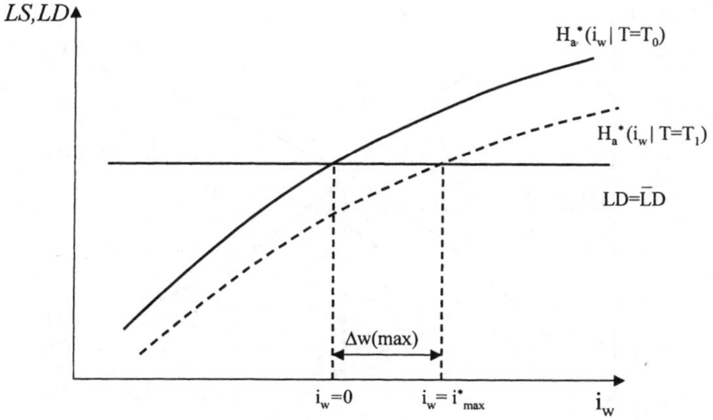

Figure 12.3: A Shift in the Supply Response Schedule: Inelastic Demand

12.3. Suppose that the tax system shifts from T_0 to T_1 following a policy reform in a way which causes the aggregate supply response schedule to shift downwards. That is:

$$H_a^*(\mathbf{i_w}|T = T_1) < H_a^*(\mathbf{i_w}|T = T_0) \text{ for all } \mathbf{i_w} \tag{12.6}$$

With demand fixed at $LD = \overline{LD}$, the supply shift increases the distribution of wages by $\mathbf{i}^*_{\max}$. This factor may be used to adjust each individual's wage before being fed back into a revised behavioural simulation, as explained above, to produce the third-round simulation results.

With a flexible demand response schedule of the sort shown in Figure 12.4, the same inward shift in aggregate supply produces movement both in the wage distribution and equilibrium supply. Under these circumstances, the third-round shift in aggregate supply corresponds to the difference:

$$\Delta H_a = H_a^*(\mathbf{i}^*_\mathbf{w}|T = T_1) - H_a^*(\mathbf{0}|T = T_0) \tag{12.7}$$

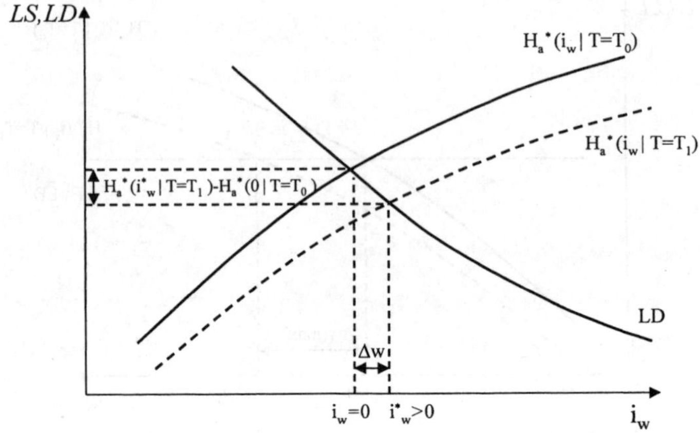

Figure 12.4: A Shift in the Supply Response Schedule: Flexible Demand

where $\mathbf{i}_{\mathrm{w}}^{*}$ is the difference in the intersections of the aggregate supply response schedules under T_0 and T_1 and the aggregate demand response schedule.

The approach can also be applied to separate groups, distinguished for example by education or occupation. This would produce a set of adjustment terms, enabling a change in the dispersion of wage rates to be modelled. A given policy change may produce wage increases for some groups while wages may fall for others, depending on the labour supply and demand effects. The wage adjustment model used here is only one among a range of possible models including, for example, search-theoretic, insider-outsider and efficiency wage models which factor unemployment into the market structure. The method proposed in this chapter could be extended to incorporate these alternative models of labour market adjustment.

12.3 An Illustrative Application

This section demonstrates the use of aggregate supply response schedules in behavioural microsimulation. In view of the difficulty of obtaining disaggregated data on demand functions, the results should be regarded as illustrative of potential orders of magnitude and the way in which third round effects can be obtained. The examples are obtained using MITTS together with data from the 1997/98 Survey of Income and Housing Cost (SIHC). See Appendix C for brief details on MITTS. A simple policy reform is examined in which the Australian income tax system of January 2000 is modified: the initial income tax rate is increased from 20 per cent to 25 per cent.[7]

12.3.1 Simulated Aggregate Supply Response Schedules

The aggregate supply response schedule for the full sample of working-age households was constructed using the formulation in (12.4). Labour supplies both under the baseline January 2000 system and the reform system were produced. The simulated average labour supply under the January 2000 system at the observed distribution of wages is broadly equivalent to the observed overall average labour supply, of around 19 hours per week. In Figure 12.5, this corresponds to the point on the first aggregate supply response schedule at which $\mathbf{i_w} = 0$. Varying $\mathbf{i_w}$ under the January 2000 system produces the aggregate supply response schedule.

Figure 12.5 shows that this empirical schedule is positive and monotonic over the range $\mathbf{i_w} = \{-0.5, 0.7\}$. The empirical wage elasticity at the distribution of wage rates observed in the data ($\mathbf{i_w} = 0$) was found to be around 0.62 for the full population, rising slightly as the distribution of wages increases beyond the observed level, before eventually falling for larger perturbations.

[7] Although the tax and sample years are not the same, the tax system in January 2000 is similar to that in 1998.

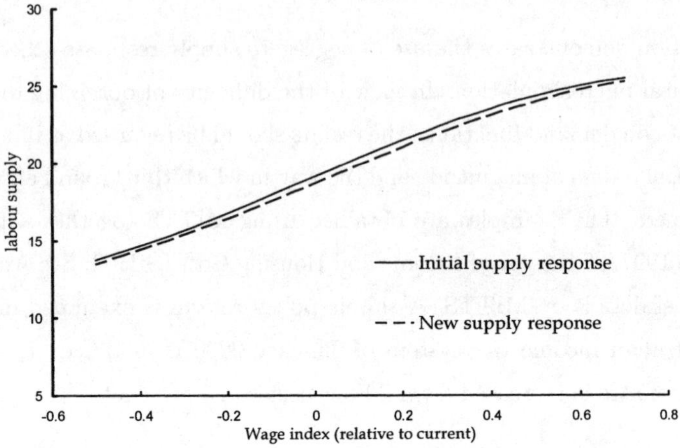

Figure 12.5: Simulated Supply Response Schedules

At lower wage rates (corresponding to negative $\mathbf{i_w}$), the aggregate wage elasticity falls, and is around 0.35 when all wages are halved. This decline in the aggregate wage elasticity might be caused in part by an increased reliance on transfer payments, particularly among low-wage workers.

The formulation in (12.7) is used to simulate a shift in the aggregate supply response schedule following the increase of 5 percentage points in the basic income tax rate. In Figure 12.5, the post-reform schedule (the dashed line) is everywhere below the first schedule. At equivalent wage rates for all individuals in the sample, aggregate labour supply falls following the increase in taxes. At the observed distribution of wages, the average reduction in labour supply is around 0.36 hours (equivalent to around 2 per cent).[8]

[8]This might appear small when compared with an apparent reduction of around 7 per cent in the marginal wage (from $w_i(1-0.2)$ to $w_i(1-0.25)$ for a basic rate taxpayer). However, this tax change is not realised by those below the tax-free threshold and those not in work.

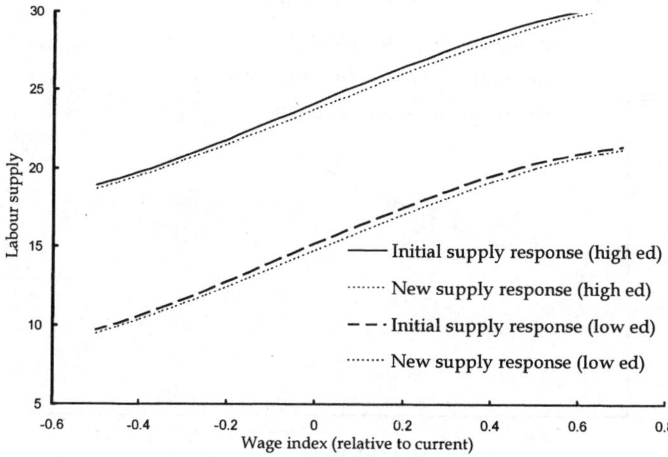

Figure 12.6: Shifts for High and Low Education Groups

12.3.2 Disaggregated Supply Response Schedules

It was suggested above that the approach can be applied to particular demographic groups, by averaging individual responses over target groups within the sample rather than over the sample as a whole. Figures 12.6 to 12.8 show several supply response schedules.

Figure 12.6 in this series of simulations shows the comparative aggregate supply schedules of high- and low-education individuals, displaying systematically higher labour supply on average among the higher educated group. The high-education group corresponds to those with more than the basic (compulsory) level of education. This comparison was designed to proxy the relative supply response schedules of high- and low-skill labour in the absence of observations on skill levels for non-working individuals in the sample. The corresponding elasticities are higher for the low-education group. This could be a manifestation of Heckman's (1993) observation that higher labour sup-

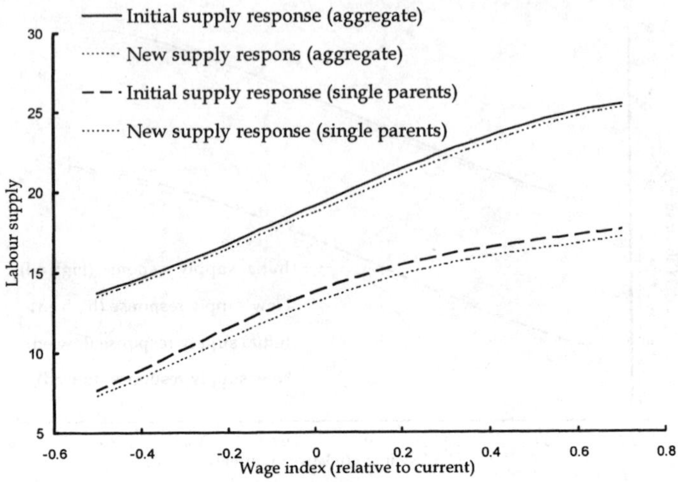

Figure 12.7: Shifts for Sole Parents and The Full Sample

ply responses are found at the extensive (participation) margin.

Figure 12.7 compares the supply response schedules of sole parents with those of the full sample. Average labour supply is systematically lower, a function in part of lower participation rates among sole parents. The shift in the supply response schedule for sole parents is proportionately larger, reflecting a higher sensitivity among this group to changes in the net wage. This is borne out by the wage elasticities, which are higher for sole parent households as wage rates fall. Similar patterns emerge when comparing the supply response schedules of women and men, as shown in Figure 12.8.

12.3.3 Simulating Wage Responses to a Policy Change

The previous section described a method by which to simulate the proportional effects on the wage distribution following a shift in the aggregate supply schedule. Under assumptions regarding the equivalent aggregate labour demand schedule, the intersections of simulated demand and supply might

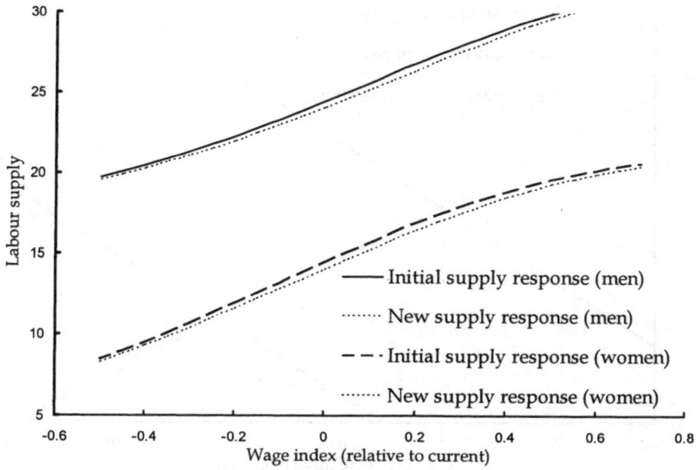

Figure 12.8: Shifts for Men and Women

be used to model the extent to which wages might adjust following a policy reform. With inelastic labour demand, the extent of the proportionate shift in wage rates could be simulated by measuring the horizontal distance $\mathbf{i}^*_{\max}$ between the two aggregate supply schedules at the pre-reform level of aggregate supply; see Figure 12.3. With a flexible demand response schedule, the full effect of the policy reform comprises shifts both in the wage distribution and in the equilibrium level of supply and demand; see Figure 12.4. Both cases are examined here.

For the simulations described earlier, the third-round effects of the 5 percentage point increase in income tax can be measured under alternative hypothetical specifications of aggregate labour demand. Consider two alternatives: the first assumes that demand is completely inelastic, so that $L_d(\mathbf{i_w}) = L_0$ in the earlier formulation. The second assumes that $L_d(\mathbf{i_w}) = L_0.(1 + \mathbf{i_w})^{\varepsilon_d}$ with elasticity $\varepsilon_d = 0.5$, a central figure in the range of labour

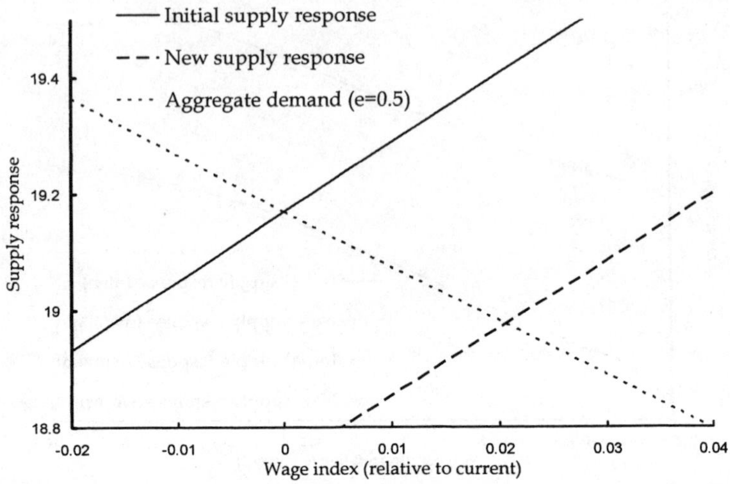

Figure 12.9: Demand and Supply Response Schedules: Detail

demand elasticities typically reported in the empirical literature; see Hamermesh (1993).

Figure 12.9 shows the relevant detail (focusing on the locality of the intersection) of the simulated aggregate supply response schedule, which applies to all individuals combined, and an aggregate demand schedule with elasticity $\varepsilon_d = 0.5$. For an inelastic labour demand schedule, the wage effect $\mathbf{i}^*_{\max}$ is measured to be around 3.7 per cent (the horizontal distance between the aggregate supply response and supply shift schedules, measured from the point of intersection of the pre-reform labour supply schedule at $\mathbf{i_w} = 0$). The second assumption is that labour demand is responsive to changes in the wage distribution, with an elasticity of 0.5. From Figure 12.9, the effect of the tax policy change, on wages and labour supply/demand under the assumption of a clearing labour market, can be measured. The third-round response combines a simulated increase of 2.07 per cent ($\mathbf{i_w} = 0.0207$) in the

Table 12.1: First, Second and Third Round Effects of Tax Reform

Percentage change in:	First round	Second round	Third round $\varepsilon_d = 0$	Third round $\varepsilon_d = 0.5$
Income tax revenue	+9.1	+7.9	+13.4	+11.7
Allowance costs	–	+2.8	−0.5	+0.1
Aggregate labour supply	–	−1.9	−0.1	−1.0
Wage rates	–	–	+3.7	+2.1

wage distribution with a reduction of 1.0 per cent in aggregate labour supply.

To summarise the successive effects of a change in the tax system, Table 12.1 shows the first, second and third round effects of the hypothetical tax change. The percentage change in income tax revenues, aggregate labour supply and wages at the three stages of simulation are reported. For the third round effects, results are reported for inelastic labour demand (providing an upper limit to the potential wage response), for an aggregate demand elasticity of 0.5 (providing a more central simulation of the potential wage response), and the second round results provide a lower limit for the potential wage response of zero.

The first column of Table 12.1 shows the first round effects of the income tax increase, with income tax revenues increasing by around 9 per cent. The second column includes labour supply responses in the simulation. As reported in earlier sections, labour supply is predicted to fall on average by 1.9 per cent in response to this tax reform. These behavioural responses have further effects on government revenues and costs; the reduction in labour supply results in a lower increase in income tax revenues than in the first-round simulation (from 9.1 per cent to 7.9 per cent). There is an increase in the cost of allowance payments, of around 2.8 per cent, as earnings fall.

The final two columns of Table 12.1 show how the earlier responses might change following potential adjustments in the distribution of wage rates. For a perfectly inelastic labour demand schedule, the shift in aggregate supply results in a proportionate increase of around 3.7 per cent in the distribution of wage rates. Feeding these wage increases back into an adjusted behavioural simulation, income tax revenues rise by 13.4 per cent compared with the status quo. The cost of allowance transfers actually falls by 0.5 per cent, since earnings increase with the adjustment in wages. As expected, aggregate labour supply remains effectively unchanged relative to the status quo, as is implied by the assumption of a fixed level of labour demand. (The value of 0.1 per cent, rather than 0, arises because few iterations were used in obtaining feedback effects.) Assuming an aggregate labour demand elasticity of 0.5, the adjustment is smaller. Wage rates are modelled to increase by 2.1 per cent, and aggregate labour supply falls by around 1 per cent overall. These effects combine to generate an increase of 11.7 per cent in the revenue from income tax and an increase of 0.1 per cent in the cost of allowances. The same percentage wage change is applied to all individuals. However, if demand information is available for subgroups of the population, the method can also be used at a more disaggregated level to allow for different effects across subgroups. After applying the method on subgroups the results can again be aggregated to the population level, with the difference that the relative wage rate in one subgroup versus another subgroup may now have changed.

12.4 Conclusions

The main aim of this chapter has been to explore an extension of behavioural microsimulation modelling, allowing for endogenous changes to the distribution of wage rates resulting from the labour supply responses to tax changes. These are called the third-round effects of a policy change. This has involved the concept of an aggregate supply response schedule which identifies the extent to which average labour supply responds to a proportional change in wage rates. Disaggregation, by using supply response schedules for particular demographic or education groups, provides the possibility of introducing an endogenous change to the form of the distribution of wage rates as well as shifts, since different groups may experience different labour supply responses to a given tax change, and therefore experience different endogenous wage rate changes.

The use of the concept of the aggregate supply response schedule was illustrated using a behavioural microsimulation model of the Australian economy. An increase in the lowest marginal income tax rate was found to reduce labour supply in the second round and consequently raises wages. Several assumptions were used regarding the pattern of aggregate demand. After re-running the microsimulation model with a suitable modification to individuals' wage rates, the third-round effects were found to generate substantially larger increases in income tax revenue than were suggested by initial non-behavioural costings. The results demonstrated the potential importance of allowing for such third round effects in microsimulation.

Appendix A

Newton's Method

This appendix explains the method used to solve maximisation (or minimisation) problems as discussed in chapters 4 and 6. In general, suppose a function $F(x)$,with first derivative $f(x)$, needs to be maximised with regard to a single variable, x. To find the maximum, the first-order condition $f(x) = 0$ needs to be satisfied. Most iterative methods are based on some form of Newton's method. Consider finding the root of the equation $f(x) = 0$, where $f(x)$ takes the form shown in Figure A.1. Take an arbitrary starting point, x_0, and draw the tangent, with slope $f'(x_0)$.

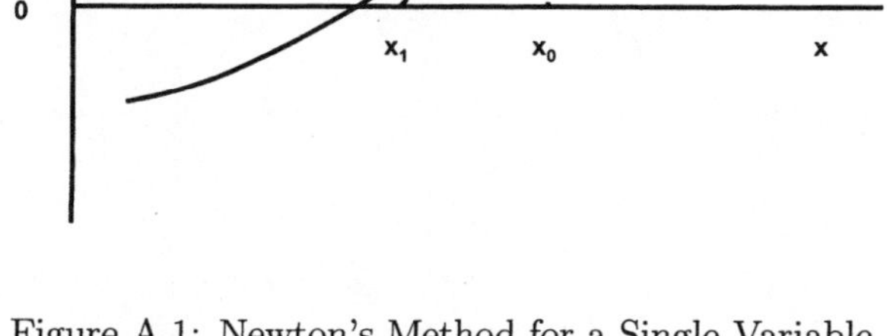

Figure A.1: Newton's Method for a Single Variable

By approximating the function by the tangent, the new value is given by the point of intersection of this tangent with the x axis, at x_1. It can be seen that selecting x_1 as the next starting point and drawing the tangent at this new point on f with slope $f'(x_1)$ leads quickly to the required root. From the triangle in Figure A.1, it can be seen that:

$$f'(x_0) = \frac{f(x_0)}{x_0 - x_1} \tag{A.1}$$

Hence, starting from $I = 0$, the sequence of iterations is:

$$x_{I+1} = x_I - \{f'(x_I)\}^{-1} f(x_I) \tag{A.2}$$

Convergence is reached when $x_{I+1} - x_I < \varepsilon$ and ε depends on the accuracy required.

Newton's method is easily adapted to deal with a set of equations, $f_i(x)$, where x is now a vector. The method involves repeatedly solving the following matrix equation, where $x^{[I]}$ denotes the vector in the Ith iteration and $f(x)$ is a vector containing the $f_i(x)$ values:

$$x^{[I+1]} = x^{[I]} - \left[\frac{\partial f_i(x)}{\partial x_\ell}\right]_{x^{[I]}}^{-1} [f(x)]_{x^{[I]}} \tag{A.3}$$

This procedure works best when the function is smooth. It is necessary to check, by picking different starting points, that there are not multiple roots, in which case convergence could be at a local rather than a global maximum. In addition, the second derivative $f'(x)$ needs to be negative at the maximum.

Appendix B

Labour Supply Calibration and Simulation

This appendix provides a formal description of the calibration and simulation processes used in MITTS.

Assume an individual is observed to work at the discretised hours level, h_i. In the calibration stage, for a given set of preference function parameter values, suppose it is required to obtain k sets of draws from the error distributions (for each hours level) for which the individual's optimal hours are equal to the observed hours. A total of up to K attempts, or 'tries' are allowed to generate each draw. There are n discrete hours levels.

Define the following terms and consider the generation of a single draw. Let:

$$v^{(j)} = \left[v_1^{(j)}, ..., v_n^{(j)}\right]' \tag{B.1}$$

denote the jth vector of n random variables (the jth 'try') drawn from the Extreme Value Type I distribution, representing the random utility component. Let:

$$U^b = \left[U_1^b, ..., U_n^b\right]' \tag{B.2}$$

denote the n-vector of deterministic utilities corresponding to the hours levels, calculated using the tax and transfer system to obtain the associated net incomes for each discrete hours level under the base (or pre-reform) system.

Finally, let $U^{*b(j)}$ denote the vector of utilities:

$$\begin{bmatrix} U_1^{*b(j)} \\ \cdot \\ \cdot \\ U_n^{*b(j)} \end{bmatrix} = \begin{bmatrix} U_1^b \\ \cdot \\ \cdot \\ U_n^b \end{bmatrix} + \begin{bmatrix} v_1^{(j)} \\ \cdot \\ \cdot \\ v_n^{(j)} \end{bmatrix} \tag{B.3}$$

For each 'try' a check is made to see if $U_i^{*b(j)}$ is the maximum value among $U_\ell^{*b(j)}$ for all other $\ell \neq i$. If so, this means that the individual chooses to work at h_i, which corresponds to the observed discrete hours for this individual. In this case, the vector $v^{(j)}$ is stored for use in the simulation stage; this corresponds to a 'draw'. If $U_i^{*b(j)}$ is not the maximum value, $v^{(j)}$ is discarded and another set of n random values from the error distribution (another 'try') is selected. This process is repeated until a successful 'draw' has been found. If, after K tries, no set is found for which optimal and observed discretised hours are equal, hours are held fixed at the observed hours for this draw. This process is repeated k times. For most individuals, k draws are obtained using far less than the K tries for each.

Simulation of a policy reform proceeds as follows. Let $U^r = [U_1^r, ..., U_n^r]'$ denote the n-vector of utilities after the tax reform. Then calculate $U^{*r(j)}$, based on the jth stored vector $v^{(j)}$, for $j = 1, ..., k$:

$$\begin{bmatrix} U_1^{*r(j)} \\ \cdot \\ \cdot \\ U_n^{*r(j)} \end{bmatrix} = \begin{bmatrix} U_1^r \\ \cdot \\ \cdot \\ U_n^r \end{bmatrix} + \begin{bmatrix} v_1^{(j)} \\ \cdot \\ \cdot \\ v_n^{(j)} \end{bmatrix} \tag{B.4}$$

For each $j = 1, ..., k$ a check is made to see which $U_\ell^{*r(j)}$, for $\ell = 1, ..., n$, is the maximum value in the vector $U^{*r(j)}$. This determines the discrete hours level after the reform for the jth set of draws, given that the individual was at h_i in the base system. The k draws thus generate the probabilities of being at each of the discrete hours points after the reform by counting the number of times for which a draw results in a particular hours point, and dividing this number by the total number of draws k. As mentioned before, for some individuals, a number of the k draws may be replaced by an assumption that labour supply is unchanged as a result of the tax reform. In that case, the discrete hours level after the reform is the same as the observed discrete hours level before the reform.

Appendix C

The Melbourne Institute Tax and Transfer Simulator

This appendix provides a brief description of the Melbourne Institute Tax and Transfer Simulator (MITTS), a behavioural microsimulation model of direct tax and transfers in Australia. Since the first version was completed in 2000, it has undergone a range of substantial developments.[1] Indeed, any large-scale model requires constant maintenance (involving, for example, re-estimation of econometric relationships as new data and methods become available, or the introduction of new ways to make simulations more efficient), as well as enhancements such as the extension of 'front end' and 'back end' facilities.

MITTS is based on the Australian Survey of Income and Housing Costs (SIHC). The SIHC is a representative sample of the Australian population, containing detailed information on labour supply and income from different sources, in addition to a variety of background characteristics of individuals and households. In the present version of MITTS, SIHC data from 1994/95, 1995/96, 1996/97, 1997/98, 1999/2000 and 2000/01 can be used. The econometric estimates of preferences underlying the behavioural responses are based on data observed between 1994 and 1998. Details of the

[1] A detailed description of this first version can be found in Creedy *et al.* (2002).

current wage and labour supply parameters used in MITTS can be found in Kalb and Scutella (2002) and Kalb (2002).

All results are aggregated to population levels using the household weights provided with SIHC to represent the population level effects of policy changes. Furthermore, data from the Household, Income and Labour Dynamics Australia (HILDA) survey were transformed so they could be used as the base data for MITTS; see Kalb, Cai and Vu (2004). However, the disadvantage of using the HILDA data is that it is not straightforward to aggregate results up to the population level.

Pre-reform net incomes at alternative hours levels are based on the MITTS calculation of entitlements, not the actual receipt. Hence it is assumed that the take-up rates are 100 per cent. Furthermore, MITTS applies only income tests, as there is at present no asset imputation in the model. However, income from assets is included in the income tests.

MITTS consists of two components. MITTS-A is the arithmetic tax and benefit modelling component or the static microsimulation component and MITTS-B is the behavioural component, which allows for labour supply responses as a result of policy changes. The next two sections describe these two components in turn.

C.1 MITTS-A

In MITTS, the arithmetic tax and benefit modelling component is called MITTS-A. This component also provides, using the wage rate of each individual, the information needed for the construction of the budget constraints that are crucial for the analysis of behavioural responses to tax changes.

The Tax System component of MITTS contains the procedures for applying each type of tax and benefit. Each tax structure has a data file containing the required tax and benefit rates, benefit levels and income thresholds used in means testing. Unfortunately, actual tax and transfer systems are typically extremely complex and contain a large number of taxes and benefits which, being designed and administered by different government departments, are usually difficult to integrate fully. The complexity increases where several means-tested benefits are available because of the existence of numerous eligibility requirements. It is only when a great deal of detailed information about individuals is available that it becomes possible to include the complexities of actual tax and transfer systems in a simulation model.

However, it is unlikely that household surveys contain sufficient information to replicate realistic tax systems fully. In some cases, for example where asset values are required in the administration of means tests, it may be necessary to impute values, although imputations may not always be possible.[2] Furthermore, regulations regarding the administration of taxes and transfers often leave room for some flexibility in interpretation. In particular, the administration of means tests or other benefits may allow a degree of discretion to be exercised by benefit officers who deal directly with claimants. Changes in the interpretation of (possibly ambiguous) rules, or the degree to which some rules are fully enforced, can take place over time. Furthermore, there may be changes in people's awareness of the benefits available and the eligibility rules, thereby affecting the degree of take-up.

In view of these limitations, even large-scale models may not be able to replicate actual systems entirely. Similarly, the same problems may give rise to distortions in measuring the extent to which redistribution occurs. Thus, in view of these data limitations of the SIHC (or any other data set), it is not possible to include within MITTS all the complexity of the tax and transfer system. However, all major social security payments and income taxes are included in MITTS, ensuring a reasonable approximation to net income by MITTS. Pre-reform net incomes at the alternative hours levels are based on

[2]MITTS assumes that if individuals or households are eligible after the income test, they are still eligible after the assets test. Kalb, Kew and Scutella (2005) checked this assumption empirically using wave 2 of the HILDA data, which collected information on wealth in addition to income. The assumption was found to be reasonable.

the MITTS calculation of entitlements, not the actual receipt. Hence, in the calculations of net income it is assumed that take-up rates are 100 per cent.

Changes to the tax and benefit structure, including the introduction of additional taxes or benefits, can be modelled by editing the programmes in this component. MITTS stores several previous Australian tax and transfer systems, which can be used as base systems for the analysis of policy changes. Alternatively, it is often possible to generate a new tax system by introducing various types of policy change interactively within MITTS by making use of the 'front end' menus. This enables a wide range of new tax structures to be generated without the need for additional programming.

MITTS assembles the various components of the tax and benefit structure in the required way in order to work out the transformation between hours worked and net income for each individual under each tax system. For example, some benefits are taxable while others are not, so the order in which taxes and transfers are evaluated is important.

MITTS-A contains the facility to examine each household, income unit and individual in the selected base data set in turn and generate net incomes, at the given hourly wage rates, for variations in the number of hours worked. Thus the changes in effective marginal tax rates (EMTRs) and labour supply incentives faced by households at various levels of the wage distribution can be compared, in addition to calculating the aggregate costs of different reform packages. This allows comparisons to be made with results obtained from other Australian non-behavioural tax-benefit models. In addition, distributions of effective marginal tax rates, for a variety of demographic groups, can be produced for pre-reform and post-reform tax systems, as well as distributions of gainers and losers or poverty and inequality measures, for various demographic characteristics. Hypothetical households can also be constructed and examined.

C.2 MITTS-B

The behavioural component of MITTS is called MITTS-B. It examines the effects of a specified tax reform, allowing individuals to adjust their labour supply behaviour where appropriate. The labour supply responses generated by MITTS-B are based on quadratic preference functions where the parameters are allowed to vary with individuals' characteristics. These parameters have been estimated for five demographic groups, which include married or partnered men and women, single men and women, and sole parents; see Kalb (2002). Labour supply responses in MITTS-B are modelled using a discrete hours approach, as described in Part II. Individuals are considered as being constrained to select from a discrete set of hours levels, rather than being able to vary labour supply continuously. Different sets of discrete hours points are used for each demographic group. For singles, 11 discrete points are distinguished. For the couples in the labour supply estimation, two sets of discrete labour supply points are used. Given that the female hours distribution covers a wider range of part-time and full-time hours than the male distribution, which is mostly divided between non-participation and full-time work, women's labour supply is divided into 11 discrete points, whereas men's labour supply is represented by just 6 points. The joint labour supply of couples is estimated simultaneously, unlike a popular approach in which female labour supply is estimated with the spouse's labour supply taken as exogenous. Thus for couples there are 66 possible joint labour supply combinations.

For those individuals in the data set who are not working, and who therefore do not report a wage rate, an imputed wage is obtained. This imputed wage is based on estimated wage functions, which allow for possible selectivity bias, by first estimating probit equations for labour market participation, as described in Kalb and Scutella (2002, 2004).

As explained in chapters 5 and 9, the simulation is essentially probabilistic, as utility at each discrete hours level allowed is specified as the sum of a deterministic component (depending on the hours worked and net income) and a random component. Hence MITTS does not identify a particular level of hours worked for each individual after the policy change, but generates a probability distribution over the discrete hours levels used. However, some individuals are fixed at their observed labour supply if their imputed wage or their observed wage, obtained by dividing total earnings by the number of hours worked, is unrealistic. Furthermore, some individuals such as the self-employed, the disabled, students and those over 65 have their labour supply automatically fixed at their observed hours.

The behavioural simulations use the method of calibration described in Appendix B. The behavioural simulations begin by recording the discrete hours level for each individual that is closest to the observed hours level. The deterministic component of utility can be determined using the parameter estimates of the quadratic preference function, which vary according to a range of individual and household characteristics. Then to generate the random component of utility, a random draw is taken from the distribution of the error term for each hours level. In MITTS the error distribution used is the Extreme Value Type I distribution. The utility-maximising hours level is found by adding the random to the deterministic component of utility for each discrete hours level and choosing the hours level with the highest utility. The set of draws from the error terms is rejected if it results in an optimal hours level that differs from the discretised value observed. The accepted drawings are used in the determination of the optimal hours level after the policy change. A user-specified total number of 'successful draws' (those generating the observed hours as the optimal value under the base system for the individual) are produced.

Given a random set of draws from the error term distribution, once the deterministic component of utility at each of the labour supply points is calculated, the optimal choice for each draw can be determined conditional on the relevant set of error terms. For the post-reform analysis, the new net incomes cause the deterministic component of utility at each hours level to change, so using the same set of successful draws from the calibration stage, a new set of optimal hours of work is produced. This gives rise to a probability distribution over the set of discrete hours for each individual under the new tax and transfer structure. For example, in computing the transition matrices showing probabilities of movement between hours levels, the labour supply of each individual before the policy change is fixed at the observed discretised value, and a number of transitions are produced for each individual, which are equal to the number of successful draws specified. As a result, MITTS-B does not generate a single net income for each individual after a policy reform.

In some cases, the required number of successful random draws producing observed hours as the optimal hours cannot be generated from the model within a reasonable number of total drawings. The number of sets of random variables tried per draw, like the number of successful draws required, is specified by the user. If after the total number of tries from the error term distribution, the model fails to predict the observed labour supply for a draw, the individual is fixed at the observed labour supply for that draw in policy simulations. In a few extreme cases labour supply is fixed for all draws of an individual. The use of such a probabilistic approach means that the run-time of MITTS-B is substantially longer than that of MITTS-A. In MITTS, the default value for the maximum number of tries per random draw is set to 1000 with 100 successful draws required.

When examining post-reform average hours of work in MITTS-B, the labour supply after the change for each individual is based on the average value over the successful draws, for which the error term leads to the correct predicted hours before the change. This is equivalent to calculating the expected hours of labour supply after the change, conditional on starting from the observed hours before the change. In computing the tax and revenue levels, an expected value is also obtained after the policy change. That is, the tax and revenue at each of the discrete hours levels are computed for each individual, and the average of these is taken, using the computed probability distribution of hours worked.

Appendix D

Welfare Changes

This appendix provides further details regarding welfare changes discussed in chapter 7. The expenditure function is obtained from the direct utility function $U(x, y)$ by first deriving the indirect utility function $V(P, m)$; this is produced by substituting the expressions for optimal Marshallian demands x and y into U. The function $E(P, U)$ is then produced by inverting V to express m in terms of P and V. However, these operations can be carried out for only a limited number of utility functions.

An example is the Cobb-Douglas case, where $U = x^{\alpha}y^{1-\alpha}$ and the optimal demands are $x = \alpha m/P_x$ and $y = (1-\alpha)m/P_y$. Hence:

$$V(P, m) = m\left(\frac{\alpha}{P_x}\right)^{\alpha}\left(\frac{1-\alpha}{P_y}\right)^{1-\alpha} \tag{D.1}$$

so that:

$$E(P, U) = kUP_x^{\alpha}P_y^{1-\alpha} \tag{D.2}$$

with $k = 1/\left\{\alpha^{\alpha}(1-\alpha)^{1-\alpha}\right\}$.

Using the concept of the expenditure function, the Hicksian demand function can be obtained from the expenditure function using:

$$x^H(P, U_1) = \frac{\partial E(P, U)}{\partial P} \tag{D.3}$$

Here the Hicksian demand traces the quantity change as $E(P, U)$ is varied, by changing P and keeping U fixed, which is equivalent to moving along the indifference curve.

For the Cobb-Douglas utility function, which implies constant expenditure shares, the Marshallian demands all have an own-price elasticity of -1. However, the Hicksian demand functions are, after differentiating the expenditure function above, given by:

$$x^H = k\alpha U \left(\frac{P_y}{P_x}\right)^{1-\alpha} \tag{D.4}$$

Hence the price elasticity is:

$$\eta = -(1-\alpha) P_x^{-(1-\alpha)} \tag{D.5}$$

The EV area measure is the integral of the Hicksian demands between the two prices. This gives the difference between the two values of the expenditure function needed to evaluate the equivalent variation. Hence the equivalent variation is given by:

$$EV = E(P_1, U_1) - E(P_0, U_1) = \int_{P_0}^{P_1} x^H (P, U_1)\, dP \tag{D.6}$$

For an extensive discussion of the duality properties used here, see Cornes (1992).

A money measure of utility can be defined as the total expenditure (budget) that, at some reference set of prices, places the individual on the same indifference curve as the actual expenditure and prices. Welfare changes can be expressed in terms of this money measure, and it is clear that there is a different value depending on the reference prices used. The equivalent and compensating variations are effectively such welfare measures, using pre-tax and post-tax prices respectively as the reference prices.

Consider obtaining welfare changes when an estimate of the Marshallian demand function is available. One method makes use of the relationship between Hicksian and Marshallian demands, given by:

$$x(P, m) = x(P, E(P, U)) = x^H (P, U) \tag{D.7}$$

Combining this with the property mentioned earlier, that $\frac{dE(P,U)}{dP} = x^H(P,U)$, gives the following differential equation to be integrated:

$$\frac{dE(P,U)}{dP} = x^M(P, E(P,U)) \tag{D.8}$$

Integration, along with an appropriate initial condition for the constant of integration, gives the expenditure function, $E(P,U)$. A numerical procedure was suggested by Vartia (1983); for further discussion see Creedy (1998).

For welfare changes involving price changes of several goods, $i = 1, ..., n$, so the vector P now has n elements, the equivalent variation is:

$$EV = E(P_1, U_1) - E(P_0, U_1) = \sum_{i=1}^{n} \int_{P_{0,i}}^{P_{1,i}} x_i^H(P, U_1)\, dP_i \tag{D.9}$$

The summation over goods raises no problems for equivalent variations, but introduces the 'path dependency' problem for Marshallian consumer's surplus measures, whereby the order in which price changes are taken affects the result.

Appendix E

Labour Supply Derived from the Quadratic Utility

This appendix provides further details regarding the derivation of labour supply from quadratic utility functions and labour supply for individuals and couples respectively.

E.1 Individual Labour Supply

Let h denote the number of hours devoted to labour supply and let c denote an index of consumption, with the price index normalised to unity. The framework of analysis is one in which individuals are allowed to vary their hours of work continuously. The quadratic direct utility function can be written as:

$$U(h, c) = \alpha c^2 + \beta h^2 + \gamma ch + \delta c + \varepsilon h \tag{E.1}$$

In empirical work, the parameters can be specified as functions of a variety of personal characteristics. The form in (E.1) is more convenient than expressing utility in terms of leisure, $T - h$, where T is the total number of hours available for work and leisure. This approach means that $\varepsilon < 0$.

For decreasing marginal utility, it is required to have $\alpha < 0$ and $\beta < 0$. However, further restrictions on the range of c and h for which (E.1) is applicable are needed for marginal utility to be positive and (more importantly) to have decreasing marginal rates of substitution along indifference curves. The parameters of (E.1) are also affected by the units of measurement of c and h. Suppose, for example, that a change of units means that all prices, income tax thresholds and the wage rate facing the individual increase by a proportion, θ. For the optimal choice of hours to remain unchanged, new values α', and so on, are required whereby: $\alpha' = \alpha/(1+\theta)^2$; $\delta' = \delta/(1+\theta)$; $\gamma' = \gamma/(1+\theta)$; $\varepsilon' = \varepsilon$; and $\beta' = \beta$.

With a piecewise-linear budget constraint any tangency or corner solution can be regarded as being generated by a simple linear constraint of the form:

$$c = wh + \mu \tag{E.2}$$

In the case of tangency solutions, w and μ represent the appropriate net wage rate and virtual income respectively. Virtual income is the intercept (where $h = 0$) corresponding to the relevant segment of the budget constraint and associated net wage; it is therefore distinct from actual non-wage income. In the case of corner solutions, the appropriate virtual income is the value generated by a linear constraint having a net wage, the virtual wage, equal to the slope of the indifference curve at the kink. The concept of the virtual wage is the same as that of the virtual price used in the theory of rationing.

The marginal rate of substitution is given by:

$$\left.\frac{dc}{dh}\right|_U = -\frac{\partial U/\partial h}{\partial U/\partial c} = -\left\{\frac{2\beta h + \gamma c + \varepsilon}{2\alpha c + \gamma h + \delta}\right\} \tag{E.3}$$

Equate the marginal rate of substitution and the slope of the budget constraint, given by:

$$\frac{dc}{dh} = w \tag{E.4}$$

Then substitute for c using (E.2) and solve for h, giving:

$$h = \frac{2\alpha\mu w + \delta w + \gamma\mu + \varepsilon}{-2\left(\alpha w^2 + \gamma w + \beta\right)} \tag{E.5}$$

It is convenient to write:

$$\begin{aligned} A &= \alpha w^2 + \gamma w + \beta \\ B &= 2\alpha w + \gamma \\ C &= \delta w + \varepsilon \end{aligned} \tag{E.6}$$

Rewrite (E.5) as:

$$h = \frac{B\mu + C}{-2A} \tag{E.7}$$

Substituting h in the direct utility function U, given in (E.1), and inverting this to obtain the expenditure function would produce a quadratic in μ. The expenditure function is then obtained as the root of a quadratic.

E.2 Labour Supply of Couples

In the static model with no saving, total net income is equal to total expenditure, c. The hours of work are h_1 and h_2, while net wage rates are w_1 and w_2. Utility is:

$$\begin{aligned} U(c, h_1, h_2) &= \alpha c^2 + \beta_1 h_1^2 + \beta_2 h_2^2 \\ &\quad + \gamma_1 c h_1 + \gamma_2 c h_2 \\ &\quad + \beta_{1,2} h_1 h_2 \\ &\quad + \delta c + \varepsilon_1 h_1 + \varepsilon_2 h_2 \end{aligned} \tag{E.8}$$

Hence:

$$\frac{\partial U}{\partial h_1} = 2\beta_1 h_1 + \gamma_1 c + \beta_{1,2} h_2 + \varepsilon_1 \tag{E.9}$$

$$\frac{\partial U}{\partial h_2} = 2\beta_2 h_2 + \gamma_2 c + \beta_{1,2} h_1 + \varepsilon_2 \tag{E.10}$$

$$\frac{\partial U}{\partial c} = 2\alpha c + \gamma_1 h_1 + \gamma_2 h_2 + \delta \tag{E.11}$$

Marginal rates of substitution are:

$$\left.\frac{dh_1}{dh_2}\right|_U = -\frac{\frac{\partial U}{\partial h_2}}{\frac{\partial U}{\partial h_1}} \tag{E.12}$$

and so on. The budget constraint is:

$$c = w_1 h_1 + w_2 h_2 + \mu \tag{E.13}$$

where μ is non-wage income. Hence various slopes are given by:

$$\tfrac{dc}{dh_1} = w_1 \quad \tfrac{dc}{dh_2} = w_2 \quad \tfrac{dh_1}{dh_2} = -\tfrac{w_2}{w_1} \tag{E.14}$$

Equating the marginal rates of substitution and the appropriate slopes of budget constraint gives:

$$w_1 = -\frac{2\beta_1 h_1 + \gamma_1 c + \beta_{1,2} h_2 + \varepsilon_1}{2\alpha c + \gamma_1 h_1 + \gamma_2 h_2 + \delta} \tag{E.15}$$

$$w_2 = -\frac{2\beta_2 h_2 + \gamma_2 c + \beta_{1,2} h_1 + \varepsilon_2}{2\alpha c + \gamma_1 h_1 + \gamma_2 h_2 + \delta} \tag{E.16}$$

$$\frac{w_2}{w_1} = \frac{2\beta_2 h_2 + \gamma_2 c + \beta_{1,2} h_1 + \varepsilon_2}{2\beta_1 h_1 + \gamma_1 c + \beta_{1,2} h_2 + \varepsilon_1} \tag{E.17}$$

From (E.17) substituting for c from (E.13) gives:

$$\begin{aligned} & w_2\left(2\beta_1 h_1 + \gamma_1 w_1 h_1 + \gamma_1 w_2 h_2 + \gamma_1 \mu + \beta_{1,2} h_2 + \varepsilon_1\right) \\ = \; & w_1\left(2\beta_2 h_2 + \gamma_2 w_1 h_1 + \gamma_2 w_2 h_2 + \gamma_2 \mu + \beta_{1,2} h_1 + \varepsilon_2\right) \end{aligned} \tag{E.18}$$

Collecting terms in h_1 and h_2:

$$\begin{aligned} & h_1\left[w_2\left(2\beta_1 + \gamma_1 w_1\right) - w_1\left(\gamma_2 w_1 + \beta_{1,2}\right)\right] \\ = \; & h_2\left[w_1\left(2\beta_2 + \gamma_2 w_2\right) - w_2\left(\gamma_1 w_2 + \beta_{1,2}\right)\right] \\ & + \left(w_1 \varepsilon_2 - w_2 \varepsilon_1\right) \end{aligned} \tag{E.19}$$

Rewrite (E.19) as:

$$h_1 = A h_2 + B \tag{E.20}$$

where:

$$A = \frac{w_1\left(2\beta_2 + \gamma_2 w_2\right) - w_2\left(\gamma_1 w_2 + \beta_{1,2}\right)}{w_2\left(2\beta_1 + \gamma_1 w_1\right) - w_1\left(\gamma_2 w_1 + \beta_{1,2}\right)} \tag{E.21}$$

and:

$$B = \frac{w_1 \varepsilon_2 - w_2 \varepsilon_1}{w_2 \left(2\beta_1 + \gamma_1 w_1\right) - w_1 \left(\gamma_2 w_1 + \beta_{1,2}\right)} \tag{E.22}$$

Substitute (E.20) and (E.13) into (E.16)

$$-w_2 = \frac{2\beta_2 h_2 + \gamma_2 w_1 \left(Ah_2 + B\right) + \gamma_2 w_2 h_2 + \gamma_2 \mu + \beta_{1,2} \left(Ah_2 + B\right) + \varepsilon_2}{2\alpha w_1 \left(Ah_2 + B\right) + 2\alpha w_2 h_2 + 2\alpha\mu + \gamma_2 h_2 + \delta} \tag{E.23}$$

Collecting terms in h_2 gives:

$$h_2 = \frac{F - D}{C - E} \tag{E.24}$$

where:

$$C = -w_2 \left\{2\alpha \left(w_1 A + w_2\right) + \gamma_2\right\} \tag{E.25}$$

$$D = -w_2 \left\{2\alpha \left(w_1 B + \mu\right) + \delta\right\} \tag{E.26}$$

$$E = \left\{2\beta_2 + A \left(\gamma_2 w_1 + \beta_{1,2}\right) + \gamma_2 w_2\right\} \tag{E.27}$$

$$F = \left\{B \left(\gamma_2 w_1 + \beta_{1,2}\right) + \gamma_2 \mu + \varepsilon_2\right\} \tag{E.28}$$

Hence:

$$h_1 = A \left(\frac{F - D}{C - E}\right) + B \tag{E.29}$$

Substitution into the direct utility function, and inversion in order to obtain the expenditure function, would produce a quadratic in μ.

Appendix F

Inequality and Poverty Measures

This appendix provides expressions for the inequality and poverty measures used in chapter 9, for the alternative approaches.

First, the **Atkinson measure** for relative inequality aversion of unity is for all combinations:

$$1 - \sum_{m=1}^{k^n} p_{h_{1m},1} p_{h_{2m},2} \cdots p_{h_{nm},n} \frac{\exp \frac{1}{n} \sum_{i=1}^{n} \ln(y_{h_{im},i})}{\frac{1}{n} \sum_{i=1}^{n} y_{h_{im},i}} \tag{F.1}$$

The sampling approach is similar, where a sample is drawn from all possible combinations and the probability of drawing a particular combination m is equal to the probability $p_{h_{1m},1} p_{h_{2m},2} \cdots p_{h_{nm},n}$. Using expected incomes:

$$1 - \frac{\exp \frac{1}{n} \sum_{i=1}^{n} \ln(\sum_{h=1}^{k} p_{hi} y_{hi})}{\frac{1}{n} \sum_{i=1}^{n} \sum_{h=1}^{k} p_{hi} y_{hi}} \tag{F.2}$$

Using the pseudo approach:

$$1 - \frac{\exp \frac{1}{n} \sum_{i=1}^{n} \sum_{h=1}^{k} p_{hi} \ln(y_{hi})}{\frac{1}{n} \sum_{i=1}^{n} \sum_{h=1}^{k} p_{hi} y_{hi}} \tag{F.3}$$

Second, the **Gini coefficient** for all combinations is expressed as:

$$\frac{n+1}{n-1} - 2 \sum_{m=1}^{k^n} p_{h_{1m},1} p_{h_{2m},2} \cdots p_{h_{nm},n} \frac{\sum_{i=1}^{n} \rho_{l_{im}} y_{h_{l_{im}} m l_{im}}}{n(n-1) \frac{1}{n} \sum_{i=1}^{n} y_{h_{im},i}} \tag{F.4}$$

with l_{im} indicating the index for the household with the ith ranked income in the mth combination and $\rho_{l_{im}} = \rho_{l_{i-1,m}} + 1$. Using expected incomes it is:

$$\frac{n+1}{n-1} - 2\frac{\sum_{i=1}^{n} \rho_{l_i^*} \sum_{h=1}^{k} p_{hl_i^*} y_{hl_i^*}}{n(n-1)\frac{1}{n}\sum_{i=1}^{n}\sum_{h=1}^{k} p_{hi} y_{hi}} \tag{F.5}$$

with l_i^* indicating the index for the household with the ith ranked expected income and $\rho_{l_i^*} = \rho_{l_{i-1}^*} + 1$. Using the pseudo method the Gini measure is:

$$\frac{n+1}{n-1} - 2\frac{\sum_{i=1}^{n}\sum_{h=1}^{k} \rho_{v_{h(i-1)+h}, \widehat{l}_{h(i-1)+h}} p_{v_{h(i-1)+h}, \widehat{l}_{h(i-1)+h}} y_{v_{h(i-1)+h}, \widehat{l}_{h(i-1)+h}}}{n(n-1)\frac{1}{n}\sum_{i=1}^{n}\sum_{h=1}^{k} p_{hi} y_{hi}} \tag{F.6}$$

with $\widehat{l}_{h(i-1)+h}$ indicating the index for the household with the $(h(i-1)+h)$th ranked income within the nh possible incomes, $v_{h(i-1)+h}$ indicating the index for the discrete hours point with the $(h(i-1)+h)$th ranked income and $\rho_{v_{h(i-1)+h}, \widehat{l}_{h(i-1)+h}} = \rho_{v_{h(i-1)+h-1}, \widehat{l}_{h(i-1)+h-1}} + p_{v_{h(i-1)+h}, \widehat{l}_{h(i-1)+h}}$.

Third, the **headcount measure** for all combinations is:

$$\sum_{m=1}^{k^n} p_{h_{1m},1} p_{h_{2m},2} \cdots p_{h_{nm},n} \frac{1}{n} \sum_{i=1}^{n} 1(y_{h_{im},i} \leq y_{pov,m}) \tag{F.7}$$

where $y_{pov,m} = 0.5 \times y_{h_{l_{im}} m l_{im}}$ and l_{im} indicates the index for the household with the ith ranked income in the mth combination, where $i/n = 0.5$. Using expected income it is:

$$\sum_{i=1}^{n} 1(\sum_{h=1}^{k} p_{hi} y_{hi} \leq y_{pov}) \tag{F.8}$$

where $y_{pov} = 0.5 \times \sum_{h=1}^{k} p_{hl_i^*} y_{hl_i^*}$ with l_i^* indicating the index for the household with the ith ranked expected income, where $i/n = 0.5$. Using the pseudo method it is:

$$\sum_{i=1}^{n}\sum_{h=1}^{k} p_{hi} 1(y_{hi} \leq y_{pov}) \tag{F.9}$$

where $y_{pov} = 0.5 \times y_{v_{h(i-1)+h}, \widehat{l}_{h(i-1)+h}}$ with $\widehat{l}_{h(i-1)+h}$ indicating the index for the household with the $(h(i-1)+h)$th ranked income within the nh possible incomes, $v_{h(i-1)+h}$ indicating the index for the discrete hours point with the $(h(i-1)+h)$th ranked income, where $h(i-1)+h$ indicates the income where $\sum_{k=1}^{h(i-1)+h} p_{v_k,\widehat{l}_k} = 0.5$.

Fourth, the **Poverty Gap measure** for all combinations is:

$$\sum_{m=1}^{k^n} p_{h_{1m},1} p_{h_{2m},2} \cdots p_{h_{nm},n} \frac{1}{n} \sum_{i=1}^{n} \left(1 - \frac{y_{h_{im},i}}{y_{pov,m}}\right) 1(y_{h_{im},i} \leq y_{pov,m}) \tag{F.10}$$

where $y_{pov,m} = 0.5 \times y_{h_{l_{im}} m l_{im}}$ with l_{im} indicating the index for the household with the ith ranked income in the mth combination, where $i/n = 0.5$. Using expected income it is:

$$\sum_{i=1}^{n} \left(1 - \frac{\sum_{h=1}^{k} p_{hi} y_{hi}}{y_{pov}}\right) 1(\sum_{h=1}^{k} p_{hi} y_{hi} \leq y_{pov}) \tag{F.11}$$

where $y_{pov} = 0.5 \times \sum_{h=1}^{k} p_{hl_i^*} y_{hl_i^*}$ with l_i^* indicating the index for the household with the ith ranked expected income, where $i/n = 0.5$. Using the pseudo method it is:

$$\sum_{i=1}^{n} \sum_{h=1}^{k} p_{hi} \left(1 - \frac{y_{hi}}{y_{pov}}\right) 1(y_{hi} \leq y_{pov}) \tag{F.12}$$

where $y_{pov} = 0.5 \times y_{v_{h(i-1)+h}, \widehat{l}_{h(i-1)+h}}$ with $\widehat{l}_{h(i-1)+h}$ indicating the index for the household with the $(h(i-1)+h)$th ranked income within the nh possible incomes, $v_{h(i-1)+h}$ indicating the index for the discrete hours point with the $(h(i-1)+h)$th ranked income, where $h(i-1)+h$ indicates the income where $\sum_{k=1}^{h(i-1)+h} p_{v_k,\widehat{l}_k} = 0.5$.

Fifth, the **Foster, Greer and Thorbecke measure** with $\alpha = 2$, can be expressed, for all combinations, as:

$$\sum_{m=1}^{k^n} p_{h_{1m},1} p_{h_{2m},2} \cdots p_{h_{nm},n} \frac{1}{n} \sum_{i=1}^{n} \left(1 - \frac{y_{h_{im},i}}{y_{pov,m}}\right)^{\alpha} 1(y_{h_{im},i} \leq y_{pov,m}) \tag{F.13}$$

where $y_{pov,m} = 0.5 \times y_{h_{l_{im}} m l_{im}}$ with l_{im} indicating the index for the household with the ith ranked income in the mth combination, where $i/n = 0.5$. Using expected incomes it is:

$$\sum_{i=1}^{n} \left(1 - \frac{\sum_{h=1}^{k} p_{hi} y_{hi}}{y_{pov}}\right)^{\alpha} 1(\sum_{h=1}^{k} p_{hi} y_{hi} \leq y_{pov}) \tag{F.14}$$

where $y_{pov} = 0.5 \times \sum_{h=1}^{k} p_{hl_i^*} y_{hl_i^*}$ with l_i^* indicating the index for the household with the ith ranked expected income, where $i/n = 0.5$. Using the pseudo method it is:

$$\sum_{i=1}^{n}\sum_{h=1}^{k} p_{hi}\left(1 - \frac{y_{hi}}{y_{pov}}\right)^{\alpha} 1(y_{hi} \leq y_{pov}) \tag{F.15}$$

where $y_{pov} = 0.5 \times y_{v_{h(i-1)+h},\widehat{l}_{h(i-1)+h}}$ with $\widehat{l}_{h(i-1)+h}$ indicating the index for the household with the $(h(i-1)+h)$th ranked income within the nh possible incomes, $v_{h(i-1)+h}$ indicating the index for the discrete hours point with the $(h(i-1)+h)$th ranked income, where $h(i-1)+h$ indicates the income where $\sum_{k=1}^{h(i-1)+h} p_{v_k,\widehat{l}_k} = 0.5$.

Appendix G

Random Draws from a Multivariate Normal Distribution

This appendix describes how random draws from a multivariate normal distribution may be obtained, given a vector of means and a variance-covariance matrix. The method is used in chapter 11.

In the univariate case, if η is a random draw from an $N(0,1)$ distribution, a random observation, x, from a univariate normal, $N(\mu, \sigma^2)$ is given by:

$$x = \mu + \sigma\eta \tag{G.1}$$

The corresponding result for an n-element vector x from a multivariate normal, $MN(\mu, \Omega)$, is:

$$x = \mu + \Omega^{\frac{1}{2}}\eta \tag{G.2}$$

where μ and η are n-element vectors and Ω is an n by n variance-covariance (symmetric positive definite) matrix:

$$\begin{aligned}\Omega &= E(x-\mu)(x-\mu)' \\ &= \begin{bmatrix} \sigma_{11} & \dots & \sigma_{1n} \\ \cdot & & \cdot \\ \cdot & & \cdot \\ \cdot & & \cdot \\ \sigma_{n1} & \dots & \sigma_{nn} \end{bmatrix}\end{aligned} \tag{G.3}$$

To generate a random set of draws from the multivariate distribution requires the matrix $\Omega^{1/2}$, which is the square root of Ω, and η, which consists of n draws from the standard normal distribution $N(0,1)$. The matrix $\Omega^{1/2}$can be obtained using the Cholesky factorisation, which states that a symmetric positive definite matrix Ω can be expressed as:

$$\Omega = LL' \tag{G.4}$$

where L is a lower triangular matrix. Given $\Omega^{1/2} = L$, (G.2) can be rewritten as:

$$x = \mu + L\eta \tag{G.5}$$

Confirmation of this result can be obtained by examining the mean and variance, as follows. The mean is:

$$\begin{aligned} E(x) &= E(\mu + L\eta) \\ &= \mu + LE(\eta) = \mu \end{aligned} \tag{G.6}$$

while the variance:

$$\begin{aligned} E\left[(x-\mu)(x-\mu)'\right] &= E\left[L\eta(L\eta)'\right] \\ &= LE[\eta\eta']L' \\ &= LL' = \Omega \end{aligned} \tag{G.7}$$

The Cholesky factorisation, that is the solution for L in (G.4), can be achieved using the following recursive algorithm:

Start with:	$L_{11} = \sqrt{\sigma_{11}}$
Then calculate for $i = 2, ..., n$:	$L_{i1} = \sigma_{i1}/L_{11}$
For all $j = 2, ..., n$:	
First calculate:	$L_{jj} = \sqrt{\sigma_{jj} - \sum_{k=1}^{j-1} L_{jk}L_{jk}}$ (G.8)
Then for all $i = j+1, ..., n$:	$L_{ij} = \left(\sigma_{ij} - \sum_{k=1}^{j-1} L_{ik}L_{jk}\right)/L_{jj}$
For all $i < j$:	$L_{ij} = 0$

where L_{ij} denotes the element in the ith row and the jth column of L.

Bibliography

[1] Aaberge, R., Colombino, U. and Strøm, S. (1999) Labour supply in Italy: an empirical analysis of joint household decisions with taxes and quantity constraints. *Journal of Applied Econometrics*, 14, pp. 403-422.

[2] Aaberge, R., Dagsvik, J.K. and Strøm, S. (1995) Labor supply responses and welfare effects of tax reforms. *Scandinavian Journal of Economics*, 97, pp. 635-659.

[3] Alogoskoufis, G.S. (1987) On intertemporal substitution and aggregate labor supply. *Journal of Political Economy*, 95, pp. 938-960.

[4] Altonji, J.G. (1982) The intertemporal substitution model of labour market fluctuations. *Review of Economic Studies*, XLIX, pp. 783-824.

[5] Altonji, J.G. (1986) Intertemporal substitution in labor supply: evidence from micro data. *Journal of Political Economy*, 94, pp. s176-s214.

[6] Amiel, Y., Creedy, J. and Hurn, S. (1999) Measuring attitudes towards inequality. *Scandinavian Journal of Economics*, 101, pp. 83-96.

[7] Anderson, P.M. and Levine, P.B. (1999) Child care and mothers' employment decisions. National Bureau of Economic Research Working Paper, 7058.

[8] Andersson, C. and Nordberg, L. (1998) A User's Guide to CLAN 97. *Statistics Sweden.*

[9] Apps, P.F. (1994) Female labour supply, housework and family welfare. In *The Measurement of Household Welfare* (ed. by R. Blundell, I. Preston and I. Walker), pp. 140-163. Cambridge: Cambridge University Press.

[10] Apps, P.F. and Rees, R. (1996) Labour supply, household production and intra-family welfare distribution. *Journal of Public Economics*, 60, pp. 199-219.

[11] Apps, P.F. and Rees, R. (1997) Collective labor supply and household production. *Journal of Political Economy*, 105, pp. 178-190.

[12] Apps, P. and Rees, R. (1999) On the taxation of trade within and between households. *Journal of Public Economics*, 73, pp. 241-263.

[13] Apps, P. and Rees, R. (2000) Household production, full consumption and the costs of children. *IZA Discussion Paper* 157.

[14] Auerbach, A.J. (1985) The theory of excess burden and optimal taxation. In *Handbook Of Public Economics, Vol.1* (ed. by A.J. Auerbach and M. Feldstein), pp. 61-127. Amsterdam: Elsevier.

[15] Auerbach, A.J. and Hines, J.R. (2002) Taxation and economic efficiency. In *Handbook Of Public Economics, Vol.3* (ed. by A.J. Auerbach and M. Feldstein), pp. 1347-1421. Amsterdam: Elsevier.

[16] Banks, J. and Johnson, P. (1994) Equivalence scale relativities revisited. *Economic Journal*, 104, pp. 883-890.

[17] Becker, G.S. (1965) A theory of the allocation of time. *Economic Journal*, 75, pp. 493-517.

[18] Bell, P. (2000) Weighting and standard error estimation for ABS household surveys. *Paper prepared for ABS Methodology Advisory Committee: Australian Bureau of Statistics.*

[19] Bergmann, B.R. (1990) Micro-to-macro simulation: a primer with a labor market example. *Journal of Economic Perspectives*, 4, pp. 99-116.

[20] Bingley, P., Lanot, G., Symons, E. and Walker, I. (1995) Child support reform and the labor supply of lone mothers in the United Kingdom. *Journal of Human Resources*, 30, pp. 256-279.

[21] Bingley, P. and Walker, I. (1997) The labour supply, unemployment and participation of lone mothers in in-work transfer programmes. *Economic Journal*, 107, pp. 1375-1390.

[22] Bingley, P. and Walker, I. (2001) Housing subsidies and work incentives in Great Britain. *Economic Journal*, 111, pp. C86-C103.

[23] Blackorby, C. and Donaldson, D. (1988) Money metric utility: a harmless normalization? *Journal of Economic Theory*, 46, pp. 120-129.

[24] Blackorby, C., Laisney, F. and Schmachtenberg, R. (1994) Ethically consistent welfare prescriptions are reference price independent. In *The Measurement of Household Welfare* (ed. by R. Blundell, I. Preston and I. Walker), pp. 247-264. Cambridge: Cambridge University Press.

[25] Blau, D.M. and Hagy, A. (1998) The demand for quality in child care. *Journal of Political Economy*, 106, pp. 474-481.

[26] Blau, D.M and Mocan, H.N. (1999) The supply of quality in child care centers. *National Bureau of Economic Research Working Paper* 7225.

[27] Blau, D.M. and Robins, P.K. (1988) Child-care costs and family labor supply. *Review of Economics and Statistics*, 70, pp. 374-381.

[28] Blau, D.M. and Robins, P.K. (1989) Fertility, employment and child care costs. *Demography*, 26, pp. 287-299.

[29] Blomquist, N.S. (1983) The effect of income taxation on the labour supply of married men in Sweden. *Journal of Public Economics*, 22, pp. 169-197.

[30] Blundell, R. and Hoynes, H. (2001) Has 'in-work' benefit reform helped the labour market? *National Bureau of Economic Research Working Paper*, no. 8546.

[31] Blundell, R., Chiappori, P.-A., Magnac, T. and Meghir, C. (2001) Collective labor supply: heterogeneity and nonparticipation. *IFS Working Paper* W01/19, Institute for Fiscal Studies.

[32] Blundell, R., Duncan, A., McCrae, J. and Meghir, C. (2000) The labour market impact of the Working Families' Tax Credit. *Fiscal Studies*, 21, pp. 75-104.

[33] Blundell, R., Preston, I. and Walker, I. (1994) Introduction to applied welfare analysis. In *The Measurement of Household Welfare* (ed. by R. Blundell, I. Preston and I. Walker), pp. 1-50. Cambridge: Cambridge University Press.

[34] Blundell, R., Preston, I. and Walker, I. (ed.) (1994) *The Measurement of Household Welfare*. Cambridge: Cambridge University Press.

[35] Borjas, G.J. (2000) *Labour Economics*. New York: McGraw-Hill.

[36] Bourguignon, F. and Chiappori, P.-A. (1994) The collective approach to household behaviour. In *The Measurement of Household Welfare* (ed. by R. Blundell, I. Preston and I. Walker), pp. 70-85. Cambridge: Cambridge University Press.

[37] Browning, M., Bourguignon, F., Chiappori, P.-A. and Lechene, V. (1994) Income and outcomes: a structural model of intrahousehold allocation. *Journal of Political Economy*, 102, pp. 1067-1096.

[38] Buhmann, B., Rainwater, L., Schmaus, G. and Smeeding, T.M. (1988) Equivalence scales, well-being, inequality, and poverty: Sensitivity estimates across ten countries using the Luxembourg income study (LIS) database. *Review of Income and Wealth*, 34, pp. 115-142.

[39] Burtless, G. and Hausman, J.A. (1978) The effect of taxation on labor supply: evaluating the Gary Negative Income Tax experiment. *Journal of Political Economy*, 86, pp. 1103-1130.

[40] Callan, T. and Van Soest, A. (1996) Family labour supply and taxes in Ireland. Tilburg University.

[41] Chiappori, P.-A. (1988) Rational household labour supply. *Econometrica*, 56, pp. 63-89.

[42] Cobb-Clark, D.A., Liu, A. and Mitchell, D. (2000) Reassessing the role of child care costs in the work and care decisions of Australian families. *Australian Bulletin of Labour*, 26, pp. 279-297.

[43] Connelly, R. (1992) The effects of childcare costs on married women's labour force participation. *Review of Economics and Statistics*, 74, pp. 83-90.

[44] Cornes, R. (1992) *Duality and Modern Economics.* Cambridge: Cambridge University Press.

[45] Coulter, A.E., Cowell, F.A. and Jenkins, S.P. (1992) Equivalence scale relativities and the extent of inequality and poverty. *Economic Journal*, 102, pp. 1067-1082.

[46] Cowell, F.A. (1984) The structure of American income inequality. *Review of Income and Wealth*, 30, pp. 351-375.

[47] Creedy, J. (1996) *Fiscal Policy and Social Welfare: An Analysis of Alternative Tax and Transfer Systems.* Cheltenham: Edward Elgar.

[48] Creedy, J. (1998) *Measuring Welfare Changes and Tax Burdens.* Cheltenham: Edward Elgar.

[49] Creedy, J. (2000) Measuring welfare changes and the excess burden of taxation. *Bulletin of Economic Research*, 52, pp. 1-47.

[50] Creedy, J. (2001) Quadratic utility, labour supply and the welfare effects of tax changes. *Australian Journal of Labour Economics*, 4, pp. 272-280.

[51] Creedy, J. (2004a) Labour supply incentives in alternative tax and transfer schemes: a diagrammatic introduction. *Australian Economic Review*, 37, pp. 230-241.

[52] Creedy, J. (2004b) Survey Reweighting for Tax Microsimulation Modelling. In *Research on Economic Inequality, Vol. 12* (ed. by J. Bishop and Y. Amiel), pp. 229-249. Amsterdam: Elsevier JAI.

[53] Creedy, J. (2004c) The excess burden of taxation. *Australian Economic Review*, 37, pp. 454-464.

[54] Creedy, J. and Duncan, A.S. (2005) Aggregating labour supply and feedback effects in microsimulation. *Australian Journal of Labour Economics* (forthcoming)

[55] Creedy, J. and Kalb, G. (2005a) Discrete hours labour supply modelling: specification, estimation and simulation. *Journal of Economic Surveys*, 19, pp. 697-734.

[56] Creedy, J. and Kalb, G. (2005b) Measuring welfare changes with nonlinear budget constraints in continuous and discrete hours labour supply models. *Manchester School*, 73, pp. 664-685.

[57] Creedy, J. and Scutella, R. (2004) The role of the unit of analysis in tax policy reform evaluations of inequality and social welfare. *Australian Journal of Labour Economics*, 7, pp. 89-108.

[58] Creedy, J. and Sleeman, C. (2005) Adult equivalence scales: inequality and poverty. Forthcoming in *New Zealand Economic Papers.*

[59] Creedy, J. and Tuckwell, I. (2004) Reweighting household surveys for tax microsimulation modelling: an application to the New Zealand Household Economic Survey. *Australian Journal of Labour Economics*, 7, pp. 71-88.

[60] Creedy, J., Kalb, G. and Kew, H. (2003) Flattening the effective marginal tax rate structure in Australia: policy simulations using the Melbourne Institute Tax and Transfer Simulator. *Australian Economic Review*, 36, pp. 156-172.

[61] Creedy, J., Kalb, G. and Kew, H. (2004) Confidence Intervals for Policy Reforms in Behavioural Tax Microsimulation Modelling. *Melbourne Institute Working Paper Series*, WP No. 32/04, Melbourne Institute of Applied Economic and Social Research, The University of Melbourne.

[62] Creedy, J., Kalb, G. and Scutella, R. (2004) Evaluating the income redistribution effects of tax reforms in discrete hours models. In *Research on Economic Inequality, Vol. 12* (ed. by J. Bishop and Y. Amiel), pp. 199-226. Amsterdam: Elsevier JAI.

[63] Creedy, J., Duncan, A.S., Harris, M. and Scutella, R. (2002) *Microsimulation Modelling of Taxation and The Labour Market: The Melbourne Institute Tax and Transfer Simulator.* Cheltenham: Edward Elgar.

[64] Cutler, D.M. and Katz, L. (1992) Rising inequality? changes in the distribution of income and consumption in the 1980s. *American Economic Review*, 82, pp. 546-551.

[65] Dagsvik, J.K. and Karlström, A. (2005) Compensating variation and Hicksian choice probabilities in random utility models that are nonlinear in Income. *Review of Economic Studies*, 72, pp. 57-76.

[66] Danziger, S. and Taussig, M.K. (1979) The income unit and the anatomy of income distribution. *Review of Income and Wealth*, 25, pp. 365-375.

[67] Deaton, A. (1997) *The Analysis of Household Surveys; A Microeconometric Approach to Development Policy.* Baltimore: The Johns Hopkins University Press.

[68] Deaton, A.S. and Muellbauer, J. (1980) *Economics and Consumer Behaviour*. Cambridge: Cambridge University Press.

[69] Decoster, A. and Ooghe, E. (2002) Weighting with individuals, equivalent individuals or not weighting at all: does it matter empirically? *Catholic University of Leuven Centre for Economic Studies Discussion Paper* 02.15.

[70] Deville, J.-F. and Särndal, C.-E. (1992) Calibration estimators in survey sampling. *Journal of the American Statistical Association*, 87, pp. 376-382.

[71] Diamond, P.A. and McFadden, D.L. (1974) Some uses of the expenditure function in public finance. *Journal of Public Economics*, 3, pp. 3-21.

[72] Doiron, D. and Kalb, G. (2005) Demands for childcare and household labour supply in Australia. *Economic Record*, 81, pp. 215-236.

[73] Duncan, A. and Harris, M.N. (2002a) Simulating the effect of welfare reforms among sole parents in Australia. *Economic Record*, 78, pp. 249-263.

[74] Duncan, A. and Harris, M.N. (2002b) Intransigencies in the labour supply choice. *Melbourne Institute Working Paper*, no. 17/02.

[75] Duncan, A., Paull, G. and Taylor, J. (2001a) Mothers' employment and use of childcare in the United Kingdom. *Institute for Fiscal Studies Working Paper* 01/23.

[76] Duncan, A., Paull, G. and Taylor, J. (2001b) Price and quality in the UK childcare market. *Institute for Fiscal Studies Working Paper* 01/14.

[77] Duncan, A.S. and Giles, C. (1998) The labour market impact of the working families tax credit in the UK. Paper presented to International Institute for Public Finance conference, Cordoba, Argentina.

[78] Duncan, A.S. and Weeks, M. (1997) Behavioural tax microsimulation with finite hours choices. *European Economic Review*, 41, pp. 619-626.

[79] Duncan, A.S. and Weeks, M. (1998) Simulating transitions using discrete choice models. *Proceedings of the American Statistical Association*, 106, pp. 151-156.

[80] Ebert, U. (1997) Social welfare when needs differ: an axiomatic approach. *Economica*, 64, pp. 233-244.

[81] Euwals, R. (2001) Female labour supply, flexibility of working hours, and job mobility. *Economic Journal*, 111, pp. C120-C134.

[82] Euwals, R. and Van Soest, A. (1999) Desired and actual labour supply of unmarried men and women in the Netherlands. *Labour Economics*, 6, pp. 95-118.

[83] Folsom, R.E. Jnr. and Singh, A.C. (2000) The generalized exponential model for sampling weight calibration for extreme values, non-

response and post-stratification. *Proceedings of the Survey Research Methods Section: American Statistical Association.*

[84] Foster, J., Greer, J. and Thorbecke, E. (1984) A class of decomposable poverty measures. *Econometrica*, 52, pp. 761-762.

[85] Fraker, T. and Moffitt, R. (1988) The effect of food stamps on labor supply: a bivariate selection model. *Journal of Public Economics*, 35, pp. 25-56.

[86] Gerfin, M. (1993) Simultaneous discrete choice model of labour supply and wages for married women in Switzerland. *Empirical Economics*, 18, pp. 337-356.

[87] Gerfin, M. and Leu, R.E. (2003) The impact of in-work benefits on poverty and household labour supply: a simulation study for Switzerland. *Institute for the Study of Labor IZA Discussion Paper*, 762.

[88] Glewwe, P. (1991) Household equivalence scales and the measurement of inequality: transfers from the poor to the rich could decrease inequality. *Journal of Public Economics*, 44, pp. 214-216.

[89] Hagstrom, P.A. (1996) The food stamp participation and labor supply of married couples; an empirical analysis of joint decisions. *Journal of Human Resources*, 31, pp. 383-403.

[90] Hagy, A.P. (1998) The demand for child care quality. *Journal of Human Resources*, 33, pp. 683-710.

[91] Hamermesh, D. (1993) *Labour Demand.* Princeton, NJ: Princeton University Press.

[92] Hausman, J.A. (1979) The econometrics of labor supply on convex budget sets. *Economics Letters*, 3, pp. 171-174.

[93] Hausman, J.A. (1981) Exact consumer's surplus and deadweight loss. *American Economic Review*, 71, pp. 662-676.

[94] Hausman, J.A. (1985a) Taxes and labor supply. In *Handbook of Labor Economics, Vol. 1.* (ed. by A.J. Auerbach and M. Feldstein), pp. 213-264. New York: North-Holland.

[95] Hausman, J.A. (1985b) The econometrics of nonlinear budget sets. *Econometrica*, 53, pp. 1255-1282.

[96] Heckman, J.J. (1993) What has been learned about labor supply in the past 20 years? *American Economic Review*, 83, pp. 116-121.

[97] Hines, J.R. (1999) Three sides of Harberger triangles. *Journal of Economic Perspectives*, 13, pp. 167-188.

[98] Hoynes, H.W. (1996) Welfare transfers in two-parent families: labor supply and welfare participation under AFDC-UP. *Econometrica*, 64, pp. 295-332.

[99] Jenkins, S.P. and Cowell, F.A. (1994) Parametric equivalence scales and scale relativities, *Economic Journal*, 104, pp. 891-900.

[100] Johansson, P.-O. (1987) *The Economic Theory and Measurement of Environmental Benefits.* Cambridge: Cambridge University Press.

[101] Jorgenson, D.W. and Slesnick, D.T. (1984) Aggregate consumer behaviour and the measurement of inequality. *Review of Economic Studies*, 51, pp. 369-392.

[102] Kalb, G. (1999) Labour supply and welfare participation in Australian two-adult households: comparing 1986/1987 with 1994/1995. *Monash University Centre of Policy Studies Working Paper* BP-3497.

[103] Kalb, G. (2000) Labour supply and welfare participation in Australian two-adult households: accounting for involuntary unemployment and the cost of part-time work. *Monash University Centre of Policy Studies Working Paper* BP-3597.

[104] Kalb, G. (2002) Estimation of labour supply models for four separate groups in the Australian population. *Melbourne Institute Working Paper* 24/02, The University of Melbourne.

[105] Kalb, G. and Scutella, R. (2002) Estimation of wage equations in Australia: allowing for censored observations of labour supply. *Melbourne Institute Working Paper* 8/02, The University of Melbourne.

[106] Kalb, G. and Scutella, R. (2004) Wage and employment rates in New Zealand from 1991 to 2001. *New Zealand Economic Papers*, 38, pp. 21-47.

[107] Kalb, G., Cai, L. and Vu, H. (2004) *Updating the Input for the Melbourne Institute Tax and Transfer Simulator*. Melbourne Institute Report for the Department of Family and Community Services.

[108] Kalb, G., Kew, H. and Scutella R. (2005) Effects of the Australian New Tax System on income tax and benefits: with and without labour supply responses. *Australian Economic Review*, 38, pp. 137-158.

[109] Kalton, G. and Flores-Cervantes, I. (2003) Weighting methods. *Journal of Official Statistics*, 19, pp. 81-98.

[110] Keane, M. and Moffitt, R. (1998) A structural model of multiple welfare program participation and labor supply. *International Economic Review*, 39, pp. 553-589.

[111] Kennan, J. (1988) An econometric analysis of fluctuations in aggregate labor supply and demand. *Econometrica*, 56, pp. 317-333.

[112] Kimmel, J. (1998) Child care costs as a barrier to employment for single and married mothers. *Review of Economics and Statistics*, 80, pp. 287-299.

[113] King, M.A. (1983) Welfare analysis of tax reforms using household data. *Journal of Public Economics*, 21, pp. 183-214.

[114] Klevmarken, A. (1998) Statistical inference in microsimulation models: incorporating external information. *Uppsala University Department of Economics Working Paper*, 1998:20.

[115] Kooreman, P. and Kapteyn, A. (1987) A disaggregated analysis of the allocation of time within the household. *Journal of Political Economy*, 95, pp. 223-241.

[116] Kornstad, T. and Thoresen, T.O. (2002) A discrete choice model for labor supply and child care. *Statistics Norway Research Department Discussion Paper.*

[117] Kornstad, T. and Thoresen, T.O. (2004) Means-testing the child benefit. *Review of Income and Wealth*, 50, pp. 29-49.

[118] Lambert, P. (2001) *The Distribution and Redistribution of Income: A Mathematical Analysis.* Manchester: Manchester University Press.

[119] Latham, R. (1980) Quantity constrained demand functions. *Econometrica*, 48, pp. 307-314.

[120] Leibowitz, A., Klerman, J. and Waite, L. (1992) Employment of new mothers and child care choice. *Journal of Human Resources*, 27(1), pp. 112-134.

[121] Lemaître, G. and Dufour, J. (1987) An integrated method for weighting persons and families. *Survey Methodology*, 13, pp. 199-207.

[122] Lucas, R.E. and Rapping, L.A. (1969) Real wages, employment and inflation. *Journal of Political Economy*, 77, pp. 721-754.

[123] MaCurdy, T., Green, D. and Paarsch, H. (1990) Assessing empirical approaches for analyzing taxes and labor supply. *Journal of Human Resources*, 25, pp. 415-490.

[124] Maddala, G.S. (1983) *Limited Dependent and Qualitative Variables in Econometrics.* New York: Cambridge University Press.

[125] McFadden, D. (1974a) Conditional logit analysis of qualitative choice behaviour. In *Frontiers in Econometrics* (ed. by P. Zarembka), pp. 105-142. New York: Academic Press.

[126] McFadden, D. (1974b) The measurement of urban travel demand. *Journal of Public Economics*, 3, pp. 303-328.

[127] Michalopoulos, C., Robins, P.K. and Garfinkel, I. (1992) A structural model of labor supply and child care demand. *Journal of Human Resources*, 27, pp. 166-203.

[128] Moffitt, R. (1983) An economic model of welfare stigma. *American Economic Review*, 73, pp. 1023-1035.

[129] Moffitt, R. (1986) The econometrics of piecewise-linear budget constraints: a survey and exposition of the maximum likelihood method. *Journal of Business and Economic Statistics*, 4, pp. 317-328.

[130] Muellbauer, J. (1981) Linear aggregation in neoclassical labour supply. *Review of Economic Studies*, XLVIII, pp. 21-36.

[131] Nascimento Silva, P.L.D. and Skinner, C. (1997) Variable selection for regression estimation in finite populations. *Survey Methodology*, 23, pp. 23-32.

[132] Neary, J.P. and Roberts, K.W.S. (1980) The theory of household behaviour under rationing. *European Economic Review*, 13, pp. 25-42.

[133] Preston, I. and Walker, I. (1999) Welfare measurement in labour supply models with nonlinear budget constraints. *Journal of Population Economics*, 12, pp. 343-361.

[134] Pudney, S. and Sutherland, H. (1994) How reliable are microsimulation results? *Journal of Public Economics*, 53, pp. 327-365.

[135] Pudney, S. and Sutherland, H. (1996) Statistical reliability in microsimulation models with econometrically-estimated behavioural responses. In *Microsimulation and Public Policy* (ed. by A. Harding), pp. 473-503. Amsterdam: North-Holland.

[136] Pyatt, G. (1990) Social evaluation criteria. In *Income and Wealth Distribution, Inequality and Poverty* (ed. by C. Dagum and M. Zenga). Berlin: Springer-Verlag.

[137] Ribar, D.C. (1992) Child care and the labor supply of married women: reduced form evidence. *Journal of Human Resources*, 27, pp. 134-165.

[138] Ribar, D.C. (1995) A structural model of child care and the labor supply of married women. *Journal of Labor Economics*, 13, pp. 558-597.

[139] Ringen, S. (1991) Households, standard of living and inequality. *Review of Income and Wealth*, 37, pp. 1-13.

[140] Särndal, C.-E., Swensson, B. and Wretman, J. (1992) *Model Assisted Survey Sampling*. New York: Springer-Verlag.

[141] Shorrocks, A.F. (1997) Inequality and welfare evaluation of heterogeneous income distributions. *University of Essex Department of Economics Discussion Paper*, 447.

[142] Singh, A.C. and Mohl, C.A. (1996) Understanding calibration estimators in survey sampling. *Survey Methodology*, 22, pp. 107-115.

[143] Skinner, C. (1999) Calibration weighting and non-sampling errors. *Research in Official Statistics*, 2, pp. 33-43.

[144] Slesnick, D.T. (1994) Consumption, needs and inequality. *International Economic Review*, 35, pp. 677-703.

[145] Small, K.A. and Rosen, H.S. (1981) Applied welfare economics with discrete choice models. *Econometrica*, 49, pp. 105-130.

[146] Smith, P.A. (1997) The effect of the 1981 welfare reforms on AFDC participation and labor supply. *University of Wisconsin-Madison Institute for Research on Poverty Discussion Paper*, 1117-97.

[147] Statistics New Zealand (2001) *Information Paper: The Introduction of Integrated Weighting to the 2000/2001 Household Economic Survey.* Statistics New Zealand.

[148] Stern, N. (1986) On the specification of labour supply functions. In *Unemployment, Search and Labour Supply* (ed. by R. Blundell and I. Walker), pp. 143-189. Cambridge: Cambridge University Press.

[149] Tummers, M. and Woittiez, I. (1991) A simultaneous wage and labour supply model with hours restriction. *Journal of Human Resources*, 26, pp. 393-423.

[150] Van Soest, A. (1995) Structural models of family labor supply: a discrete choice approach. *Journal of Human Resources*, 30, pp. 63-88.

[151] Van Soest, A. and Das, M. (2000) Family labour supply and proposed tax reforms in the Netherlands. In *Taxes, Transfers and Labour Market Responses: What Can Microsimulation Tell Us?* (ed. by T. Callan), pp. 59-80. Dublin: Economic and Social Research Institute.

[152] Van Soest, A., Woittiez, I. and Kapteyn, A. (1990) Labor supply, income taxes, and hours restrictions in the Netherlands. *Journal of Human Resources*, 25, pp. 517-558.

[153] Vanderhoeft, C. (2001) Generalised calibration at Statistics Belgium. *Statistics Belgium Working Paper*, no. 3.

[154] Vartia, Y.O. (1983) Efficient methods of measuring welfare change and compensated income in terms of demand functions. *Econometrica*, 51, pp. 79-98.

[155] Vlasblom, J.D., De Gijsel, P. and Siegers, J. (2001) Taxes, female labour supply and household income: differences between the Netherlands and the Federal Republic of Germany. *Applied Economics*, 33, pp. 735-744.

[156] Wales, T.J. and Woodland, A.D. (1977) Estimation of the allocation of time for work, leisure, and housework. *Econometrica*, 45, pp. 115-132.

[157] Walker, J.R. (1992) New evidence on the supply of child care. *Journal of Human Resources*, 27, pp. 40-69.

[158] Whiteford, P. (1985) A family's needs: equivalence scales, poverty and social security. *Department of Social Security Research paper*, 27.

[159] Woittiez, I. (1991) *Modelling and Empirical Evaluation of Labour Supply Behaviour: Studies in Contemporary Economics.* Berlin Heidelberg: Springer-Verlag.

[160] Zabalza, A., Pissarides, C. and Barton, M. (1980) Social security and the choice between full-time work, part-time work and retirement. *Journal of Public Economics*, 14, pp. 245-276.

Index